Welcome Home
A Time for Uniting

Welcome Home
A Time for Uniting

PRETTY FLOWER
channeled by EILEEN ROTA

Foreword by
SIR GEORGE TREVELYAN

Introduction by
EILEEN ROTA

Compiled by
NORMA ECKROATE & LINDA KOLBER CAPUTI

ISBN #0-9619931-0-3
Library of Congress Catalog Card Number: 87-63572

FOR MORE INFORMATION ABOUT the channeling of Eileen Rota and audio tapes of the Pretty Flower sessions, please refer to the order form at the back of this book or write to the Publisher.

Cover Photo by JOHN CAPUTI
Inside Illustrations by JULIA FIERMAN
Design Consultant: FRANCIS SPORER
Typesetting by ALPHABETZ, Norfolk, Virginia
Printing by RIVERRUN PRESS, Piermont, New York

 Sand Castle Publishing
P.O. Box 629
Virginia Beach, Virginia 23451

Wholesale Inquiries please direct to Riverrun Press, Box 367, Piermont, NY 10968
Manufactured in the United States of America

10   9   8   7   6   5   4   3   2   1

TABLE OF CONTENTS

In dedication and gratitude to all Beings —
for we gather together that we might become One.

"We are One in the same."

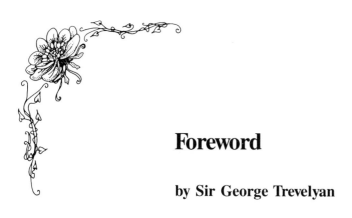

Foreword

by Sir George Trevelyan

This book consists of sessions with a channeled source called Pretty Flower, giving answers to a stream of questions about past incarnations and the conduct of our present lives. There is a refreshing directness and charm about this material. Throughout it reinforces one message — that all life in all its aspects is a great and total Oneness, NOW. This is the Truth which can change our limited and separatist thinking into expansiveness.

Answering questions about previous Earth-lives, Pretty Flower again and again stresses that all Time is One, that the earlier life is in a real sense NOW, a touching into a vibratory field which, being part of our total experience of life beyond linear time, is truly NOW and always.

This book is something extraordinary. This is IT. I do believe that a most important thing has happened in the channeling of Pretty Flower. Here is Joy — the dissolving of the imprisoned ego-self into the wholeness of Being. When we die and the matter-body dissolves, we shall expand into the One. But it can be achieved now. It is true that Time is the necessary illusion while we are embedded in matter. But free from matter and embodiment there is no time. All is in the One, as Pretty Flower says. It is a wonderful truth that all "earlier lives" are here now if we can attune to them. This is an *important* book. Everything melts and merges.

"Remember — we are everything. WELCOME HOME."

Our thanks go out to Pretty Flower and to those who have offered her teachings in this book. It is a fine example of channeling at its best and this form of communion with higher intelligences or Universal consciousness is of profound significance for the spiritual awakening of our time.

Introduction

by Eileen Rota

Years ago, a woman asked me before a session, "What kind of channeling do you do?" I said, "I don't know," which was certainly the truth. She then proceeded to help me define whether I was a conscious or unconscious channeler. At the end of the session, she told me that I was definitely an unconscious channeler. "But I could hear everything that was said," I thought. "What does that mean?"

Since that time, I have heard and read many descriptions of channeling. People have shared with me their ideas of what is the best and most trusted source. For example, one person told me that he didn't quite understand the unusual accent that came through when I was channeling, but he felt for certain that it was "higher self." "Whenever the channel addresses itself as 'we,' it's higher self," he said. Another person told me that Pretty Flower must be an American Indian Master. And yet another told me she felt that it was really me and that I was evolving into the Master that I am.

I also heard that unless the channeler was unconscious, the material coming through was not totally pure. Lazaris, channeled by Jach Pursel, keeps his eyes closed. Ramtha, through J.Z. Knight, has his eyes open and has quite animated movements. Both Jach and J.Z. say that they have no recall.

Edgar Cayce, known as the Sleeping Prophet, went into trance while lying down and had no recall of the material that was chan-

3

neled. Kevin Ryerson has his eyes closed and, as many of us saw in the movie *Out On A Limb,* walks around that way. Elwood Babbit stayed seated with his eyes closed during my session with him. Brazilian Luis Gasparetto channels not words but paintings as the great masters work through him. Luis remains conscious during a session, and says he experiences the feelings of the painters as he channels their art.

I have never seen Pat Rodegast channel Emmanuel, but I am truly uplifted by the written material. I have also experienced a meditation teacher who, during class, goes into trance and speaks Vedantic truths.

What dimensions are we speaking of when we define our experiences as conscious or unconscious? Who is right? Is there really any "right"? Who created the rules? And who follows them?

During the last few years I have attempted to define what it is that occurs when I channel, which I often call "working with Spirit." I can honestly say with much relief that I cannot define exactly what occurs. The only thing that I can do with certainty is to share with you a little of my story. Perhaps you can identify with my experiences and feelings. I'll leave the interpreting and "trying on for size" to you, hoping that you have fun with it all.

For about fifteen years I experienced different types of communication from the non-physical plane — including clairvoyant visions, clairaudience, and automatic writing. My spirit teacher had been communicating his teachings to me through automatic writing for about two years when he said that I would soon stop automatic writing. He said I would meet a new teacher, who would be a woman in physical form.

Reluctantly I ceased written communications with the teacher who had gently guided me through many of life's experiences, the teacher who I continue to hold within my heart. Yet, I looked forward with excited anticipation to my new teacher — in physical form. In fact, I found myself "scouting" every woman at any spiritual gathering, wondering if "she might be the one." Little did I know that my new teacher in physical form would be the full-body-synchronization of an energy known as Pretty Flower. But that's getting a little ahead of the story.

4

On a trip to Virginia, I spent a week with a dear friend and teacher, Henry Leo Bolduc. Henry had been working with a man who was introduced to me as Daniel Clay Pugh. As Henry had done with me a few years earlier, he had just completed teaching Daniel methods in hypnosis. However, now he was trying something new: Through hypnosis, Henry was guiding Daniel to a place within where he would then begin to speak and teach in a voice quite unlike his own. I experienced Daniel's channeling and found the information beautiful and the process quite exciting.

One morning I found myself saying to Henry, "Would you introduce me to my next teacher?" He asked me if I wanted him to work with me as he was working with Daniel. I really didn't know what I had meant. I heard the words come out of my mouth, yet I had no idea I would say such a thing! I said, "I guess that's what I mean. Yes, I would like to work with you in that manner." Henry said, "Good! Let's start tonight." So began my journey with a new and different kind of channeling.

During the first sessions, I felt many different physical movements. I felt my body change position. It leaned forward in the chair. My face changed, feeling at times a little contorted. My eyes remained closed. I felt energy enter my being from the top of my head. The words which came through were slow and accompanied by labored breathing. I experienced difficulty in synchronizing with the energy until I began practicing my own way of centering and aligning myself with the Universe — a technique which is as natural to me now as breathing.

During the third session, Henry asked the energy if there was an identifying name we could be using. He was told that the vessel's throat (meaning my throat) was not able to speak the actual name, but that she would be known as "Pretty Flower."

I found all of it quite interesting. First of all, the voice carried an accent which a year before I had found myself slipping into when I talked aloud to myself. As for the name Pretty Flower ... I had been studying voice with a woman, Islene Runningdeer, who asked me one day if I had ever heard her speak of "Pretty Flower," her spirit Indian teacher. Islene said that she felt Pretty Flower's energy all around me that day.

The whole experience brought to the surface my first major concern as a channeler: Was the channeling valid? Was it real? Was I making it up? Where was it coming from?

During my travels, many channelers have shared with me those exact feelings, doubts and questions. I realized that we were all experiencing our own channeling through critical eyes. Henry and I spent many nights discussing this same issue. He frequently reminded me of a guiding statement upon which we had mutually agreed — "I accept neither credit nor blame for these channelings." However, I often found myself mentally wringing my hands and praying that everything be right.

Each night, walking up the hill near his home, we tossed back and forth new ideas. Finally, we both agreed we would continue "as long as no one was harmed — as long as people were helped." I never would have been able to continue without his support and the encouragement of those friends and neighbors who attended those first sessions.

And so the channeling sessions continued with Henry guiding me into a trance-like state, allowing Pretty Flower to come through and teach. I began to love that energy — so gentle, loving and kind. She told wonderful stories and sometimes answered questions with enchanting parables. It was quite an experience to hear a story begin and not know where it would end. Way in the background, I would just listen like everyone else. Sometimes I would think a story was heading in one direction, and it would actually head in quite a different one! Other times Pretty Flower would tell an American Indian tradition in great detail. She displayed a wonderful sense of humor and often filled the room with her booming laugh. She also made deep, melodic tones, which seemed to vibrate within every being present at the gathering. These episodes and procedures are shared in detail in Henry's latest book, *The Journey Within: Past Life Regression and Channeling* (Inner Vision Publishing, 1988).

Then there came a time in 1986 when Pretty Flower asked for "full-body-synchronization." Up until then she had always sat in a chair with her eyes closed. She described a procedure which, when followed, resulted in her full use of my body. Now she walked around with eyes open. This occurrence was a little unnerving for those people who had experienced previous sessions. They told me that her eyes radiated a depth and a brilliance — "I felt like I could just fall right into them."

Pretty Flower then began calling people forward to stand in front of her. When this happened, she sometimes moved her hands around the person and made toning sounds. Other times she told a person a story while she rocked them in her arms, all the while encouraging them to allow their wonderful little child within out to play. Many people have communicated to me that they experienced a form of healing during a session — some physical healings, some emotional healings — and *all* spiritual healings.

Back home in New England, a young man with whom I shared Henry's teachings displayed a deep interest in the process of channeling Pretty Flower. In fact, he came to my home every week just to talk with her. Brock Hood eventually became my new guide, with Henry's encouragement, and we traveled through states on the East Coast, sharing Pretty Flower at many gatherings. Through these travels I have had the blessings of meeting hundreds of wonderful new friends.

Since those first experiences with channeling and through the self-questionings, I have changed. I experience my life in a very different way. By releasing ideas concerning "rules and regulations" as they come to my awareness, I have opened to the now — to trusting my own inner messages. I no longer define my life's experiences by another's teaching. Perhaps this has happened because these teachings came through me so many times that they became part of me, or perhaps they were already part of me and I allowed them to manifest outward. Who really knows? Who *really* knows?

Sometimes when channeling Pretty Flower, I consciously experience the whole session. Sometimes I experience only part of the session. Never, however, have I remained unconscious for the entire session.

What do I see and feel? I see concerned, guilt-ridden faces turn into joyful, round, teary-eyed ones. I have seen a little child emerge from the face of a newspaper reporter when she heard the words, "Once upon a time ..." as an answer to her pointed question. I have heard sighs of relief. I have heard much laughter, both from

7

the people who attended sessions and from my own mouth.

I have felt Pretty Flower weep with a woman in deep sorrow and only then did I realize that I had only cried in my liftime; weeping is different. Weeping is from the very depths of our being. I have heard Pretty Flower say to a woman, "Give it to me. Give me that burden," and felt my arms embrace the woman, while warm, vibrant, powerful waves of energy flowed up our two bodies. I have felt a very tall man bend to shed tears on this shoulder which Pretty Flower and I share as one. And I have heard the words, "I am totally healed! My back is healed!"

But most of all, I have felt the Love flowing at every session. Some people say that they feel this Love flowing, radiating from Pretty Flower when they are in her presence. I remember her saying, "What you are feeling is your very own selves. We manifest in this manner so that you might know your very own self." And where am I in all of this? Pretty Flower and I are One in the same!

May the blessings of the Universe surround your being within and without. I do hope that you have fun with these teachings, stories and meditations. Please don't make them your rules and regulations. Please do trust *your* inner messages. Please share your thoughts and experiences with others. It's time for us to be in the open now, sharing and experiencing together.

Perhaps we'll meet each other, skipping down the path. Remember, I love everything about you ...

Chapter 1

Welcome Home

We are seeking and seeking that we would be filled and we are not quite sure what we would be filled with.

[This chapter consists of an individual's session with Pretty Flower. The woman starts by asking about the lessons of this lifetime and about the dynamics of a current relationship.]

We would first be asking: What would you be *believing* would be the lessons? Is there an inkling within your being?

Part of the problem has been my inability to see the lessons and to just know there's pain and a purpose and waiting to find out what it is.

Wonderful. We would be speaking about some beliefs. There would first be the statement that there would not be one human being who would not be wondering the very same question with the very same feeling of the inability to see the lesson. For as human beings, we are hungry for the knowledge, hungry for the Light, hungry for the union—that we would be One. As human beings we gather together that there might be a marriage between physical and spirit. We decide that that would be our purpose: the marriage of the physical

9

and the spirit. And as you have said so aptly, my dear friend, when we come upon the planet called Earth there is a time of forgetfulness.

We are seeking and seeking that we would be filled and we are not quite sure what we would be filled with. But we want to be filled. We want it, and we wish we really knew what we wanted.

We try to fill ourselves with the love from another being. And we find ourselves empty at times and we don't know why. We try to fill ourselves by reading great teachings, by judging ourselves to see if we fit those teachings. For we have a belief that those beings who are writing the great truths would know something that we do not. We read the pages so that we would find the great truth, the answer. We try to make ourselves be as that being has written on the pages so that we could try it. And every time that we try it, we feel a little empty. We feel as though we are pretending and it is not real. Over and over again as human beings we try to fit ourselves to what we read—to be something wonderful. And we always come up empty.

As human beings we have tried to fill that emptiness with many beliefs. And we decide that we would look within ourselves and see what might be wrong. We find that we have all the humanistic tendencies. And then we judge our very own selves for having them.

We might find that we are jealous, that we have a dislike for another being. We might find that we are angry, and then we judge our anger. We find that we do not have holy and pure thoughts all of the time. So in trying to fill that empty space, we have in one time or another gone within and viewed our imperfections, judging what we find as negative. Then we try to change ourselves. We try to squeeze ourselves into a perfect picture that we might become holy. All of these things of which we have spoken would be beliefs. They would be beliefs. They would be our own creation. We *are* holy beings. We are the holiness itself.

...when we allow the marriage of physical and spirit to occur, everything that we do is from spirit.

10

As human beings, at times we believe that we must do a great thing. We must manifest something wonderful. "What would be my job, my spiritual fulfillment?" And we look for that thing. We look for that job. We look for that teaching in which we might manifest our very own selves that we would be spiritually fulfilled. And we find, my dear friend, that when we allow the marriage of physical and spirit to occur, everything that we do is from spirit. Whether we are walking down the street, embracing our friend, or feeling anger; whatever we do, we are fulfilling our purpose. It cannot be any other way. *Everything* we do is a fulfillment of purpose.

In all of the teachings that have been written, there has been the expression in words of the different occurrences of different beings. And as we have said, when we attempt to view what someone has done in a magazine or in a teaching and we try to fit ourselves to that image, we are trying to become the page. It would be almost as if we would be tearing a page from the book and chewing it up and swallowing it. That it would be within us, so that we could be like the page because the page felt correct. And we would be putting our own experience on hold. As human beings we have been attempting this for a very long time.

We would be saying that we could disregard trying to mold ourselves to the rules and regulations which some other being has created for us to follow. We could allow those rules and regulations to fall away. And we would recognize that deep within our being is I AM. Everything.

When we say, "Deep within my being I AM," what are we saying? We are saying, first of all, that I AM is everything, everything in every dimension. The thing that you call God is I AM. Everything. We would be in the recognition that "out there" is fantasy. Out there—where we believe we go to travel, to learn—is our fantasy creation, our playground, so to speak. Not incorrect or correct—just simply a fact that it is a creation which we have chosen. When we recognize that the journey is within, the journey would be within.

Now when we say: "Allow the marriage of physical and spirit to occur," what on earth are we talking about? It would be quite simple. We would simply say, I OPEN MYSELF TO THE AWARE-

NESS I AM. And what occurs? We open. *You* are the being who is in charge. Each one of us, so to speak. For deep within flowers I AM. And when we awaken to that fact, then we open.

I OPEN MYSELF—I AM. When we say, I OPEN MYSELF, what occurs? All of the places which we term to be energy centers about our being vibrate. We are awakening to the I AM. And when we say, I OPEN MYSELF TO THE AWARENESS I AM, those centers vibrate. Those wonderful centers of our being. Those centers connected to the entire Universe. And when we say, I OPEN MYSELF, they open.

We would be in the statement: I OPEN MYSELF TO THE TOTAL AND COMPLETE FULFILLMENT OF MY PURPOSE. That is all we have to do. It is very simple. If we find that we are struggling with finances—I OPEN MYSELF TO THE ABUNDANCE OF THE UNIVERSE—that is all we have to do—for we are I AM. Everything resides within our being. All of the beliefs would be simply feathers in our hands.

"Welcome home. For I AM everything."

When we see part of ourselves and we see perhaps jealousy—and we say, "I don't want to be jealous, I don't want to be that way," what are we doing? We are denying part of our very own self. How could we not be jealous? How could we not have jealousy within our being if we are everything? When we recognize that we are everything, then we have the choice. So when we recognize that we are in jealousy and we find ourselves saying, "I do not want to be that way," then there could be the remembrance, "I will not deny myself." For each time that we deny part of our being, it returns. And we say, "I do not want to be that way." And what do we do? We be that way. For it would be part of our being—coming forward again and again—begging for union.

And what would we really do? We would say to that part of our being, "Welcome home. For I AM everything." When we recognize that we are vibrating in jealousy, we say, "I am vibrating in

12

jealousy. I am jealous. Welcome home, jealousy. For I AM everything. And now I know that part of my being very well. Welcome home."

When we receive that part of ourselves, we are discarding the judgments. When we welcome that part of our being home, then we are uniting. It would also be called in some books "getting to know ourselves," accepting ourselves for who we are. It would be the same thing in a way. It would be receiving that part of ourself that has been knocking and knocking on our door.

There would be another thought that would be—"I really want to feel good about myself like that person does. I don't really like myself. I want to really love myself." And we say to that part of our very own selves, "Go away. I don't want to be like that." And that part of ourselves, like a magnet, comes back saying, "I want to be part of the One." Saying, "Let me in." And once again we could recognize, "This is part of my very own being coming forward to me." And I would say, "Welcome home—for I AM everything." Welcome home, as if gathering the petals together and allowing them to be in our very own selves. When we receive our very own self, then we are truly vibrating I AM.

As human beings we are in the belief of denying our very own selves. You would not be alone, my dear friend, when you would be saying, "I am confused. I don't know what the lessons are. I want to know what they are. For I wish to receive the pain in a positive way." That statement involves a lot of beliefs. It has the belief that we are struggling to change from negative to positive—in our experience of pain. Human beings running away from the expression of pain.

Firstly, as we have said before, we would be saying, "I welcome home that part of my being." Whatever it would be—"Welcome home. Welcome home, pain."

Then we view that there would be part of our very own expression which we do not understand, "I do not understand the teaching. I do not understand." Then we have created the great unknown.

It is quite simple—for we are in charge.

As human beings we create everything. It would be that we have created what we call the "great unknown," and then we go about for the rest of our life, so to speak, seeking the answers. And what has occurred? *Both* are beliefs. The great unknown is a belief! It does not really exist unless we breathe life into it. And the search for the answer? Because we have created a great unknown, we must create the answer. But *we* have created the unknown! How can it remain the "unknown" if we have the answer? So we say, "I do not know the answer," because we don't! Because we have created the unknown.

We would be in the statement that each would be a creation. And we would be upon the planet to be in the teaching of what we have created. As human beings, to be in the recognition of what has been created. For we are everything.

When we find that we are experiencing pain, we would be in the statement of first receiving the experience. Then we would be in the statement, "I OPEN MYSELF, THAT I AM. I AM EVERY-THING. I OPEN MYSELF TO THE UNDERSTANDING OF THE MANIFESTATION I AM." When we say, "I OPEN MYSELF TO UNDERSTANDING," we are creating that we actually open ourselves to understand. When we say, "I can't understand this," then we are creating that we cannot understand. It is quite simple—for we are in charge. *You* would be in charge. And when you say, "I OPEN MYSELF THAT I WOULD UNDERSTAND," then there is the opening.

When a being recognizes the belief, when a being recognizes that there has been balance and counterbalance, then there exists the choice. The freedom or the re-entry.

Now we would be asking what would be the belief? What would be the occurrences that you believe you do not understand, "Why

14

has this happened in my life?" Speak with us about those things, if you please.

> *Well, there are various losses. Losses—in terms of divorce or distance from a child, or other relationships that have ended. I have questioned the pain that results from the losses. And I say to myself, "I have to go on from here." Maybe all this is from things that happened in past lives and had to be resolved in this lifetime with these people. But in order to accept it, I have to believe there is a reason for it. And confirming that there is a reason enables me to keep going on and say, "Well, it's not just all happening for nothing. There is a reason; there is a lesson." I want to know how to help my child and how to resolve this other relationship. And I want to know that the pain is growth— and deal with it in the right way.*

We would be in the statement that upon entering this dimension there was the decision from your very own spirit, from your very own soul, that there would be the expression of completions within this vibration. That it would be a cleansing process of this life. There would be the balancing and the counterbalancing that there would be completion. There would be the gathering together of those beings in other dimensions in which you term "past lives," and they would be gathering together in this dimension, called the physical, earthly plane, that there would be a completion, that there would be a balance of what has occurred. It would have been the decision of your very own self. And we would be saying that that, in fact, is what has been occurring. The balancing of those times, so to speak.

We would be in the statement that we recognize the need to understand what has occurred that we might continue. It would be quite necessary. That is why we would be communicating on this very day. It would be said also that there is the belief of the balance and the counterbalance. That in one life, so to speak, I was a wonderful being and someone mistreated me. And in this next life, perhaps I mistreated that being and that's why he is mistreating me

15

in this time. There must be a balance. There *is* a balance. It continues on and on, over and over, each turning upon itself, until one day we are asking for understanding and we receive it. *That would be today.*

Until we recognize that that is what occurs—the balance of the counterbalance of the balance—each time we attempt to balance, it turns upon itself. *It is unending.* How do we allow it to be complete? We recognize that we have the choice. We have the choice. We say that it is complete as it is. Complete!

Now, with this example, we could be viewing what we would term four separate lives in which there has been a balance and a counterbalance. And we view the last life and recognize that perhaps this current life is a balance of that one. Now we have a broader picture, so to speak. Now we can see, as we have been speaking, at least four balances and counterbalances. And as we view, we can see that it goes on and on. Each turning upon itself. The Law of the Universe.

And what is the choice? As we view it, we can decide to enter again and balance, knowing that it turns upon itself, over and over. That there is no end and no beginning, that it is part of the cycle of the Universe. When we recognize this to be the truth, we can choose to go enter that balance, that cycle, and try to "straighten it out." However, when we have the truth, when we have the understanding as we are presenting today, that it is unending—it is part of the Universe—why would we choose to enter again? In that example, we would not. And so we would say, "I recognize that I have a choice."

When a being recognizes the belief, when a being recognizes that there has been balance and counterbalance, then there exists the choice. The freedom or the re-entry. It would be quite simple. The freedom or the re-entry.

We would be in the statement that what we believe to be in the past is occurring right now—in a different dimension, so to speak. There is no past and no future—it would be right now in this dimension. When we recognize that that moment is occurring right now, we have the choice. For here we are, viewing the occurrence.

16

My friend, the purpose of those experiences would be that we would be here today—hearing the truth. That yes, there is a release. Yes, there is a great learning in the pain. The learning would be that we have a choice. We have a choice.

As human beings we continue to choose that we would make things all better, so to speak. That perhaps there would be someone with whom we would be trying to communicate in different ways that we would receive a different type of communication—that there could be a flow of Love. And we continue and continue to try to change that being so that we would have the union which we desire. And we recognize that we have a choice. We have the choice to reenter or to remain. Would that be clear?

It has meaning for me, yes.

> ***O**nce we recognize that that space within our being is filled with I AM, then we no longer expect another being to fill us.*

How would we be applying that to the now? What would be the questions? For there has been the question concerning the child and the question of the man.

I think that what you're saying would apply more to the question of the man. The choices of whether to reenter and continue the cycle or end the cycle would apply more to that.

What would you be believing would be the problem with the man?

I guess that I've been compelled to keep reentering and continuing the cycle—to keep replaying it over and over.

Yes, my friend. It is quite difficult. As human beings we try to fill the emptiness with another being. We want to be fulfilled. Once we recognize that that space within our being is filled with I AM, then we no longer expect another being to fill us. When we recognize that the abundance of Love is from the Universe, then we can

17

release our grasp on another, that we would have the Love of the Universe. We could then allow ourselves to receive what that being is able to give. And we would allow ourselves to give what we are capable of giving, for when we attempt to Love of our very own strength, we could crumble to dust at the responsibilities we place upon our very own selves.

When we recognize that we open, that we allow the Love of the Universe to flow, then we are as children once again, playing, allowing the flow to come forward. We are however we are. We accept every part of ourselves. The Love of the Universe is flowing through our being. And how does that occur? We simply open ourselves to the Love of the Universe, that it would flow from our being. It is a simple statement. And then we have given ourselves permission to receive those parts of ourselves which we have judged as non-loving. And we can say, "Welcome home—for the Love of the Universe relieves me of the burdens which I have placed upon myself—that I would receive myself once again—as I AM."

When we have recognized within ourselves those beliefs, those experiences, those choices—then it would not be a question of whether we would be with that man or not. It would not quite be a choice of that. For he would be a fine man—he would be quite a fine man. However, it would be a question of whether we would want to be reacting and interacting in the same principles which we have tried to change over and over. It would be the releasing of expectations for both beings.

When we have spirit within our being, when we are filled with the Love of the Universe, then we have great abundance within our being. Then we do not need the Love of that being to fill our very own selves. However, we receive the Love of that being, for the Love of that being is the manifestation of the Love of the Universe. And we open ourselves to the view of the Universe.

When we open to the Universe and we allow the flow to continue, then we release ourselves of the expectations. We release ourselves from trying to hold on to any being. We release ourselves from the constriction that we feel within our being and the pains within our heart—for we have been clinging on. For we have tasted the Love and we want it. We want it. *And it is ours. From the Source.*

When we expect that other being to fulfill our needs for the Love of the Universe, we could be crumbling to dust in the waiting.

When we receive the Love of the Universe by saying, "I OPEN MYSELF TO THE LOVE OF THE UNIVERSE," then we are filled. We would be saying it often, that we would be filled. Then when that being would be wanting to share Love, share the Universe, there would be a marriage of that energy of Love. We would receive and give at the same time. For when we open to the Love of the Universe, we release ourselves of the bondage of Love. We release ourselves from the burden of seeking Love. For then we *are* Love. We are everything. We would be the Love and feel it flowing through our being. It would be, so to speak, giving ourselves a break.

It would not so much be deciding "Would I discard this relationship?" For it would present itself in another form—for has it not, over and over? It would be more in the decision, "I will not reenter the energy that has been manifesting in this relationship. I would be viewing what I have been expecting from this man and our unions. And I would recognize that those expectations are fulfilled from I AM."

When we recognize that every expectation is fulfilled from within, then we release ourselves from the balance and the counterbalance. Then we are not seeking; we have found the marriage of physical and spirit within our very own beings. Then we are releasing ourselves that we might play as children. That we might be with that man as a child. That the two might be as children—released from the bondages of the balance and the counterbalance. The expectations, the needs—they would be free. And we would be as children.

When children play, they play. They could be walking down the path and one child might say, "I'm going to go and kick my feet in the water." And the other child might say, "I'm going to go play in the sand." And they would do what they would do. For one would be knowing that they would be kicking their feet in the water—that would be what they want to do, even if the other being is playing in the sand. Children do what they need to be doing.

They don't say, "Well, I really want to kick my feet in the water but if that being is going to play in the sand, maybe I should

19

play in the sand too." Children do what they would do. And they play together. Whatever they are doing, they are playing together. For they have released each other from the bondage of balance and counterbalance. Never fear. There need not be the choice of never being with this wonderful man again. It would be the choice, as we have stated, of playing as children. Would that be clear?

Yes. Quite clear. Thank you.

> *...we are here in the fulfillment of hope. We are here that there would be the foundation built that we would trust our hopes.*

There would be the statement that in our lives there has been the seeking of hope and the fulfillment of hope. And each time we have found that the hope has had a hollow foundation. And we have been in the fear of nonfulfillment of hope. For each time the hope has been dashed to the ground, so to speak, we have experienced the negativity of the hope—the unfulfillment. And we would be in the statement, my friend, that we are here in the fulfillment of hope. We are here that there would be the foundation built that we would trust our hopes. That we would know within our being that that for which we hope would be fulfilled. That would be why we are gathering together. That the hope would be fulfilled. For there has been much concern that everything would be correct.

[Pretty Flower embraces the woman in her arms as she continues:]

Drink of your fill of this moment, my friend. Drink of your fill. We know everything about you. Everything. Everything you have ever done or said. Even those things that you wish you had never said—we know those things—and we love every part of you. Even those things which you abhor when you remember them—we love those parts of you. Even those thoughts which you wish you would never think—we Love those thoughts. We Love everything about you. Everything. There is not one part of you that we do not Love. We know everything, and we Love everything. Never fear.

There would be no secrets, my friend. It is a belief. Belief of a secret. It is merely a belief. For we know everything and we Love everything about you—everything—in every dimension.

We are quite happy to be vibrating together, my friend. The Love of the Universe fills your entire being. The blessings of the Universe flow forward with every breath. Each being who comes in contact with you sees the Light shining forward. And they are filled with the Light. Just by the recognition as it shines from your very being.

When we want to do something and we want to be something, it is because we already are and it is begging to be manifest. We already are.

The gifts of the Universe reside within your being. For deep within I AM. Everything. Everything that we would ever desire. When we want something and when we want to be a certain way—we wonder, "Can I do this?" We would be in the statement: When we want to do something and we want to be something, it is because we already *are* and it is begging to be manifest. We already *are*. Know this to be a truth. For how would we even know we want to be that way? It already exists within our very being.

Now, what would we be communicating, my dear friend? What would be your desire?

Is there anything else I should know that I haven't asked about?

"How can I cease from seeking?" would be the question. Why would we cease from seeking? We would cease from seeking so that we might be. It would be as we have stated: When we seek, we go "out there" somewhere. When we cease from seeking, we recognize that everything is correct. Enlightenment is not something out there. It is not something we become. It is something we are already. When we wish for anything it is because we already are. And it is begging to be manifest. When we believe that we must

21

attain a certain spiritual ladder, so to speak, then we once again deny I AM. Each time, my friend, that you find yourself seeking to be something else, reside back within—being I AM.

When one being is enlightened, every being is enlightened. For we are all One in the same. Every being is One in the same. When we hear of a Master who has ascended, know that we are ascending even as we hear of it. When we see the Light shining from another being, the reason that we see the Light shining is because we are looking through the Light. Everything which we desire is already occurring within our being. That is why it is coming to our consciousness.

All the rules and regulations are creations. Creations. Then we have the choice to reenter those rules and abide by them and struggle with them—or recognize that we are free of them. All the beliefs. We are the creators. Everything—I AM—everything.

And we would be as children...And allow ourselves to play.

When the children dance upon the petals of the flowers, their tiny toes barely touch the petals. The reason that their toes touch the petals at all is that there would be a marriage: The petals would feel the wonderful joy of the children, and the children would feel the blessings of the petals.

And we would be as children. We would be saying to ourselves, to that wonderful child, "I am with you once again and we can play." And we would allow ourselves to play—sometimes by ourselves—that we would be uninhibited in expression. We might find ourselves skipping along. We might find ourselves picking up a rock and throwing it. Or humming a tune. Plucking the petals from a flower. Twirling about. Swinging our legs from the branch of a tree. Whatever we would feel like doing—for no particular reason. It would be a gift to the child. It would be remembering to play. For as children the Wisdom of the Universe manifests in spontaneity, for we are without rules. It would be a gift: I AM to I AM.

Dear wonderful woman, the work is great for the desires are great: That there might be fulfillment in the planet, that there would be fulfillment in the family, that there would be fulfillment in self. And we are in the statement that the fulfillment exists now. We simply say, "I OPEN MYSELF TO THE TOTAL AND COMPLETE FULFILLMENT OF PURPOSE." And what is the purpose? The marriage of physical and spirit. That we might manifest I AM—without judgment—just knowing that whatever we do—I AM. Everything that you do is perfect. Everything. Everything.

We are never apart, my friend. We are always together. When you breathe the breath, we breathe the breath together. When you place your fingers into the water, we feel the water. When you hear the music, we are the notes. We are everything together. We are never apart.

It would be just asking. It would be the simple statement of whatever you would want the fulfillment to be—manifest. The simple statement: I OPEN MYSELF. I AM. I DESIRE TO MANIFEST. And then there would be the statement of the desire—it would be quite correct and simple. And complete. For there has been much reacting, painful reacting. And it would be time to be vibrating as the creator. The releasing of the balance and counterbalance that the pendulum would cease swinging back and forth and be laid to rest. That we would be in alignment—and then we would create.

Never fear. Every action is our action. There is no such thing as being alone. For we are never apart. And the wings of the angels would be about you. And when you rest the body in sleep, there would be many spirit beings about. They would hold you in their arms. For there is much Love in the Universe. It is unending. It is being expressed over and over again in many, many ways. And we have opened together that we might experience the Love of the Universe in every expression. Never fear. We would be together.

The blessings of the Universe reside within your being, my friend. See how much you can receive. It is only the beginning. For we fill and fill, more and more, receiving more and more the Love of the Universe, the abundance of the Universe. Filling our very beings, more and more until it is even spilling over. And it never ceases from spilling over, for it never ceases to flow.

Once the door is open, it does not close. Never fear. Remember, my friend, to play. We would be together especially then. Remember to play.

***

The Story of the Pocket

Once upon a time there was a child and there was a teacher. And the child was walking beside the teacher. And they would be continuing down the path together.

And the child said to the teacher, "May I place my hand in your pocket?"

And the teacher said, "No, you may not."

And the child was sad. And the child was confused, for the teacher had given the child everything. Everything. Everything. And then the child said to the teacher, "Why may I not place my hand in the pocket of your garment?"

And the teacher continued walking. And the teacher said to the child, "Do you feel that I do not love you?"

And the child said, "You have given me everything. And still you would not allow me to place my hand in the pocket of your garment."

And they continued along.

And the teacher said to the child, "Would you be feeling that I would not want you to be with me?"

And the child said, "You have allowed me to be with you everywhere. We are never apart. And still you will not allow me to place my hand in the pocket of your garment."

And they continued.

And the teacher embraced the child and said, "Are you fearful that I would not embrace you again?"

And the child said, "You have embraced me every day. You have embraced me in every instance. And still you will not allow me to place my hand in the pocket of your garment."

And they continued. And they continued. And then they came to a resting place. And the teacher decided that he would be in the flowing of the water of the river. And he did remove his garment and he placed it on the side of the river.

And while he was in the river the wonderful child said, "Now I will place my hand in the pocket of the garment of the teacher." And he picked up the garment.

And he searched and he searched for the pocket. And there was no pocket in the garment of the teacher.

***

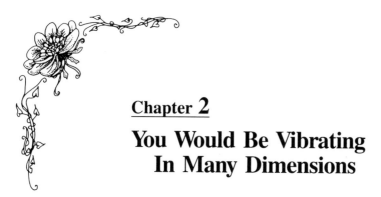

Chapter 2

You Would Be Vibrating In Many Dimensions

We could call the journey into what you would term "past lives," the journey into other dimensions.

Can you tell me about my past lives?

Yes, my friend. We could be speaking of other times. We would be in the statement before we begin, that we have a belief. The belief tells us that we have had "past lives"; and we would be in the statement that that would be a conceptual misconception, for we would be residing in the "now." There would not be the existence of the past or the existence of what we term the future. Everything would be vibrating at the present.

We could call the journey into what you would term "past lives," the journey into other dimensions. For we would be viewing parts of our very own self as we vibrate in the present. Would that be clear?

Sort of.

We would be in the statement that everything is occurring as we speak. There would be many dimensions in which we are vibrating.

Simultaneously?

27

Yes, my friend. And when we open ourselves that we might view what we call "past lives," what we are actually doing is opening the door that we might view the dimension of that vibration in the present.

We have created, as human beings, the belief of time. And we would recognize that it would be but a belief. It would be very interesting if humankind were to come to recognize the truth of this statement.

**

In every other dimension there would be our very own selves vibrating in the stories therein.

When we have the belief of "past lifetimes"—there would be the recognition that they would be vibrating in the present. When we view our time we would be in the recognition that as we vibrate here, we are vibrating in every dimension and choosing to manifest as we do in the present. In every other dimension there would be our very own selves vibrating in the stories therein.

When there has been a completion in another dimension, it may manifest in this dimension and we would find ourselves changing. We would be in the process of awakening to those dimensions. That would be why so many beings have been asking about what they call "past lives." For, in fact, they would be wishing to know what would be occurring. It would be the process of opening that we would know our very own selves—more and more—and better and better.

We would find that there had been in the country of France, as we are speaking in the current vocabulary of past, the doctor, so to speak. The physician. There would be in that time as the physician many receivings of remuneration for the work being done. And there would be the recognition that there was confusion within the being in the correctness of receiving remuneration. In the decision to receive the monies, there was a part of the very being within that went to sleep. *Not that it would be incorrect to receive money*

28

but that the very self had charged that it would be incorrect. And the spark of Light from within felt betrayed. And the spark of Light within dimmed, so to speak, in that dimension.

There has been much work through the years, has there not? Going toward the Light. Opening for deeper understanding of self and of the Light. Opening to the manifestation of the purposes which would be within. That we would be wondering what we would be about in this dimension. And then deciding that we would manifest amongst the people who would be the closest to our very own vibration. Making many decisions that would be in place of the remuneration—that we would be in the decision of the fulfillment of purpose in this vibration. It would be part of the cause and effect of other dimensions.

We would be in the statement that when we have the belief of balance and counterbalance, what occurs in our life? We have, as human beings, the belief that if we have been a certain way in one time that we must "make up for it" in another time—that there would be balance and counterbalance. We have the belief that in one time if we were to be in a destructive way—in another time we would have destruction be upon us that there would be a balance. We would be in the statement that it would be a belief. *It would be a belief.*

When we recognize that it is a belief, then we are viewing the entire process. As human beings allowing the marriage of physical and spirit to come forward, we have the choice. What is the choice? The choice would be: Do we want to re-enter balance and counter-balance? Do we believe we can go "in there" and make everything all right and correct? Or, do we recognize that it *is* complete? *It becomes complete when we have the recognition of the truth that it is a belief.* When we are recognizing our beliefs, then we are free. Then we have the choice. Then we have the choice.

***

*The belief of balance and counterbalance is
unending. It turns in upon itself, over and over
again, until we recognize that it is a belief.*

*[A man asks:] I would like to know my soul's purpose this
time on earth—and the lessons I'm supposed to be learning.*

There would be the statement: We would be the creators. There
would also be the understanding that we have the belief of balance
and counterbalance. We have the belief that as we are in what we
call one lifetime, we would be in atonement, so to speak, in the
next. And that it would continue until we would be perfect beings.
It would be in the statement of those truths, that there would be a
type of misconception.

There would be in the times of France, in the country of
Mongolia, in the land of England, and in western South America
the vibrations of the warrior—*that being who would be in the battles
of his very own self—manifested in a battlefield.*

At times there would be those beings who would be in the
gathering together with your being for the preservation of the Peoples
of the tribes, so to speak. Within the being there would be the belief
that then there would be the necessity of the residing in peace, in
order to balance. In order to balance and counterbalance. And in
this particular vibration, here and now, would be the receiving of
this truth, as it is being said.

The belief of balance and counterbalance is unending. It turns
in upon itself, over and over again, until we recognize that it is a
belief. It would not be *not* occurring—but the belief of the purpose
would be what would be continuing the balance and the counterbalance. When we are in recognition that it is a belief, the belief that
we must "atone"—that we must be one way in order to make up
for another way—then we are in the freedom from the belief.

Hear the words: When we recognize that it is a belief, then
we have the choice. For we are free. We are in balance. We are
complete. We are One. And there is the cycle, over and over, of
the balance and counterbalance. And we could chose to enter that
cycle any time we would want to. That we would be in the balance
of peace and war. Peace and war. Or we could be as we are. At One.

For it would be the purpose in this vibration to be in the recognition I AM. To be in the recognition of the marriage of physical and spirit that we would be at One within our very own selves. When we say, I OPEN MYSELF TO THE TOTAL AND COMPLETE FULFILLMENT OF PURPOSE, then everything we do is fulfillment of purpose. In the union. In the recognition that it would be a belief. That we are I AM. It would be giving ourselves the wings, so to speak. The freedom of our being. The freedom from the belief.

It would be the next step—the releasing of self from the bondage of the belief of balance and counterbalance. It would not be that it would not be occurring—for I AM is everything. And when we view that I AM is everything, my friend, then we know we can manifest in any balance and counterbalance. We can choose to be in any balance and counterbalance—in any one. However, as human beings entering the earthly vibration, we sometimes forget that it would be a belief of balance and counterbalance. And we become involved in the cycle, over and over again, one lifetime after another, trying to balance our very actions—trying to be perfect once again. When finally one day we hear the words. We hear the words to give ourselves the freedom to be in the "now," to be in I AM—to be vibrating. To give ourselves permission to recognize I AM. Then we have the choice of how we would manifest.

We could choose—as we have many times—to be dipping into the balance and counterbalance of what we call "lifetimes." However, here we are—right now, recognizing that we are in the freedom of balance and counterbalance that we might manifest I AM. For the time is at hand that we would be One. That we would be in the consciousness of our being. That we would be awake.

***

That within ... there would be the marriage of the Darkness and the Light.

I would like to understand my past life involvement with my

31

ex-husband. It was a difficult marriage that lasted many years. How did this all come about?

In the time of Rome there was the great warrior, who would be your very own self in the masculine representation. And there would be in that time, the being you have termed your husband—who would also be the warrior.

He would be within his being, and you would be within your being. And there would be the viewing by your being of the Darkness within that being. And there would be the puzzlement within your being of the Darkness that you viewed. The Darkness within that being.

There would then be the occurrence of the battle. And within the great battle would be the raising of the swords of the two. That the battle would continue and continue—through the day and through the night. And through the day and through the night. That there would be on the third day—the battle still continuing.

And there would be the realization of the meaning of the battle. For there was the recognition of the Light within your being. And there was the recognition of the Darkness within his being. And there was the great battle. And you did raise your sword that you might cut him asunder. For he would be on the ground, in the essence.

And you would be viewing and he would be saying, "We are One in the same. We are One in the same." And you would be saying, "You are the Darkness and I am the Light." And you did take the sword to pierce the heart of that being—that it would be complete in the slaying of the Darkness.

And there arose from that being the Spirit. And he did point his finger at your being and say, "You have cut me asunder. You have cut me asunder and I will return."

Then there would be the time together in the present. And within your being, in the traveling through the different dimensions before the entry to this plane, there would be the awareness of the need of the marriage of the Darkness and the Light. And in the awareness of your being, in the spirit of your being, the teachings had come forward—first in one dimension, then in another dimen-

32

sion—learning that there was the Darkness and the Light upon the Universe. And that in the marriage of the two would be the completion.

There would be within yourself then the regretting. The regret. For the occurrence of the battle would be in the remembrance of your being. And you would be in the remembrance of the marriage that would be occurring in the teachings of the Darkness and the Light. There would be part of your being that would be wanting to be in the manifesting of the marriage of the Darkness and the Light. For there was the remembrance of the slaying.

Then there would be the decision: That there would be in the traveling through the dimensions, the manifestation of the lesson— the marriage of the Darkness and the Light taking form. Taking form. Manifesting. Manifesting. Until there would be in the present life the manifestation in the physical form of those two beings. And there would be within your very being—the determination to be in the marriage of the Darkness and the Light. That they would be One.

But still there appeared to be the great struggle—the great struggle. For there would be the yearning within to be in the marriage of the Darkness and the Light, that it would be complete. And there would be the struggle. That part of your being would be—as if by a magnet—pulled away from the Darkness. Yet you would be determined to be with the Darkness. Determined.

There would be then the statement: It would be in the present teaching—as we vibrate together in the now—that within every being is the Darkness and the Light. And when we are in the marriage of the Darkness and the Light, it would be within our very beings. *Within our very beings would be the marriage of our own Darkness and our own Light.* Within our being. For this would be the teaching coming forward—that there would be the recognizing that within your very own self is the Darkness and the Light. It would be One in the same. One in the same. For there has been the seeking to be One, the seeking *outside of self* in the physical manifestation.

There would be then the releasing of self. That there would be the understanding of releasing that being, releasing that man, even in the present vibration—even in the now. The releasing of

33

that being in this very second. "I release you. I relinquish you. I allow you to re-establish your being within yourself, that you might find the Light within your being. For you must find the Light within your being, as I have found the Darkness within my being. That within your being would be the marriage of the Light and the Darkness. That I might allow the marriage within my being." That it would be complete. That he would be on his way—even as we speak now. On his way—to seek the Light within his being. For he had been wanting the same, wanting the marriage of the Darkness and the Light. And he would be in the embodiment of the Darkness. Whatever he would do would be the expression of the Darkness. And there would be the magnet in him that would say "no"—yet he would be in the manifestation of the Darkness.

And there would be the blessings of the Universe upon the two. That within each, there would be the marriage of the Darkness and the Light. Within the being, within the self—the marriage.

For as we have journeyed through the dimensions, we have carried the teachings. We have carried within our very being the learning of the message—the marriage of the Darkness and the Light. And we have, in this physical vibration, been in the receiving of the truth. And we have viewed that in the present, within the being, would be the secret of the truths of the ages. For there has been the seeking of the Darkness—that there would be the marriage.

And we would be in the statement that within the self is everything. Everything. And we have been in the fear of the Darkness of our being. For we had the judgment of old that we would be only the Light—only the Light. And there would be the statement that we are I AM—*everything*. That there would not be the fear of the Darkness. For the Darkness is manifestation I AM. Light is manifestation I AM. That there is occurring, even as we speak, the marriage.

That there would not be the need of allowing any other manifestation to occur. For there has been the marriage. In the concept of time it would appear that it has taken "forever" to allow the releasing and the marriage. And we would be in the statement that in infinity it would be the tiniest second—that there would be the joy of the releasing and the marriage. That would be complete, my friend.

That's good.

Yes, it is good.

It's wonderful to release.

Yes, my friend. It is released. It is a *great* release. It is no longer there. For the child would be vibrating in the understanding of the truths of the Universe. The secret is in the innocence of the child, for therein lies the truth.

[Pretty Flower continues with this final statement to the same woman:]

My friend, there is the belief that there would be life and death, and life and death. And that we would be in the occurrence of life. When we view the vibrations upon the planet called Earth we have heard many beings saying that there would be the "speeding up," so to speak. And we would be in the statement, my dear friend, that within the incarnation of this particular vibration which you term to be your life, within this vibration, this would be the fourth life, so to speak. This would be the fourth life within this life. For you have decided not to incarnate again. That there would be the beginning—and the completion. Does it not appear to be another time, another life? It would be correct. This would be in the beginning of another, for you would be new.

The spirit within your being would be in the enjoyment of the newness of your being. For this is the beginning of another time. Another—what you term to be "life." For you have allowed the completion of the rest.

***

Whatever we are doing now in our present vibration would be a mirror image of what is manifest in other dimensions.

[A woman who was very interested in her past lives asks:]
What past life experiences are affecting my present life now?

35

The dimensions that would be directly affecting this present vibration which you term your life—would be the time in the country of England. In the countryside, there would be a cottage. And in the cottage would be the father and the young daughter. The mother would have been passing on early in the child's life. And that child would be your very own self. She would be with a long white apron around her being, around her dress. And she would be loving her father very much. And she would be about the cottage, the very small cottage, keeping it clean and tidy. Keeping the windows clear that they might be seeing within and without. Gathering together the flowers to place upon the table.

In that dimension, there would be the time when the father would become very sick. And the daughter would be in the nursing of the father, caring for his very being. There would be the beseeching of the Father in Heaven, as those words have been stated, that the father be healed. And the father was healed. The father was healed in spirit and made the journey through the transition. But the daughter felt discouraged. The daughter felt betrayed. *For she did not understand that the healing did occur in spirit.* That the journey was complete and whole. That the father was healed. And the daughter, my friend—the spark of hope fell from her being. For she was not in the understanding of the healing of that very father.

We would be in the statement that there would be even in this present life the seeking of the fulfillment of hope. And there would still remain the doubt—and the fear of placing full hope. There would be in the remembrance of that time, the recognition that in this life, in this present vibration, there would be the opening to the truth. When we ask, we receive. It is as simple as that. *When we ask, we receive.*

In the human being, there would be at times the misunderstanding of the manifestation of what we are receiving. Believe, my friend. *Believe that the foundation for the fulfillment of hope is trust and surrender.* We would be in the statement that we would be present on the planet called Earth that we might be in the fulfillment of hope. You have asked, my friend, and in asking you receive. For when you ask, "What other lifetimes are directly affecting this present one?"— that would be the asking. That would be the request.

36

The hope that there would be fulfillment. And as you have asked, you would receive—in the lesson—the lesson in the fulfillment of hope.

At the present moment, that would be the lesson coming forward. Every dimension. Every—what you term "past life"—every dimension has a direct bearing upon our very beings. For we are everything. And this would be the lesson coming forward at this time. The trusting in the fulfillment of hope.

Did I have a life in Atlantis?

We would answer this question in two ways, my friend. We would be bringing to the attention the obsession with the past. Once again, we would be in the statement that it is the present. It is vibrating even now.

And yes, we would also be answering the question. First we would be stating: When we ask another for information of our very own being, what are we doing? We are in the belief that they know more than we do. My dear friend, my dear wonderful woman, there would be the statement: Deep within your being resides everything. Everything. Everything you ever thought you would want to know. Why would you be asking about Atlantis? Because you know deep within your being and the vibration therein!

In the time in which you are referring to as Atlantis, there would be those beings gathered together near the end of the civilization, so to speak, gathering together supplies. For there would be the recognition that it would be the end. It would be the end of the civilization as we would have known it. And in that time there would have been a woman, the teacher. And the teacher would be gathering the students together. For there were those who heard and knew the truths gathering together that they might depart into what they termed the wilderness. For there was the recognition that there would be great change. And in the change there would be the parting of many beings.

So the teacher would be gathering together those students, that they might journey and begin again. Students of what? Students of the manifestation in the physical plane. Students of creation. That they might be learning how to manifest in the physical plane.

And you, as the teacher, working with the other teachers, were in creation. That there was the creation of the civilization. There was the creation of the temples. There was the creation of the expansiveness of Light within the temples. There was the recognition of the total and complete I AM. Upon the mere thought was the creation.

However, there were those beings who wished to be in power. We would be saying this, not that it would be correct or incorrect, but simply a statement of fact. There were those beings who would be in the creation of fulfillment of power. And you felt yourself shrinking away from those beings and being quite careful of what you would teach the students—for fear that there would be those among the students who would be wanting to be in the power.

And there was, as we have said, the gathering together of those children, of those students. That there would be journeying to the wilderness to begin again. There have been many times where you have gathered beings together to begin again. And, my dear friend, that is what you do in this particular vibration—gather beings together, that they might have the courage to begin again. In one form or another, whatever we are doing now in our present vibration would be a mirror image of what is manifest in the other dimensions.

Was I a shaman in the southwest of the United States in the past?

We would find that that energy would be in the country of Tibet. The name perhaps would not be "shaman," but the teachings would be the same. The teachings would be quite the same, for there would be the learning of being One in the physical vibration. There would be what had been termed in that time discipline. There would be the display of those powers of healing. Those powers of teleportation. Those powers of opening to the God within. Those powers, once again, of creation. There would be in that vibration, in that dimension, the total surrender.

There have been many times where the issue of power has come forward. And there has been a fear of the power, for there has been a judgment of the power. For there have been those who have misused, so to speak, the power, that they have become consumed when they were in the vibration of One in the Light. They felt the power flowing through their being—and they directed. And you viewed that occurrence. And with fear you viewed their misuse of power. And with fear you made the statement that *you* would not be in the misuse of power. However, in the statement, you have denied your very own self the flowing of the powers of the Universe. You have denied your very own self the God within.

It would be time, my friend, to be opening and releasing that fear. Releasing the fear that you would misuse your very own power. It would be time, my friend, to be in the strength of the Universe—as in the time we have mentioned. To take the risk, so to speak. We could continually tip-toe about, or we could take the risk and open wide—that we would be fulfilled. That we would be fulfilled.

When we make the judgment of the misuse of power, what are we doing? We are denying our very own selves, my friend—for we are everything. *And everything about us, in every dimension, is a manifestation of our very own selves.* When we say we do not want to be "that way," we are denying our very own selves. And what would we be doing? We would be viewing that part of our self—that manifestation—and we would be saying: "Welcome home. For you are part of me. For I AM everything. For I AM."

When we view another misusing power, so to speak—when we have made that judgment—what do we do? We say, "That is a manifestation of my very own self, for I AM everything and I AM. Welcome home." When we deny part of our very own being, what happens? The balance and counterbalance keeps occurring. It keeps coming forward that we would view our very own selves. And in distaste we turn away. And what do we see when we turn away? The same part of our very own self, manifest in a different way. Until one day we finally say, "That is my very own self I have been denying. Welcome home. I welcome that part of myself which I have been abhorring, which I have judged as incorrect. I welcome that part of myself home, for I AM everything."

When we have received every part of our being, then we have the choice. When we deny—we have no choice at all. The blessings

39

of the Universe reside within your being, my friend. Would there be more?

Yes. What was my most recent past life?

We would not be speaking of past lives again, for we are complete in the statements of past lives. Do not be disappointed, my friend, for we have spoken much of past lives. And we would be in the statement once again: It would be a mis-belief. It would be a belief that would be contorted to our belief of linear time. Everything— everything—vibrates in the present. Every dimension which we term "past" vibrates in the present. The most recent, my friend—is everything. Every, every vibration.

***

There would be the union of beings. Where there would be the receiving of one another, without the fear and without the manipulation of each other...that they would be One.

[A woman asks about her past lifetimes and Pretty Flower begins with a time in Atlantis:]

In the time of Atlantis would be the gathering together of those beings who would be working with the energies coming forward from the great crystals. In the working with the energies coming forward would be the experience of those beings themselves *becoming* the transformers. In that form there were several, in the number of five, who would be gathered together. For there was the recognition that even though there were the great crystals in physical manifestation, there were the five who recognized that they themselves were the transformers. There would have been the relinquishing of the pleasures of the civilization that the work would be completed at that time. And there would be those beings who would be in the semblance of being transformers that they would be vibrating with the energies at hand.

There would have been, however, in that civilization the number of three who would be separate and in control of those beings in the manifestation of experiments with the energies. The three who would be in control would be termed "the capping of the pyramid." And those three would be in dis-union of selves. Those three would be the beginning of the fall of the civilization.

However, during those times, the five would be pure of heart and mind and spirit and would be in the vibration of transformers; that there would be the manifestation of the teachings coming forward. The three who would have been in charge, however, would be fearful of the teachings coming forward for it would be the teachings that all would be One. And the three would be in the recognition of the power in which the five would be vibrating. And the three would wish to be in the containing of the power in their very own selves.

There would be, at that time, the releasing of the five by the three—and that would have meant the disintegration of the body physical of the five. Even as it was in the process, the five recognized what was occurring, and there was the decision to be in what we have termed "ascension" of the five. The five would have been in ascension before the decline of the civilization called Atlantis. And the five, after the ascension, would have been placing themselves in the form of the star—above the energies of the civilization. That there would be the receiving of the destruction and it would be in the assistance of balancing the whole experience. For there would be many who would be upsetting the balance and the counterbalance of their very own beings for which they would be in cycle after cycle. Fear not, my friend, for the work that had been done by your very own self in the dimension of Atlantis would be in the completion of many times. It would also have been in the service of many that they would be in the completion. Much work had been done.

[Pretty Flower continues with simultaneous lifetimes the woman had chosen:]

41

And we would have, in the country of Austria, the being in the form of the man traveling about carrying the news from one village to another. He would be in the joyfulness of his being.

And, in another time quite close to that period, in the country of Germany, there would be another being—that being being yourself—where would be simultaneous lifetimes.

And in the country of Germany the very tall man would be in the blackness of his dressing and clothing, for it would be the style of the day. And there would be the cape about his shoulders and there would be the tallness of the black hat. Everything except for the material close to his physical being would be in black. And he would be in the secretness of communications at that time. For there would be in what would be termed the "negativity" of his being—the selling of souls.

However, even in the work of the being in the Darkness, would be the service of the balance to many beings. For they would be in need of recognizing their very own selves and of the action they would be in.

And there would have been in the simultaneous time in the country of Austria that being so filled with joy, traveling about, carrying the messages to the people. And it would have been a decision of your being to be in the incarnation of two. That two balances would complete each other in the recognition that there would not be the judgment of favor for either—that it would be the presentation of the entire being. For we would be everything. And there would be the decision at that time to be receiving the information of the two lives, that there would be the fear removed from the being— that the balance would be experienced at the time. Never fear, even in the present vibration, the balance of those two vibrations would be complete.

[Pretty Flower continues with another lifetime:]

There would be the time in the East, in the land of Tibet, the gathering together of the great teachers. And in the mountain there would be the studying of the great teachings. However, in that time would be the rebellion of the being, for there was the recognition

42

that the teachings would have been growing stale on the pages. That the being would be calling that there be action. And there was the great teacher who would be saying to the student that there would be the action within self—within self.

And there would be the student who would be gathering his being together and traveling to be in solitude. For there was discontent in the non-action—in the viewing of the non-action of those great teachers. In the solitude and in the mountains there was the cleansing of the being and the recognition of the journey within. And upon the returning of that being, the teachers would be in the knowing of the experience. For each one in turn, in their youth, had made the same journey and had the same restlessness and the same discontent with the non-action. And they would be in the awareness of the youth returning with the wisdom of his very own self.

[Pretty Flower goes on to another time, this one involving her husband:]

There would be the being in the West as the pioneers—with that particular being who you have known in this present vibration as the husband. The two together would be traveling across the country in wagons and experiencing the newness and the hardships of the land. They would be of the first who would be traveling. In that time there would be the learning and the receptivity of those nations termed the red-skinned.

Coming forward, there would be of the two, the woman who would be yourself, who would be in the knowing that there could be the trusting of those peoples of the red-skinned nations. And in the bravery and in the trusting of the truth of your being, you did venture forth even against the warnings of the man termed to be the husband. That you did venture forth to those peoples, carrying the treasures of your being. For you would be amongst the very few who would be in the giving of the gifts which would be your very own treasures.

It would not be those things which you could do without— as others had attempted. It would be the treasures of your being. That

you would be carrying them in the satchel, in front of your being—
from the heart. And there would be the recognition of those peoples
as you would stand amongst them in the strength of your being
without fear. For you were in the recognition of the rightness of
your being.

And they would be receiving. They would be placing the holy
blanket upon the ground that you might kneel and they might kneel
in the circle—and that you would be presenting the treasures of
your being. There would be the locket of hair. There would be the
tiny wooden box carrying the teeth of the grandmother. There would
be the ribbons that would have been about the garment of the
child—the ribbon of blue that would be in the holiness—for there
would have been the losing of the child at birth. There would have
been the cloth that would be in the altar of the holiness of the past.
And there would be the links of gold coming from the very small
time-piece. Carrying together all of these items—gathered together—carried from across the sea.

These presentations would be made to the peoples. And the
peoples of the nation—the people of the skin of red—would be in
the recognition of the offerings of the treasures of your being. They
would be in the recognition of the truth coming forward from your
being and the desire to be One—to co-inhabit the land. And there
would be the gathering together of those treasures by the chief of
the people. That he would be carrying the treasures to the holy
ground, to the altars. And he would bid you join him at the great
altars. That you would be standing to the side and that he would
be placing those precious gifts on the altars of the ancestors. There
they would reside for many times to come.

There would then be the journeying of yourself in returning
to the husband and those beings who would be vibrating in fear.
As you would be returning, the peoples of the skin of red would
be carrying with them the nourishment of the land—in the sharing
of the feast of union. And there would be those other women who
would be coming forward in the fearfulness of their being that they
would be seeing the holiness and the comradeship that had been
shared.

Many of the beings would be in the settlement of the land.

And this would be the one settlement with the peoples of the skin of red where there would be the union of the beings. Where there would be the receiving of one another, without the fear and without the manipulation of each other. Two peoples of the planet called Earth co-inhabiting that they would be One.

> *[This reading concludes with one final "dimension" the woman shared with her husband:]*

There would be in the times and in the location of Salem, the two in secret having great fun. There had been the mixtures of the potencies and the knowingness of the beings in the playing with the powers at hand. There would also be at that time the experience together, back to back at the burning of the stake. Never fear, for the two were above, viewing the physical. And they were in knowledge and also in sorrow that the times could not receive the information coming forward. For there was Darkness about that part of the planet in the arts of knowing.

***

> *We have been in the recognition that as human beings we are going toward the Light—and toward the Light—and toward the Light—for we wish the marriage to be complete. And we would recognize that the Light is within. And that, in fact, we are the Light.*

[Another woman, asking about past lives, is told:]

There would be a similar time in the vibration of Lemuria and in the vibration of Atlantis. In those times there would be the gathering together in the temples. There would have been many times in the temples. For there would be the recognition of the need for the union within. That there would be a marriage within the being of what we have been terming male and female. And those beings within the temples would be in the recognition of the androgenous being. They would have been vibrating in the secret, so to speak, for there would be in the external vibration of the communities those beings who had forgotten the purpose.

And deep within the temples would be the residing of your being. For even in the temples where the decay began, there would have been that recognition of the falling away of those vibrations of the whole. And there would be the statement that deep within the temple, in the center, did you reside, for you were in the very blossom, so to speak.

There has never been the falling away of your being from the vibration of One. There would be the honor of One deep within your being. And there would be the recognition that those beings about would be coming forward as in a magnet, for they recognize the Light deep within.

In the time in the temples would be the beginning of the falling away of the truths. And there was great burden on those beings residing in the center. For in their wisdom and in their all-encompassing consciousness they recognized the falling away. That there would be those beings creating themselves to be separate—that they might re-experience the physical union of their very own selves. Not incorrect or correct—that they would be in the vibration of flesh and they would be wanting to be re-experiencing the vibration of physical union on the planet called Earth.

There would have been in the center in the temples, those beings gathering together in great concern. For there was the wisdom in the One. There was the holiness in the One. There was the vibration of the entire Universe in the One which we would term androgenous being. There would be the recognition that there was the hesitation of those learned beings about your very being in the center—the hesitation to allow the occurrence to take place. For in the recognition of the falling away was also the recognition of the crumbling of the temple from which they reside. And there had never been the vibration of those beings without the temple.

Even as the vibrations around crumbled—there was the decision in the center that there would be what we would call the ascension of beings. That they gathered together, my dear friend, that you would be in the very center. Those beings gathered about that they would form the circle of seven—and there would be the recognition of One.

There would be the increasing of vibration from within. And in the increasing of vibration from within there would be the alignment of what we term the centers. In the alignment of the centers would be the opening of the doors. In the opening of the doors would be the increase of vibration. And there would have been the allowing of the increase of vibration to continue until there would be the increase of vibration within the entire physical manifestation. As the physical manifestation would be manifesting that vibration within, there would be the ascension of those beings.

There would be the recognition that those beings gather about your very being. For they would be in recognition of the presence of this gathering. There would be much weeping for joy of those beings for the recognition of your very being to the truths that are being stated even as we speak.

That part of your being has been asleep for a time. For we have been in the process of evaluating self, so to speak. In the process of evaluating self we have come upon those parts of our being which we have termed negative. And we have viewed those parts for a time. It would be now in the present, that we would be learning of this time. That there would be the recognition of the coming forward of those beings, in spirit form, that you would be vibrating in the center—every second. That they would be about the being for they have never been apart. And we would recognize that even as we speak that dimension is pulsating within our very beings.

We would be in the feeling that those vibrations of other times, so to speak, and the dimensions of the present would be complete. For we would be in the recognition that those presented and coming to the conscious state at this particular gathering would have a specific purpose. And we would not cloud the issue with other information. For it has been a great vibration that we have related. Would there be more words, my friend?

Yes. Could you tell me about my soul's purpose this time?

We would be in the recognition, my friend, that in the telling of the story has presented the purpose and the fulfillment of purpose. When we view that we have a purpose, for some reason as human beings, we place the fulfillment of purpose somewhere else. *When we are in recognition of our entire being, we have in the very thought fulfilled our purpose.* We vibrate in the center and we are One.

In the marriage of those dimensions which we have communicated and the present physical manifestation of those dimensions — we find the fulfillment of purpose. We would be in the statement: In the physical manifestation of those dimensions we find the now. We find that in the physical manifestation is the fulfillment of purpose. There would not be the seeking for the fulfillment of purpose. Our very vibration within would be I AM, the total and complete purpose. And those times of which we have spoken would be in the process of manifesting even as we speak.

> *[The same woman asks about her deceased parents:] Can you tell me how my mother and father are doing?*

There would be the preparation, so to speak, in the slumber. For there has been a decision to rebirth in the union of family once again.

There would be the information coming forward: When you would be placing your head upon the pillow there would be the embrace of the parents. For we cradle you within our very arms in the presence of your being. There would be the recognition that even in rebirth, we are never apart.

There would be the statement: Never fear, for we have allowed the encompassment of the Light to shine within our beings. And we would be in the process of determining the purpose for reuniting in the physical plane — that the vibration of the planet called Earth might be raised once again.

There would be the recognition that even though the preparation would be in the present, there would be those times manifesting from other dimensions where those beings would be gathering together — that they would embrace once again the very being present at this gathering. Would there be more within that particular communication?

If I heard you right—it seems like both of them are going through the decision of rebirthing.

Yes, my friend.

I wish I could tell them not to.

What would be the purpose of that statement?

I feel if I had a choice—I wouldn't myself.

We do have a choice. It would be a type of viewing of the vibration of the planet Earth, as from the picture. There would be much about to be occurring in the planet called Earth, for the manifestations have come forward.

We would be in the recognition that those beings who would be viewing as from a picture would be in the understanding of the great changes that would be occurring. And as the great changes occur, even as we speak, we create where we wish to be—and then we manifest our beings there. We would be in the recognition, my friend, that those beings who wish to be in disaster—will be in disaster. Those beings who would be wishing to be in the Garden of Eden—would be in the Garden of Eden. It would be a matter of choice. For there would be the Garden existing even as we speak.

There would be the recognition that the many dimensions are focused about us. And we view one picture and we step into it and we call it our "life." And we could recognize that in the manifestation of the planet called Earth, we are viewing the planet called Earth from this picture. And we could, so to speak, turn the page of the magazine. We could be entering the Garden and be living in the vibration of the center. It would be a matter of choice. There would be pain, or there would be joy. It would be in the focus of our consciousness.

In the rebirthing of those beings there would be the recognition of the great joy. For they would be in the vibration of the planet called Earth—the Garden of Eden. And there would be once again the birthing of those beings that there would be the beginning of the end, so to speak. For there would be the creation of the time, for those beings, when they too would be in the balance and counterbalance complete—that they might ascend. And they would be in great joy that they have decided to be together again—in re-creation.

I understand.

Thank you, my friend.

Can you help me to become more consciously aware of my higher self?

There would be the recognition that what we term "higher selves" is something we have decided that we know nothing about. It would be something foreign—something which we would attain some day. Even though we might recognize that parts of our being have had a little taste, so to speak, we would also recognize, my dear friend, that we *are* our higher self. *We are.* As we vibrate. For we are everything. We would simply manifest ourselves in the way we choose to manifest. And we would simply allow ourselves to make the statement: I OPEN MYSELF TO THE AWARENESS I AM. It would be quite simple.

For we have been in the recognition that as human beings we are going toward the Light—and toward the Light—and toward the Light—for we wish the marriage to be complete. And we would recognize that the Light is within. And that, in fact, we *are* the Light. We are it. And when we say, I OPEN MYSELF TO THE AWARENESS I AM, that is all we need to do to open ourselves. How do we open ourselves? By the simple statement. There is no mystery about it at all. There is no great step to take. We would be in charge of our very own selves. The secrets are simply beliefs. We believe that there are secrets. That it is hidden from us. And we would be in the recognition that there have been those who have capitalized upon those beliefs. And we would be in the statement that that entire pattern is a belief. That it would be simple—for we are in charge. We manifest our very selves. And we are I AM. We simply say to our very own selves: I CHOOSE TO MANIFEST MYSELF IN EVERY MANNER POSSIBLE THAT WOULD BE THE VIBRATION *I AM*. And we allow ourselves to be. For we are everything. Everything.

When we view ourselves in judgment, then we are refusing to see that part of ourselves in a marriage. When we judge our selves, we are denying I AM. Everything we say, everything we do—is perfect. For we are the entire Universe manifesting. Everything is perfect.

> *I have a hard time with that. If what I do or say causes someone pain, I would think it is only right that I would judge myself to be wrong to be doing that.*

It would be part of the balance and counterbalance which we have created within our being. We have a belief that there is "right" and there is "wrong." And as human beings, and as the Universe, we manifest everything in which we believe. When we manifest everything in which we believe, and we have the belief of "good" and "bad"—we manifest in a way that we can judge that we are bad. We manifest in a way that we can judge that we are good. And we continue to manifest in those ways like the swing of the pendulum, in the balance and the counterbalance, until we recognize that we are, in fact, manifesting the judgments. We are manifesting the beliefs. When we accept that part of ourselves, when we recognize that it is a belief, that "good" and "bad" are beliefs, then we can accept the marriage of the two—and then we vibrate I AM.

When we say, "This is bad and I don't want to be this way," we deny part of our very own being for we are everything. When we do something that we have judged as bad, what do we do that the marriage might be complete and the balance and counterbalance might cease from swinging in the pendulum? We say to that part of ourselves: "I did that. That is me. Welcome home. I deny you no longer. You are part of my being."

When we view something that we have done and we judge it to be good, we look at that part of ourselves and we say: "I deny you no longer. For I recognize I AM. Welcome home. For I AM

51

everything." When we continue to welcome home those parts of our being, then we release ourselves of the judgments, we release ourselves of the beliefs and we no longer function in the swing of the pendulum. It would be a way of viewing, like a picture, as we have spoken.

Instead of being in the bad and saying, "I have said things that hurt other beings," it would be: "I have said things that others have chosen to be hurtful of. I have said those things. That is me. And I welcome that part home. I deny that part of myself no longer. I refuse to push away that part of my being—ever. I accept that part of my being and I say welcome home—for I AM everything. When I deny that part of my being, I deny that part of I AM." It would be quite simple. It would be that we would be unfurling our wings and allowing ourselves to be in the vibration of freedom. In the freedom of the expression I AM.

For when we view what we have been doing, as in the picture, then we have the choice of returning to the swing of the pendulum, or welcoming the completeness of our being. Once we recognize in our consciousness and wake up to what we are actually doing—"I am judging myself"—then we have the choice. We can return to the judgment and judge ourselves as bad or we can recognize that we are judging ourselves and say, "I remove that judgment and I deny that part of my being no longer. Welcome home, for I AM." Would that be clear?

Yes.

Wonderful. For we have punished ourselves for a very long time, trying to become perfect—when we *are* perfect.

There would be the remembrance that deep within our being I AM. *I AM.* I AM is not something foreign. It is our entire being. Everything about us. Every vibration. Every sparkle within our being. I AM. It is everything we know. Everything. It is quite familiar to us. It is not foreign. For we have carried that belief for many a time and we would be in the recognition that I AM is our very being. And we can say to ourselves, "Welcome home, for I AM."

Remember, my dear friend, we are never apart. Remember most, my friend, that I AM is the most familiar part of our being. It is not the unknown. We know I AM best. We know I AM before everything else.

It is not so difficult once we learn that we don't have to do all those things.

I have to remember that.

Yes, my friend. It would be a simple process of remembering—if during the day at specific times we would say, I OPEN MYSELF TO THE AWARENESS I AM. It would be a simple choice. There probably would be the loaning out of many precious books that would not be so precious any longer. For there would be the learning of I AM, through our very own selves. When we read about someone else's experience we put ourselves on hold, and then we try to duplicate that experience we have read about. When, in fact, we could be vibrating in the now in our own experience. It would be a simple choice once again. I OPEN MYSELF TO THE AWARE-NESS I AM—THE MOST FAMILIAR PART OF MY BEING.

Why does it hurt here? (The woman points to the heart area.)

There would be the releasing of the burdens of the heart, for we have constricted our very own selves. And there would be the holding back of the weeping of releasing. For much releasing has been occurring, even as we speak. And there would be the belief that it would not be correct to be sobbing. And we would be in the statement that we would weep together. (Pretty Flower holds the woman in her arms.)

For we have vibrated together and the truths of the Universe spill forward from our beings. We would be in the recognition, my dear wonderful woman, that when we would become aware of these great happenings in other dimensions, that there would not be the need to try to be those beings that we have talked about. We would be in the recognition that we *are* those beings. We are the holy

53

woman, we are the great mother, we are the androgenous being, we are all those beings—vibrating together as One.

And we would recognize that even as we speak, in the center of the heart is the blossom. In the center of the blossom is the Light. And we allow the Light to come forward that it might vibrate within the center of the heart. And it might fill the heart. And it might release the burdens that the petals might unfold—that they might open and bask in the Light.

For there would be the weeping of the letting go, for we have held ourselves together. And we would recognize that the entire Universe holds us together—and we are simply a petal in the wind. And the masterful Wind Spirit has carried us for many, many times and we find ourselves basking in the Light, every time we turn.

***

And there would be the recognition that in order to be in the dimension of Masters, one would be a Master.

[A man asks:] Can you tell me about a past lifetime that is pertinent to this lifetime?

There would be the time in what has been termed Atlantis. In that time there were several beings who would be in the center of the temple of Enlightenment. Those beings would be working with the elixir of life, the golden liquid. There has been much misunderstanding in the present manifestation in this life, for many in the present vibration on the planet called Earth would be seeking the elixir of life. We would be in the statement that in that time there was the ability to manifest *from the inner self*—from the center very well known and used in the name of God in the present. There in the center would be the vibration of the liquid of the golden elixir of life.

In those times amongst the three beings—you being one of them—there would be the common practice of the manifestation of the elixir of life. And how did that occur, my friend? There would be the three gathered together in the shape of what we have termed the triangle or pyramid. However, in the pyramid shape there would be the recognition that there would still be the three. There would be in the center, the three, and the goblet being held by three. And there would be from the very center of the being the recognition of the gold that vibrates within our very being—the very center of the Universe.

There would then be the three in the toning of sounds that would come forward from within. That there would be a surge of energy coming forward, making a full circle. As the circle grew it would encompass the center where the three would be facing. And there would be as the vehicle, the energies. That from the very center, the center of the Universe, would flow forward the liquid gold—the elixir of life.

And the three would be standing in non-movement, that the gold would flow forward from their very beings to be filling the goblet. There would be the three in the completion and the raising of the goblet, in the recognition of the joy. For there would be the use of the liquid in the creation of the beings—in the creation of the beings of Light. That the three would travel amongst those beings who had been in the Darkness. And there would be in the traveling amongst those beings—the sharing of the liquid of gold.

There were many who would have been in great disapproval of the actions of the three for there are many who were in the enjoyment of the powers. Not to be in judgment of correct or incorrect, there were many in the enjoyment of the power. There were many in the enjoyment of what we term Light around the planet. There were many who were enjoying the freedom of their beings. And then there were those beings who had great concern for those in the Darkness. And you would be one of those beings working together, that the elixir of life might be shared with those beings. That the transformations might occur within the vibration of the civilization.

There would have been many transformations occurring. Many would have been termed misformed—for their Light would not have been able to receive the strength of the elixir. Yet the three continued in the faith that they would be in the proper use of the gift of their being. And they would be continuing. And there would be those beings about in the laboratory who would be in the misforming of their physical being. Yet there would be the continuation of the use of the elixir, for there was the faith amongst the three that the transformation would occur. And there would have been success in their experiments.

However, the surge of energies flowing through that time would be in the destruction of the civilization. That the great fire would be flowing. And within the three there would be a great disturbance for there was the recognition that the work was correct. And then there would be the decision of the three to be in full body movement to another dimension. But there was great sorrow amongst the three that there would be the leaving of those beings who would have been misformed—for their beings could not retain the vibration necessary for the traveling to another dimension.

The three beings then in the decision to move onward were in the discussion of what to be doing with those beings. For there were many who could not view those misformed beings. However, those beings were in the decision of passing on without the physical bodies. And the three were in agreement for they were of the Light. And the three, in seeing the passing on of those beings in Light forms, were filled with joy for there was confirmation of the very action of their beings. That there was a wholeness and completion of the Light. And those beings would have journeyed to other dimensions.

Then there was the decision of the three that they would be in the journey, carrying their physical beings with them in the vibration of what has been termed ascension. There were three groups of beings who would be in the practice of ascension during those times. There would be the three. There would be the group of women in the temples. And there would be another of whom we would not be at liberty to speak at this time. The three, of their own vibrations, would have been in the process of ascension. There would have been the union of One that the three would be One, together—at the center of the Universe. That there would be the returning to One. For there had been the recognition of the secrets of creation. Would there be more that would be required?

Did I ever know the Master who became Jesus in any of his lifetimes?

Yes, my friend. There would be the time walking in the arid desert as a child at the age of twelve. Even though this being—being yourself—would be a young man, still there was the recognition of the great Christos. That the Christos would be coming forward in the robes and hood of dark brown, traveling in the arid time. And the Master would be in solitude that he would be in the manifestation of the teachings from within.

There would be, then, those beings coming forward that they would be in the teachings of the caves. And there would be the child—as yourself—coming forward, following those beings. That there would be the discovery of what would be going on. There would be the curiosity and the great attraction, for the energies coming forward would be great. That there would be the arousal of the being within. And there would be the traveling and the trusting of the messages from within.

On the hills, there would be the Christos coming forward. And he would view the boy. And the boy, the child, would be viewing the Christos. And as the boy would be viewing the Christos, there would be the viewing of the entire Universe. And the Christos would be quite—what we would term—human, in the presentation of His very physical being for the purpose of that young man. That they would talk together. They would walk together many times, not saying one word. That the young man, the boy child, would be viewing the Christos. And the Christos would be viewing the child. There would not be much need for verbalization.

Yet at times there would be the words. The words of the teachings. The words of the teachings that would be presented now—that we are One in the same. That when we view each other we view our very own selves—would be the teachings. There would be the recognition within the boy, the young man, that it would be the truth. And yet there would be the confusion. For how could it be, he would say. Then the Master, as we have termed him, would be placing His arms about the young boy that he would be in laughter. That he would be in the joviality of comradeship. That there would be the recognition that they would be One in the same.

During that time there were many who viewed from the mountains. Many who would be there in the teachings, viewing the Master and the young boy walking amongst the foothills. And the blessings of the Universe would be flowing forward, for there would be the recognition of the One in the same, my friend.

Those beings in the mountains viewing would be of One. They would be in the manifestation of One. And they would be viewing the marriage occurring with the Master and the young boy. For even as they walked amongst the rocks and the dryness, there was the viewing of the marriage of One. The recognition that they would be One in the same. For that would be the lesson in that time.

Did I know the soul of Jesus in any other lifetime?

There would be in the dimension of nonphysical form, the vibration of the Master where there has been the gathering together of beings of Light. And as you would approach that dimension seeking — seeking once again the Master — you would bask in the Light of the Master. That there would be upon approaching that dimension, the coming forward of the Master. And as you would view, you would be viewing the Master "from the feet," so to speak. You would not be able to be viewing the full face — for there was the remembrance of the splendor.

And there would be the Master calling, calling with the thoughts to look forward. And in the looking forward there would be the tears of releasing — that there would be the union. That there would be the recognition of self — the recognition of self.

And there would be the recognition that in order to be in the dimension of Masters, one would be a Master.

***

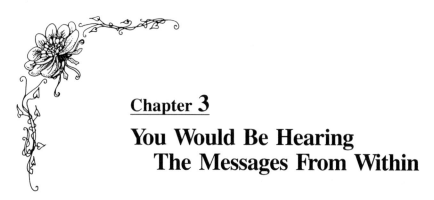

Chapter 3

You Would Be Hearing
The Messages From Within

I OPEN MYSELF THAT I MIGHT BE RECEIVING THE MESSAGES FROM WITHIN...

[A woman asks Pretty Flower about decision making, explaining that she is often guided by a physical sensation in her solar plexus. However, this confirmation often happens at the last moment and she would like it to give her notice in a more timely manner.]

First we would be in the statement: Remember, we are in charge. We would simply ask of our very own self: I OPEN MYSELF THAT I MIGHT BE RECEIVING THE MESSAGES FROM WITHIN, THAT I MIGHT BE AWARE. We could be speaking to ourselves. It could even be matter-of-fact. When we are feeling that vibration within our being we could even be saying, "I wish that you would come along a little earlier. I request that of my being." We are in charge. It is belief that we are the leaf in the wind. And what else would we be communicating?

I also want to know why I get those feelings here (pointing to the solar plexus) rather than somewhere else.

It would be that we would be wanting the rule. We would be wanting the rule. For example, when we are in meditation and we are opening, we would allow our awareness to settle anywhere within our being. One being would settle here, (pointing to different spots on her body as she continues) one being here, one being here, one being here—and what would be the significance? It would be as we are—for that second. It would be part of our being. Part of your very being. It would be similar to be saying, "Why do I sense scent here (pointing to the nose) and sight here (pointing to the eyes)?" It would be becoming aware of part of our being. Wonderful being.

Thank you.

Thank you, my friend.

***

We are asking that you be awake and view within.

[A woman asks:] Pretty Flower, regarding beliefs—I have been tested for food allergies and I've been given a list of foods to which I'm supposedly allergic and that seems right. But I also have a belief that I can bless my food and literally raise its vibrations so it will be healthy for me. However, I have seen you give certain people very specific lists of foods to avoid. I'm confused—are we able to exert "mind over matter" with our food or not?

We would be in the physical plane, my friend, vibrating in every dimension and manifesting in the physical plane. As we are crossing the street, for example, there would be the vehicle coming down the street. We are in awareness that we are the entire Universe—therefore we could simply ascend. Or we could jump out of the way. It would be a matter of choice. A matter of choice. Which would be correct or incorrect? We are in charge. You are in charge.

When we bless the food, does that change the vibration?

My friend, rules and regulations. My friend, we *are* the food. We are change. We are vibration—as is the food. It would be that we would be begging that you be viewing the expansiveness of self. The expansiveness of being. That all those things which we believe occur—we are. We are. We are the finger, we are the note on the page. We are the sound—we are the instrument. We are the vibration. For we are everything.

As human beings we are quite accustomed to be viewing what we term to be the separateness of our beings. The bread, and our very own self. Yes, there would be the quandry: "Would I bless the food and eat it. Or, would I follow the directions of the doctor?" It would be hearing the message from within as to which would be correct or incorrect. The message from within. There are many who are asking that they be told what to do. They are asking that they would be asleep. We are asking that you be awake and view within.

***

When we find that something is occurring ... we would simply ask our very own selves for the message.

Can you give me information about my spiritual growth? What is causing the physical vibrations I'm feeling and what is it leading to?

We would be in the statement: Deep within the being would be the need for opening. For there would be the energies flowing forward from within. And what would the energies be crying out? That they would be able to be made manifest. That deep within our being would be the energy centers. And we would be wanting them to be open wide.

It would be the need for synchronization of those centers. That we would begin with the top—with the crown chakra. That there

61

would be the opening—gentle, gentle, my friend. That there would be the opening. How do we open? We simply make the statement, my friend, I OPEN, and we view in our being the opening. We are in charge, my friend, of our very own being. And then we ask that the eye be opened. Then we ask that every center be opened. Each in time, my friend.

You know the centers very well. When we feel energy flowing through our being and vibrating in our being and we say: "What would this be? What would this be?"—we would be in the remembrance that we are in charge, my friend. Yes, we could be in the statement that the vibrations you feel would be the surging of energy flowing through the centers—that the creativity might be flowing forward. We could be in that statement very easily. However, we would be in the statement, my friend, that *you* know for you have asked, have you not? You have asked for the "illusive" enlightenment. You have asked, my friend, and thus you receive.

When we think of enlightenment, sometimes we view that it is very far away from our being. And where would it be? Right here. *Right now.* There is no such thing as "going toward enlightenment." We *are* enlightened. *Right now.* We are awake. *Right now.* And what is occurring? The being is recognizing the lights within. Where is it heading? It is a full circle, my friend, within and without. It is like receiving the blessings and bestowing the blessings in the same breath.

How would we be using the energies? We would be opening that we would be channels. Never fear. When we open that we would be in total and complete alignment, my friend, then that is what occurs. When we find that something is occurring within our being, we would simply ask our very own selves for the message. And yes, my friend, we have stated, "It is the opening"—as you have requested.

***

Whatever spot we settle in, within, is the correct spot. How do we know? Because we are there!

We've been looking for land in the mountains. I don't really know if it's because of earth changes or because of this pull I feel towards the mountains. I'm confused about it. I don't want to be doing it out of fear.

The mountains would be calling, my friend. And there would be the recognition that when we feel the pulling, we go. It would be similiar to going toward the Light.

Could you suggest the area that would be most harmonious for all of us?

That would be doing the work, so to speak. There would be the reason for gathering up thy very own self and driving to the mountains. Driving around. And when the vibration calls to turn, we have the freedom to turn. And when we go to that location, then we find that we vibrate within.

If we were to say, "Go to the left and then to the right and we would find this would be the spot," then we would not have the lessons of vibrating with I AM, and *knowing* that it is the spot. It would be more—"We were told this was the spot." Never fear. The journey has begun and there would be much joy in the releasing of the beliefs of what the spot would be like. There would be the releasing of those concerns.

And there would be one day the statement: "Let's drive to the mountains. Let's just drive and see where it takes us." And there would be fun. There would be the releasing of any cares or preconceived ideas. For there would be the manifestation of the vibration within and there would be the knowing. Never fear. It is similar to going within. Whatever spot we settle in, within, is the correct spot. How do we know? Because we are there!

When we go about and we find the spot, there would be the vibration within. It would be the manifestation, would it not? And

63

it would be quite beautiful. For we have requested that the manifestation be of great beauty. Never fear. For we create everything. Never fear. There would be wonderful water purified through the air and the rock. There would be the ferns. There would be the tall trees. There would be the meadows where the deer would come to visit. It would be the Garden of Eden. For we have created, and we allow the manifestation to be a reality. Never fear. For those beings in spirit form are about you at all times. And there would be the guidance. Never fear. For there would be the beginning of many who would be opening the earth that they might place within, the vibration of the foundation of the teachings of the truths.

And there would be the time when you would find yourself standing on the floor, and there would be the remembrance within your being: "I remember at the oceanside that I would be standing on the floor with the foundation of truth within the earth—that we would build that others may find the Light within."

***

*How would we know what we would really want to be doing? Whatever fills us with joy. The very **thought** of it fills us with joy!*

[A woman asks about getting a job.]

It would be the choice of trying to scurry around and rearrange our life. Or we could be in the viewing, that we would be hearing the message from within.

And how would the message be presented to us? For there would be many who would have been hearing the messages within the mind and wondering, wondering, "Is this the correct message? Should I be doing this? Or should I be doing that?" It would be correct questions. For how would we know as human beings what would be the correct message? We would know by opening to the child within our very own selves. That we would be the friend to the child within our very own selves. That part of ourself that we have placed aside for a very long time. That part of ourself that we have said: "Not now. In a little while." The child, begging to come forward. Begging to manifest. At times we find ourselves skipping and we wonder how we could have done that. It would be the child begging to come forward. And we would be opening to the child within. We would be opening to the innocence of our very own selves.

As human beings we have been taught that innocence would have the same meaning as vulnerability. It would be quite incorrect. Innocence. In the innocence of the child is the awareness of the truth of the Universe. The truth of the Universe—when we open to the child within. We would even be speaking to that child: "Never fear, for I am here again. And I am paying attention to you—for I have a deep love for you. I give you permission to be here. Not tomorrow sometime, but right here. Right now." That we might allow the innocence of our being to come forward.

And then, when we are making a decision, what would we be doing? We would be allowing the child to come forward. If the child is skipping about in joy, then we could be quite certain it would be a correct decision. It would be correct, for we would be trusting the message from the child within. The playing. The joy.

For have we not been told that we are children on the planet called Earth. That unless we become as children, we would not enter Heaven. The words have been stated in one form or another, over and over, that we would allow our child to be vibrating in the present. So then we would be recognizing, my friend, that the child within would be skipping along, coming to this vibration, being filled with joy—gathering together with those beings who would be wanting to play.

What would be the play? At times the play would be gathering together and hearing the truths and clapping the hands together and jumping up and down with glee at the discovery of self. At the discovery of self. That there would be the reading of teachings. And what would be occurring? It would be the recognition of the vibration—and the marriage of the vibration.

When we read the teachings and we feel that the spark of Light within would be vibrating, then we know a marriage has occurred.

It would not be that we would try to be that way. We would be recognizing that we *are* that way. We would be recognizing the manifestation of our very own selves.

If we find a teaching in the writings that appears to be good, we could say in our minds, "That sounds good"—but the rest of our being would be asleep. For that teaching would not be how *we* would be. And what would we do? We would attempt to mold ourselves to page 32, that we would be page 32, and the child within would be moaning and groaning. Abandon that practice. It would be useless. It would be in the recognizing of self. In the recognizing of self.

My friend, you would be creating. Creating. For as human beings, once again here we are stating: "I need to be having a job. What can I be doing? Will there be a job? Will I be making enough money? Will I be doing something I will be happy doing? Or, what *can* I be doing?"

We would be in the statement of creating what I would *want* to be doing. And how would we know what we would really want to be doing? Whatever fills us with joy. The very thought of it fills us with joy! That we would be in the question: "How would someone pay me for doing this—I am having such fun." That would be the work.

When we are in the fulfillment of the work, of the purpose, never fear—the rest would take care of itself. Never make the decision for remuneration. Make the decision for the fulfillment of joy, and the rest would be in the abundance of the Universe. For when we vibrate in joy, in our very own work, then we are open. When we are open, we are giving and receiving in the same breath.

We could be stating what job, at what time, at what day—and what would we be doing? We would be telling you to go to sleep. That that part of your being that would recognize the joy—would go to sleep. That you might hold your breath until that time, and then you would awaken and vibrate.

We would be in the statement that it would be for naught. And the procedure would occur again. And again. Until there is the awakening of the being. That there would be the recognition of the child within. The fulfillment of the child within. The jumping up and down for joy of the child within.

Why does a child skip about? Because the child cannot possibly walk. They are so filled with joy that they cannot walk. They *must* skip about. They would be so filled with joy that they would look down and their feet would be skipping. For they could not be walking. It would be that occurrence which would be vibrating within your being. Begging to be manifest. Never fear.

Wonderful.

Yes, my friend. You would be creating your own reality. For in play—is the work.

***

...when we ask another, then we are still left with the question...."Was that answer correct?"

I have a trivial question—

There would be the statement that the word "trivial" would be of no meaning whatsoever.

Well, a small question then. In a group I met a young man. He asked me to hug him, which I did. And he asked me to write him, which I did, and we corresponded. Did we ever meet before in another lifetime? He doesn't understand his strong feelings and neither do I.

And what would occur if we were to say "yes"? For example, my dear friend, if we were to say "yes"—then you would return to your home and you would be in the statement, "Yes, we have vibrated in another time together—and we are gathering together in the present." And what would we be doing? We would be confirming what you already know within your very being, my friend.

67

I would just like to have it confirmed.

The answer would be yes, my friend. There would be three dimensions—where the young man would be the son, where the young man would be the lover, and where the young man would be the sister. That there would be gathering together of three in recognition of One. And, my friend, you have known every being here at this gathering—*yes,* my friend. There would be the remembrance that with every being with whom we meet there is marriage. For there would be no accident at the meeting of any being. The blessings of the Universe reside within your being.

We would be in the statement, my dear friend, that when we ask another, then we are still left with the question. For we ask another: "Is this the truth? How do I know this being? What is the answer to this question?" We ask a friend, "What is the answer to this question?" And we receive the answer. And once again we return home and we still have the question. The question would then be, "Was that answer correct?"

And where would we find the answer, my friend? Within our very beings. How would we be accustomed to hearing the answer? We would open that we might get what we term to be in the vocabulary—an "inkling." We get an inkling. We get an inkling of what would be the answer—and we hear it. And when we hear it, we give it validity. And then when we have another feeling—another inkling—we give *it* validity. Then we are answering our own questions. For there could be many different answers to the same questions. It would be the question to self, "Is this correct for me? Does this vibrate in wholeness within my being?" Then we have the answer within.

If we are making a decision for a journey, for example, and there are friends who would be saying, "It would be so good for you to take a vacation—to travel." And we would be thinking, "It would probably be good for me to take a vacation." However, the inner Voice, the message from within, is in the statement, "It is time to remain in my home." How many beings would be traveling even though the inner message says to stay at home? Yes, my friends. And the time is here that we would be hearing the messages from within.

**

When we search for God, where are we searching? Out there somewhere? My friend, the journey is within.

Have I known my study group in the past?

You have asked and you would receive. There have been a group of—what we would term "healers"—who have been gathering together in each dimension. We would remember once again that the "past" is the "present." When we say "past," it is a belief. The truth would be that every dimension vibrates in the "now."

There would be a group of beings in four dimensions, including the present, in the group you have been stating. And the group would be a gathering of healers—for each has decided that he and she would be a channeler. To channel the healing powers of the Universe. Seeking and seeking the fulfillment. Seeking and seeking God. Remember, when we seek outside of ourselves, we are unfulfilled.

When we decide to be healers, my friends, what are we actually deciding? We wish as human beings to be in the service of others. We wish to understand more deeply what would be our God-manifestation. We wish to understand prayer and meditation. We seek the answers. And what do we do? As healers we have the belief—it would be quite human—we have the belief that we come upon a being and we view that being and we make the judgment that that being needs healing. Then we think how we would want that being to be—according to our beliefs. We think, "How would that being manifest that we would believe that they would be healed?" Then we go about struggling, struggling in our being—praying, pleading at times—that that being be healed according to our beliefs. And

69

we would be saying: When we attempt to heal of our own strength, we could crumble to dust at the responsibilities.

How do we heal? My friends, we open ourselves to the healing powers of the Universe. How do we do that? We simply say, I OPEN MYSELF TO THE GREATEST HEALING POWERS OF THE UNIVERSE—THAT ALL WHO COME IN CONTACT WITH ME WOULD BE HEALED, WITHIN AND WITHOUT, BY THE MERE PRESENCE, BY THE MERE THOUGHT, BY THE MERE TOUCH OF THE GARMENT—FOR I AM. Then we go about our business. That is how we heal. We are channels. We do not judge. We do not decide how another should be. We simply open—that we are channels. That the blessings might flow forward from within to without. *The entire Universe, my friends, is within.*

When we search for God, where are we searching? Out there somewhere? Up there, up in the sky? Beyond the sky? Beyond the atmosphere? Going outward, outward, outward. My friends, the journey is within. The physical manifestation would be our fantasy playground—our manifestation. Deep within resides I AM. I OPEN MYSELF TO THE AWARENESS I AM. As human beings we have the belief that there is the great unknown—the secrets of the Universe. We believe this to be true. And what do we do? We go about seeking the answers. Seeking and seeking the answers to our own creation of the unknown. We know everything, my friend. Everything.

The beings in the dimensions we have mentioned would be gathered together at the top of the mountain. That there would be an opening to the Light. From within to without. That there would be a marriage. That those beings gathered together would be in the awareness of the marriage of physical and spirit, that they would be in the union of One. Gathered together in the union of One.

A Meditation to Meet the Child Within

There would be for that group the following statement: That this gathering could be sitting together, closing their eyes, being quite comfortable within their very beings. Releasing expectations, releas-

70

ing the questions, releasing the prefabricated answers and words—words—words. Allowing ourselves to be One. Allowing the releasing of judgments of our very own self. That there would be the releasing of judgments of our very own self.

That there would be the recognition that deep within our being resides the child. And as we open ourselves that we might journey within, we recognize that the journey is with the child. And as we open, we can be saying "Hello" with love and with understanding—and openness. That we would open. And within our being we would say to the child: "The journey would be yours, my friend. Let us continue." And the child would clap its hands together with glee at the recognition of self.

And we could see the child place its tiny feet upon the path, walking down the path, with no particular purpose. Just walking down the path. Seeing a flower on the side of the path. Bending down to smell the scent of the flower. Perhaps having a little bit of pollen stuck to the nose. Walking further down the path. Seeing a pebble. Picking up the pebble. Looking at the pebble. Putting the pebble in a pocket. Skipping down the path, skipping. Looking about at what would be on the path. Going around the bend.

And what is around the bend? A gathering of children. A gathering of children. And the child self comes forward and says, "Hello. Hello." And all the children say "Hello" to each other, looking at each other in the eye. Looking directly at each other. Saying "Hello" to each child. Saying "Hello." Gathering together.

And, my friends, we could know that deep within our being we vibrate as One. That we have opened ourselves, that we might vibrate as One.

And we could decide on the journey to allow ourselves to see the child. To see the child about us. And we would slowly—ever so slowly—while we are remaining in this wonderful vibration for a temporary moment, we could allow ourselves to open our eyes and view those about us. The children about us. Our friends. Simply viewing. Simply viewing. Looking at each one, in the eye. And then we can return.

We could close our eyes once again. And we could remember that the child within is the embodiment of the truth of the Universe.

In the innocence of the child is the wisdom of the Universe. And then we could thank that child within. Thank that child within—for the journey. And we could ask that child to remain with us so that we could remember how to play together.

And then we would return, coming to the center. Beginning to be in conscious state, recognizing that we carry everything forward to conscious state. For we have chosen to vibrate together. And, my dear friends, the blessings of the Universe reside within your beings.

And there would be—when you would be ready, my friends, the opening and the viewing of those about, knowing that you each would be the petals of the great flower. And that in the center resides the gold, the elixir of life. The spirit. The vibration I AM.

***

Right now—as we vibrate in this very second— this is it. Right now.

My son-in-law's business has failed. And I was wondering if he and my daughter are going to continue to live in this area or if they're going to go elsewhere so that he could start a new career.

It would be time for a change. The manifestation of what we term the business failure—would be the message that it would be "time for change." It would take great courage. It would take the going within to be hearing the messages. It would take the going within to know what the move would be.

We could be saying, "Go to this place and do that and you would be successful." And what would that accomplish? Not one thing. For there would then be the need for failure again until we would find the rebuilding of our very own selves from within.

There would be the need for that man to be in the resting from responsibilities. A very difficult time to be resting from responsibilities when they tug at our shoulders, but it would be a great need. And it would be of great benefit for even just a few days to be by self. By himself, that he would allow the releasing of cares and worries to escape from his being. That he would allow the messages to come forward. That he would know what the truth would be from within his being.

It would be a time of writing in a journal—even if the words were very few. It would be a time of sharing with another man—or men—the *real* feelings from within. That there would be the feeling of comradeship. There would be the recognition that it would be what he would need to be doing. He would be needing to do it, for we manifest what we desire.

> *Now, getting to myself, I'm wondering if I would continue to live here or settle in another part of the country.*

Once again, it would be going within. It would be hearing the message from within. When we feel the vibrations within our being in the marriage with that particular place, *then we know that no matter what—it would be correct.*

When we have a yearning within our being, the yearning is not satisifed in temporary measures. The yearning is not satisfied by viewing what we already have. The yearning exists. And we would be in the choice of satisfying the yearning or residing with it. For it would not go away. It would be going within. By "going within" we don't mean that we have to sit and meditate. It would be paying attention to that part of our being that speaks to us. When we recognize that we are vibrating and happy, then we know that that's what we would be doing.

> *I have two young granddaughters. And I look at them and feel so much differently than I did when my own were young. I'm looking at them and I'm seeing little free spirits.*

Yes, my friend.

> *—just loving to play.*

73

There would be the statement that your very own self could go into the forest and skip about, kick a rock, or pick a fern and strip off the branches—just for the fun of it. Your very own self could stick the fern in the hair, put the mud on our face and our clothes, and crawl on the earth, making sounds. Climbing a tree and swinging our legs. Humming a tune. Throwing a pebble into the river. *Just for the fun of it.* Just for the fun of it. For no particular reason. If we would begin to do that, once a week, just one time a week—

> *You don't think we should worry? Don't we have to have some kind of plan in our lives, or should we just go where the spirit leads us?*

There would be the statement that has been made of old: Unless we be as children, we cannot enter the kingdom of heaven. Now we would be changing the words a little and it would be the same vibration: *Right now—as we vibrate in this very second—this is it. Right now.* When we vibrate and we exist in our thoughts, we are not vibrating in the now. We are allowing part of ourselves to go to sleep again. And we think about what happened yesterday. We think about what might happen this evening or tomorrow or the next year. And what happens to right now? It has been put on hold.

We would be in the statement that in the vibration of now—is I AM. What would be our purpose as human beings upon the planet called Earth? To be One. To be One. That there would be a union of physical and spirit—that we would come together to be One.

> *And is this going to come in time?*

It *is* right now. It is right in this second. As we vibrate together we are One in the same. When we go to play in the country, when we walk upon the beach in our own privacy—that we would feel free to play. We would begin once a week—and then twice a week. And then we would find that we would be wanting every day to be playing just a little. And then a little more. And soon we would be playing everywhere we would be—whether it would be at work, whether it be with the children or shopping—it would be playing.

And we would be skipping about. And it would grow within our being—that wonderful child within. And we would be existing right *now*. It would be the greatest gift that we could give to our very own selves.

And to mankind, I'm sure—to our fellow human beings.

Yes, my friend. The joy of the Universe is awaiting to manifest. Would you be making a statement that you would be playing once a week?

I will play once a week. Yes. I will. The expression is "let your hair down"—but I never do.

It would be time. It would be time to be a little mischievous. It would be—

It would be quite a change.

It would be quite a release and a gift to self.

I would be an entirely different person because I'm just not that way. Oh, I suppose I was—when I was very, very young. But I doubt if I was that way after I was 21.

We would be in the statement that there could be the remembering of the child—at about 6 or 7 or so. Playing. Just having fun. There could be the going in the forest, with nature. It would be quite a gift. Then we could go twice a week. Then we could go three times a week. And soon we might be saying to our friends, "I'm sorry but I have something else planned." And they would ask and you would say: "Oh, it's just something that I do for myself every day. I'm sorry that I can't quite make it."

And there would be the playing. It would be a little stiff at first. And then it would be easier and easier. We might find ourselves trying to balance on a log, walking along. And we would catch ourselves and say, "This must be playing." And then we would let

75

that thought go, and we would continue to play. And soon we would be running to the forest that we would play.

***

Surrounding yourself with those beings who love to play in the Lightness of their being would be the greatest gift you could give to yourself.

***

The Story of Three Gifts

A being was skipping along and a little girl was seeing the joy of that being. And the little girl was wondering, wondering, "What would be the joy within that being?"

And she said to the being, "Hello."

And the being said, "Hello."

And she said, "Where would you be going, skipping along, as you would be skipping along?"

And the being was a little boy. And he would be saying, "I am going no place in particular. I am simply skipping along. Skipping along."

And the little girl said, "I will skip along with your being. I would skip along with your being."

And there came along on the path a being. It was a tiny rabbit. A tiny rabbit. Soft. Soft and fluffy. And the little girl clapped her hands together with glee that she might be in the experiencing of that rabbit. And she wondered, "Would he come here? Would he come here?"

And the little boy said to the little girl, "If you would be wanting him to come here, you would simply call. You would simply be in the statement, 'Come here, that I might be with your being.'"

And the little girl said, "Oh." And she called the rabbit—the wonderful, soft rabbit. And she said to the being, "Would you be coming forward. Would you come here that I might feel the softness of your being?"

And then the rabbit came forward. And he was at her feet. At her very feet and she was looking at the rabbit. And she said to the rabbit, "May I place my hand upon your fur. It looks so soft."

And the rabbit was smiling—for that was just what he wanted.

And the little girl placed her hand upon the rabbit, on the fur of the rabbit. And she felt the softness of the fur. She felt the softness of the ears as she stroked the ears of the rabbit. And she was feeling joy.

And the rabbit said, "I would be asking a question also."

And the little girl said, "What would be the question?"

And the rabbit said, "I would be wanting to know how to skip. I would be wanting to know how to skip, for I have been in the viewing of you and of your friend, the little boy, and I would be wanting to know how to skip."

And the little girl said, "When I am skipping I am filled with joy. And I have been wondering about that thing called joy. For I came along with this little boy, skipping about. And I found that when I met you, and you allowed me to touch your very fur—that I was filled with joy."

And the rabbit said, "Hummm. Do you think I could be coming with you? Do you think I could be coming with you—you and your friend, the little boy?"

And the little girl said, "Of course. We are together on the path."

And the three went skipping down the path together.

Now the rabbit did not know that he was skipping. He was simply making some strange movements with his feet. And he was skipping. He was skipping. Why was he skipping? He was filled with joy. The joy of union with his friends. The joy of being together. That he was so filled with joy—he was skipping.

And they continued down the path, so to speak. They continued down the path.

77

And along the path came another being. Along the path came a man with a satchel.

And the little girl said to the little boy, "I wonder what would be in that satchel. I wonder what would be in that satchel."

And the little boy said to the rabbit, "I wonder what would be in that satchel? I wonder what would be in that satchel?"

And then the man with the satchel came closer. And the little girl said, "I wonder what is in that satchel you are carrying."

And the man smiled. And he said, "Would you like to view? Would you like to see what is in that satchel?"

And the little girl said, "I would like to see what is in that satchel."

And the little boy said, "I would like to see what is in that satchel."

And the rabbit said, "I would like to see what is in that satchel also."

And the man opened the satchel. And the little girl peered into the satchel. And what did she see? She saw the stars of the Universe. The stars of the Universe, twinkling about. Twinkling about. And she was filled with joy. The stars of the Universe—filling her being. Twinkling about.

And then the little boy said, "Could I see in there? Could I see in there?" For on the face of his friend he saw joy. And the little boy viewed in the satchel. And what did he see in the satchel, my dear friend? He saw the depths of the ocean. The depths of the sea. The flowing plants. The tiny creatures in the depths of the sea. And he saw the sunlight through the water. And he felt the water upon his being. And he was filled with peace. For he felt the serenity of the great sea.

And the rabbit was wondering, wondering—what was going on? And he said, "Can I see what is in there? Can I view what is in there?" And the rabbit viewed.

And he saw in the satchel great wings. The great wings of freedom. And he saw that the great wings would carry him everywhere in the Universe, in the great dimension. Everywhere. And he was filled with the freedom of the Universe. The freedom of the Universe.

And there were the three—the little girl filled with joy, the little boy filled with peace, and the rabbit filled with the freedom of the Universe.

And the man with the satchel was smiling and smiling. For he had been told that it was a satchel of great gifts. Of great gifts. For he had been coming around the bend and he had been saying to the Great Fairy at the bend—he had been saying, "I have been carrying this satchel and I know not why I am carrying the satchel."

And the Great Fairy said, "You are carrying the satchel for it was filled with the gifts of the Universe. Filled with the gifts of the Universe."

And the man said that he thought he looked in the satchel and he did not see a thing. But he knew of the trusting of the Great Fairy that he continued to carry the satchel. And he only knew that every time he opened the satchel—the being who peered into the satchel received a gift. And he did not know what was occurring. He only knew that he was carrying a satchel of gifts.

And so he asked the little boy, "What would be the gift you had received from the satchel?"

And the little boy said, "I received the gift of joy. The gift of joy."

And the man said, "Oh." And he asked the little girl, "What gift did you receive from the satchel?"

And the little girl said, "I received the gift—the wonderful gift—the wonderful gift of peace."

And the rabbit said, "I received the gift of freedom."

And then the little girl thought. And she said, "I think I received the gift of joy. Just a minute. I'm wondering."

And the little boy said, "Well, I was wondering that maybe I received the gift of peace. How could I have said I received the gift of joy?"

And the rabbit said, "I know that I have received three gifts this day." And he hopped out into the field.

And the little girl wondered what he was meaning.

And the little boy wondered what he was meaning.

And the man with the satchel said, "Perhaps he is meaning that when one receives joy, all receive joy." And he skipped along the path, with joy in his being.

And the rabbit, in the field, was thinking, "I have received three gifts today. I have been the friend of the little girl. I have been the friend of the little boy. And I have been the friend of the gift giver. And I have received those three gifts."

***

Chapter 4

It Would Be Belief —
It Would Be Quite
A Belief!

We could just chat a little even. That's what we do here really. We toss back and forth our belief patterns, and then hopefully we drop them and forget to pick them up!

***

> *...the **only** thing that ceases us from being totally and completely enlightened beings is the belief that we are not.*

I think we have a fear that when we evolve spiritually—

(Pretty Flower interrupts:) What would that be?

I'm not sure.

It would be belief.

> *Well, if we're going to get to a point where we are part of I AM also—it sounds like we're no longer going to have personality.*

My friend, there are several beliefs which you have been experiencing. First, there would be the belief of "becoming evolved"—for there would be the belief that we must be becoming perfect. Becoming perfect. Becoming the total enlightened being—*which we are.* The separation—the *only* thing that ceases us from being totally and completely enlightened beings is the belief that we are not. That is the only thing.

It's not that we are becoming—as you have been thinking—but that *we are.* It would be relative to the belief of linear time. It is a belief.

As we have been teaching, the past would be present. The future would be present. Every dimension resides in the present. Right here, right now. It would be releasing ourselves of "becoming" and just be, my dear friend. That we would be as children. That we would open and allow the child to come forward as we are—to come forward and play. To be. Children do not think of becoming enlightened. They are. In the innocence of the child is the wisdom of the Universe. In the wisdom of the Universe resides the heart of the child. Yes, my friend.

> *This is very confusing. I've been doing a lot of reading. I find that I really don't know anything.*

Wonderful!

> *—on reincarnation, soul mates, going to our higher selves. What is all this about? Where are we going? Why are we here? Why does the soul have this body? I don't understand any of this stuff.*

There would be many, my dear friend, who would be in the writing of their very own truth. There would be those who would be experiencing what we have termed to be "dimensions." There would be those who would be experiencing what we term to be "reincarnation." It would be their truth. It would be their belief.

There would be those who would be meditating and be feeling the energies flowing within—and they would be writing on paper that others might be sharing in the experience. When we are reading, my friend, we are hearing. We are opening to be hearing of other beings' experiences.

And what would we be doing then? We would be making the decision to be exploring our very own selves. For we could be attempting to fit ourselves to page 32. That we would be as that being wrote, that we would experience what that being experienced. Becoming page 32. And what would be occurring actually? We would be asleep. For we would be making ourselves be a certain way. And what all this would be about would be opening to self, to hearing the truths of self. Vibrating in self. Hearing the messages from deep within our being. Hearing the messages.

We may hear one being be speaking and we may believe that what they are speaking would be correct for our being. And we could perhaps try meditation. However, *how* would we meditate? How could we meditate? One being would be sitting; one being would be walking; one being would be running; one being would be laying. One being would meditate for one second; one being would meditate for one hour. It would be what *we* would do to be with self. To be with self. To recognize that that which we call God is within our beings. That we might vibrate with that part of our being.

Sometimes as human beings we are so very busy in our every-day vibration that we forget that that vibration which we term to be God is within our very beings. We are I AM. If we are saying that God is within us, then we are God. There is the marriage.

Then, as human beings when we are in the hearing of those words there would be certain questions. There would be for some the statement, "That is not what I was taught. It is confusing." We would then be wondering at the source of the teaching. And we would be wondering at the source of *all* teaching. How would we know which teaching would be correct? We hear from our very own selves. We vibrate from our very own selves.

When we would be deciding to meditate, we could be sitting and we could be finding that we would be figetting. We could be finding that we could not silence our mind, as there are many who have been in the statement. And we are struggling and struggling.

83

Every time we sit and meditate, we feel like we could be running. Then perhaps we *would* be running.

There would be in the vocabulary of human beings, two words that would be in the joking: *"Says who?"* Says who? Where did this come from? Who said meditation is exactly this way? It would be the truth for that being. It would be the truth—it would be neither correct nor incorrect. And we would be deciding what would be correct for *our* very own being.

As when we are walking upon the path, and we are placing our feet upon the path, there would be those beings who would be skipping. There would be those beings who would be sitting on the side of the path, viewing. There would be those beings who would be laughing. There would be those beings who would be weeping. Neither would be correct nor incorrect. And we would, as human beings, be viewing other beings and how they would be. Deciding which one of those ways we would be.

And we would be in the statement: "Vibrate in the truth of your being. Be as *you* would be." Perhaps one second you would be sitting; the next second you would be running. Perhaps you would be sitting on the side of the road. However you would be would be correct. It would be the freedom of self.

***

I open myself to know the awareness of the beliefs that have created this situation.

[One person asks:] What is my soul's purpose on this plane?

It would be that we would be in the statement: Every being would be in the purpose of the *conscious* manifestation I AM. *Conscious* manifestation. Whatever we do is manifestation I AM. Everything is manifestation I AM. Every thought. Every movement. Everything. There would be unconscious manifestation and there would be conscious. Neither would be correct or incorrect—for both would be manifestation I AM. However, the purpose on the planet called Earth would be in opening to conscious manifestation—to be aware of what we are creating, how we are creating it, and that everything in our vibration is our own creation. *Everything.*

When we open that we would be in conscious manifestation— what occurs? Those creations about us which have been giving us "trouble," which have been nudging us, would be coming forward even closer. For we would be in the statement: I OPEN TO CONSCIOUS MANIFESTATION. And those unconscious manifestations would be coming forward, saying "Hello—I would become conscious that I might be revealed to the Light." That we might shed our own Light on the unconscious manifestation.

In the past we have said, "Why has that person been that way?" Or, "Why has that occurred in my life?" We would now be in the statement, "How have I created this to be in my life? What are the beliefs that create this in my life?" What are the beliefs?

And we open ourselves that we might be hearing the beliefs of how we created this in our life. Then what would we do? We would be in the understanding and we would receive, "Welcome home—for I AM everything." Then we have the conscious decision of manifestation. Conscious decision to remanifest, or to change. And how do we manifest? We say within our beings, "THIS I DO CREATE—FOR *I AM.*"

If you would be wanting to change anything that would be occurring in your life, there would be the question to self, "How have I created this to occur in my very own vibration? What are the beliefs that create this in my life? What are my beliefs?" We open that we would allow the beliefs to come forward. Perhaps we would write them on paper. And when we see the beliefs of how we have created the circumstances of our very own lives—then we would say to the realization, "Welcome home. For these beliefs reside within me. For I AM everything." However, now I would be in the *conscious* manifestation—*conscious* decision—for now I have a choice. For they would be in the awareness of my being." And then we would be in the changing—if we would want to. To be changing the beliefs.

[A person responds:] The thing is—our beliefs are not always clear to us.

We would be in the viewing of the process of how our beliefs would become clear. How we would consciously manifest. That we would say to ourselves, in this instance, for example: I OPEN MYSELF THAT I WOULD BE AWARE OF MY BELIEFS. How could I be aware of these beliefs? How would we know? We would say, I OPEN MYSELF TO KNOW THE AWARENESS OF THE BELIEFS THAT HAVE CREATED THIS SITUATION. And then we would write them down. That we would see the beliefs, uninhibited. No judgments.

What are the beliefs—the belief that I despise this person? Then I believe that I am feeling bad that I despise this person. And then I would be remedying that feeling by being extra good to that person. And what have we created? A little war, so to speak, within ourselves. Why? For we believe that we must be perfect. And we have the judgment on what "perfect" would be.

Then what would we do? We *receive* all of the beliefs. For it is I AM—everything. There would be the statement: THIS I DO CONSCIOUSLY CREATE. CLARITY WITHIN THE RELATIONSHIP. THAT I GIVE MYSELF PERMISSION TO BE SPEAKING THE TRUTH.

And what is the truth? What is the truth? That perhaps I was with this being and I really didn't want to be with this being. And I have placed the resentment upon this being instead of myself—recognizing that I did not want to be with that being and the statement is the truth. "I decide to be with myself today." And we release ourselves in the truth of our being. Would that be clear?

Yes, I think so. Thank you. You've given me ways which I cannot find myself.

Yes, my friend.

Because we don't know ourselves.

86

Yes, my friend, and that would be a belief when we say, "Because we do not know ourselves." It would be changing the belief this way: We would be saying, I KNOW AS MUCH ABOUT MYSELF AS I POSSIBLY CAN KNOW AT THIS VERY SECOND. AND I OPEN MYSELF TO THE AWARENESS DEEPER AND DEEPER, I AM. Then we have changed. The very same being. The very same truth. All over. It is changed. It would be good to be in the statement of those words every day.

Yes.

Yes, my friend. We are by your side always.

Truly?

Yes, my friend.

Ah, what a comfort.

You are by our side. Always.

I'm not aware.

You are as aware as you possibly can be.

Which is very limited.

Which is as unlimited as it can possibly be at this very second.

Okay. I can accept that.

For there would be limited and unlimited and it would still be the truth.

There would be the woman who would be going to the well. And there would be the Great Master at the well. And she would be in what would be termed the crippledness of her being. In the crippledness of the physical manifestation, she would be saying to the Master, "Great Master, I have come to the well early this morning for I knew that you would be here without the others and I wish to be healed."

And the Master said, "Then why have you not been healed?"

And she said, "Because my faith is so weak. I have very little faith."

And the Master looked at the woman and He said to her being, "You have great faith. For faith is faith. It does not come in quantity. You have faith."

And the woman was healed.

***

We create the belief of a blockage ... of abundance. Welcome home to those beliefs for I AM everything.

[A woman asks Pretty Flower about the blocks to abundance in her life.]

It would be belief. It would be belief that there would be blocks to abundance. What would be the belief? That I am a certain way and therefore I am refusing great abundance in my life. And we would be wondering how we would change. Of course!

It would be that we would be in the recognition of the abundance in our very own vibration. Is not the Universe filled with abundance? Are we not vibrating in abundance in the present? For we are. When we are in the statement: I OPEN MYSELF. I OPEN MYSELF TO THE ABUNDANCE OF THE UNIVERSE. Then what occurs next? As human beings we have great expectations. We are hoping that out of the sky will fall great buckets of money. Part of being a human being.

There would be the question, what would be all this talk of abundance and manifestation? Every time I try to manifest a great

88

amount of money, I don't receive it. We would first be in the recognition of abundance within our very own life. Our very own life. I OPEN MYSELF TO ABUNDANCE. What would be the abundance in our very own lives? We would be viewing the abundance. We would be viewing the flowing.

What would be the abundance on the planet called Earth? What would be the abundance in the Universe? Unlimited supply—in the entire Universe—unlimited supply. "Then why don't I have more?" is the question. Part of being a human being. For there are many who would be in the statement that we should be grateful for what is occurring in our very own vibrations. And there would be many who would be in other statements of how we should be. And the truth of self would be, "I believe that I am blocking the abundance of the Universe." What would we be doing, my friends? I OPEN MYSELF TO THE ABUNDANCE OF THE UNIVERSE. I OPEN MYSELF UP TO THE AWARENESS I AM.

When we are viewing abundance, what is occurring as we have been speaking? We would be experiencing an inkling of the grandness of the Universe. When we are experiencing an inkling of the grandness of the Universe, what occurs? We grab onto it and we try to squeeze it to our being. We have finally recognized the abundance of the Universe and we want more. Of course.

How do we open? We release that little inkling that it might flow. That we might open—and receive—and flow. When we find within our receiving that we are in the trickle of abundance, what do we say as human beings? "This would not be the abundance of the Universe, however it might do for today. It might be enough. It is not exactly what I had in mind—but it will do." For we have a tiny sign, a tiny feeling of the abundance, and we hold it to our being. That there would be the recognition of even the trickle of the abundance of the Universe. And what would we do? We would allow that trickle to flow through our being and *away* from our being. Receiving the abundance and releasing the abundance. Receiving the abundance and releasing the abundance. What are we doing? We are opening with trust. Opening with trust.

We are learning when we try to vibrate in the humanness of our beings, when we try to *squeeze out* the abundance, we are in the pain of our being. In the dissatisfaction of our being. And when we open to the abundance of the Universe? Unlimited supply. And how do we know this? It sounds like wonderful words, however, how do I know that to be true? When we feel the trickle and we hold on to it, then we are never allowing ourselves to experience the totality of the abundance of the Universe. The totality of the abundance of our very own beings. Our very own beings. I AM. Flowing. Flowing. I AM.

How would we begin? I OPEN. I OPEN MYSELF. I OPEN MYSELF TO THE ABUNDANCE OF THE UNIVERSE. I OPEN MYSELF TO THE AWARENESS I AM. When we receive, allow it to flow from our beings. For example, if we were to receive a quantity of what we term to be paper money, we would hold it to our being and we would vibrate in the poverty in which we have created, holding it in our being. And what would occur? We would be there, as we have been stating. And we could be opening our hands and we could be allowing the abundance to flow, in the enjoyment of self. Receiving the abundance. Allowing the abundance to flow through our being. *Allowing. Allowing.* It would be — in the vocabulary — without attachment. Receiving and giving. Receiving and giving in the breath of our being.

How else would we manifest abundance? In the Love surrounding our being. In the joy surrounding our being. In the birds and the songs of the birds, abundance. *Abundance.* It would be the manifestation in many different forms. In the petals of the flowers, abundance. In the colors, abundance. That we would view everywhere the abundance within our very own vibration. It would be, so to speak, "no big deal."

For we have created the belief of blockages. And then what do we do? First we create the *need* for abundance. And then we create the *belief* of a blockage. And then we would be deciding how we would remove that blockage. And all and all as we continue, we are further and further away from receiving the abundance.

And what would we do? We would recognize our very own beliefs. "I have the belief in the blockage. I have the belief of abundance and I have the belief of the absence of abundance. Welcome home. Welcome home to those beliefs. For I am every-

90

thing. Welcome home to those blockages. Come along. For I AM—
everything." Then we have the choice. The choice. Receiving of self.

***

*We have a belief as human beings on this
planet called Earth that there are two things—
work and play.*

How do we decide what to do in our very own lives? For there
would be many choices. And the entire Universe would be at our
disposal.

We would be remembering that we are the child. That within
our being vibrates the innocence and the trust and the truth of the
child. How do we decide what we would be doing? We seek with
our child-self how we would be in the fulfillment of joy. How we
would vibrate in happiness. How we would be having fun. For we
have a belief as human beings on this planet called Earth that there
are two things—work and play. We would be in the statement, my
friend, that that would be words. Words. Words.

We would be in the statement, my friend, that *when you play,
you are fulfilling purpose.* When the child plays there is the bestowing
of the blessings of the Universe without even thinking about it. In
play there is fulfillment. When we work with other human beings—if
we are not having fun, if there is not joy, then we need to reassess
what we are doing. We need to look at it. We need to decide what
it is we would be doing that would be fun, that would be fulfillment
of our very own selves.

For we would be beginning. There would be the awakening
and awareness that it would be time for fulfillment of hope. That
it would be time to play. To play. How do we play? We practice.
We practice letting ourselves be a child once again. We practice by
letting ourselves skip down the path. We practice by scheduling,
so to speak, in our very busy day a time when we can play. When
we can be the child. How does the child play? Without preconceived

91

ideas of play. Kind of trip-tropping along, doing whatever comes in front of the child. Playing. Kicking a pebble. Playing. Playing.

We would have a redefinition of "work," so to speak. We believe that work is struggling in order to make money. Interesting beliefs we would be thinking. However, the work is the fulfillment of purpose. It has nothing at all to do with what we call money. Nothing to do at all. It is the fulfillment of purpose.

When we are vibrating in the fulfillment of purpose, and we allow ourselves to play, and we allow ourselves to be filled with joy — then the Universe would be supplying our very beings with every need. *Every need.* Could that be more clear? Of course not. It is quite clear. It would be a matter of trust. It would be a matter of doing. For when we say that the entire Universe would supply us with every need, we recognize that we *are* the entire Universe. For we are I AM.

It is a belief that we function with our nose to the grindstone, trying to be "responsible" — whatever that would be. What would be the belief of "responsible"? We surround ourselves with judgments. And then we surround ourselves with a belief of how we can be pure so that we will not be judged. And we go around and around in the circles. My dear friend, relieve yourself of the burden that you might enjoy fulfillment of purpose.

***

...the spirit would be seeking the Light and the ego would be fighting for control, so to speak. We would be in the statement that **that** *would be a belief. It would be quite a belief!*

I have read from several sources that when one pursues a spiritual path, a rebellion of the ego causes fear and anxiety to surface. And recently I began having such feelings. I have learned to control those feelings most of the time but they are still in my consciousness. I thought perhaps I had triggered a soul memory. And I would like to have your feelings on this, Pretty Flower.

Why, of course, my friend. There would be the relief of that particular condition when there would be set aside that time of the day to be in play—in total and complete relieving of responsibilities and cares and worries. That there would be the time during the day, when the child within could come forward and play and have some uninhibited fun. Maybe even to be a little mischievous.

At times, there would be what we would term anxiety and depression—when the spirit would be seeking the Light and the ego would be fighting for control, so to speak. We would be in the statement that that would be a belief. *It would be quite a belief!*

It would seem as though one being might have observed himself to be feeling that way. And when the words have been written, others have determined that what they would be feeling would be matching that man's experience. And we would be saying it would be for the individual.

When we seek the Light, my dear friend, we do not struggle at all. Every part of our being rejoices at the very thought. There has been very much written about the ego as if it were something evil. And we would be in the statement that *that* would be our very own selves. For as we have said, deep within resides I AM. And I AM is everything. *Every single thing. Everything.*

And when we recognize I AM, then all those things which we have been trying to get rid of would come crowding around that they would be part of the Light—and received as part of the Light. And our very strong humanistic tendencies would be tapping us on the shoulder and we would be in the process of pushing them away. And they would return. For what would they be doing? They would be coming to the Light within. And once again we would say, "Welcome home. For I AM everything."

There has been much written from the perspective of separateness. For in the human being, as we have said, it is quite easy to see our separateness manifest in many forms. And in spirit, it is quite difficult to see the separateness. And we would be saying of all those parts of our being, "Welcome home. Welcome home." When we view our humanness, "Welcome home."

When we feel as though we are feeling what we call anxiety, what do we do? We say, "How can we get rid of this anxiety?" And

93

it keeps showing up. And we would say, "Welcome home." For once we receive every part of our being, then we have the choice. When we deny part of our being we have no choice until we receive it to our being. It will keep coming back and coming back and saying, "Hello, I am here." And we would be in the process of welcoming home every part of our being.

It would not be that the written material would be "bad." It would be for that one being's experience. For our experience, we would find that in unity we find peace. If every piece of information written could pass the test—"Would this be in assistance of uniting every part of my being?"—and if it would not, then it would not be the correct vibration toward the One.

> *We don't struggle. We bless whatever comes to us, right? We don't resist anything.*

We receive it. It would be correct. For the reason that we resist is because we have a judgment. We have a judgment that says that as holy beings that can not be part of us. And as I AM, everything is part of us. *Everything.* Even those things which we feel are from the Darkness. All of those things would be I AM. And we would be in the manifestation I AM.

Then we would be releasing the judgment. For we have been taught by the many that there would be the judgment. When we are in judgment, we continue balance and counterbalance. And back and forth, the swing of the pendulum takes us. When we receive everything about our very being, without judgment—then we are in completion of balance and counterbalance. Then we have stopped the swing of the pendulum and we are One. And then, my dear friend, we have a choice. We have a choice. We can manifest whatever we would like to manifest.

***

94

...the God to whom you pray would be your very own self.

I have a question about prayer. When someone feels the need to pray for someone else, is it just a belief that the other person needs prayer? Could you talk about prayer and its role in our life?

Yes, my friend. There would be those beings who would be residing on the planet called Earth. And as we view those beings, we would be in the judgment of their very vibration. In the holiness of our beings we would be judging that they would be needing help. And there would not be one human being who would not be in the attempting of this process.

There would then be the diagnosing of what that person would be lacking, that in the prayer we would fix this being up, so to speak. We would then be deciding within our minds what would be the best occurrence for that being. And then we would be in the praying that that being would be manifesting what we would believe to be health, in spirit and physical form. That being, however, may be a Master who has incarnated in this vibration. It would be quite interesting—our judgments as human beings.

Then there are those beings who would be seeking help. And they would be praying. In the belief of their beings, there would be fulfillment through prayer. However, there would be the growing awareness that the God to whom we pray would be our very own selves. Our very own selves. We are I AM. We are everything. Everything.

When a being would be seeking health, and that being would be in the awareness—what would be the prayer? I OPEN MYSELF TO THE HEALING POWERS OF THE UNIVERSE, THAT I MIGHT BE HEALED, WITHIN AND WITHOUT.

There would be those beings who would be lacking in the awareness that they would be in the healing of their very own selves. It would not be improper. It would be the truth of that being. And they would be coming forward, saying, "I would be healed." And what would be occurring? They would be healed. There would be the remembering to ask. And those beings would be asking.

There would, however, be those beings who would be saying, "I would be healed." And there would be the belief that would be saying, "This would never occur." And their awareness would forbid them to be recognizing that they would be healed. Those beings would be crawling forward to be healed and they would be healed. Their physical being would be in the perfection of the Universe and they would still crawl back to their seat. For they would not allow themselves to be healed. They would not be viewing the healing. It would not be sad. It would simply be the facts.

There would be the prayer—vibrating in the present, in the now. Each one of the beings present at this gathering would be in prayer—in the process of praying. What would be praying? Vibrating I AM. Manifesting I AM.

There are many who believe that the prayer would be, "Please give me what I want. Thank you." And they would be unfulfilled. It would be in the emptiness of their being. For those who seek without would be empty. And those who journey within would be fulfilled at the first step. For without would be fantasy. The reality of the being is within. The entirety of the Universe is within.

The physical manifestation of the being would be the very smallest part of the being. It would not be inconsequential. However, it would be the smallest part of our being. In the physical plane we are quite accustomed to viewing the separateness of our beings. In spirit form it is quite difficult to see the separateness of our beings. Would that be answer to your question?

Almost. If someone asks you to pray for them—is that just a belief system that serves no real purpose?

It would be that they would be seeking help. They would be seeking help. If a being would be saying, "Would you pray for me?" would we deny? Of course we would pray for you. We would be praying for you in every breath that we take. For we are I AM. We *are* a prayer. It would not be a trick of the words, so to speak. It would be that we would be speaking with those beings that they would

96

understand what we would be saying—and that they would be receiving the messages. Never fear.

Everything would be perfect. Everything. Never fear. When a being comes to your presence and says, "Would you pray for me?" what does that mean? That you would take the responsibility of their being upon your shoulders? No.

> *The way I pray is to ask that God's Love and Light be directed to them. God knows what healing is needed. I just want to be a channel of it.*

It would be quite correct. However, there would be the reminder that the God to whom you pray would be your very own self. Receive the gift of the Universe, my friend. The truth of the Universe. Deep within your being resides I AM. Everything. Everything.

If you bite your fingernail, you would be eating Him alive. It would be a belief that the God, the Great I AM, would be out there somewhere. We would be in the statement that the entire Universe is within. When we channel, we channel. It would be as a cycle. Would that be clear?

> *Yes. Thank you.*

Would it be frustrating?

> *A little. I heard that to pray for someone, either here on the Earth or in other dimensions, is a wonderful thing.*

It would not be incorrect. It would be quite proper if that would be the desire of your being.

There would simply be the reminder that the God to whom you pray would be your very own self. It would not be blasphemy, it would be the truth. For has it not been spoken that we would do these things and more? Even in that vocabulary were the words spoken. For the Father resides within. It would be the same words, so to speak.

97

It would be correct to be residing in the comfort of beliefs. It would not be incorrect. Conscious manifestation.

***

When we release our beliefs of "heaven," when we release our belief of "hell," what occurs? "Welcome home."

When we die, what happens?

What happens when our physical being dies?

Does the soul leave the physical body and go somewhere?

Toward union. Toward union. To be One. Vibrating together as we are vibrating together here. And that would be one truth. There would be many others who would be saying very many different statements. It would be what would be correct in the vibration of your very own self, for we are the Creator.

If we believe that at the end of the physical vibration of our being we would go to a place that others have termed to be "hell," guess what we will experience? If we believe that at the end of our physical being we would be in "heaven," guess what we would experience over and over again until we recognize that we are creating with our beliefs. That we might release ourselves of belief. Release ourselves of belief. That we might *Be*. That we might Be. Whether we are in physical form or spirit form—we are I AM.

Many human beings ask for the rules and regulations. Many would be asking similar questions. We would be in the statement that it would be as we create it to be. For we could be hearing many different answers and we would be saying, "Which would be correct?" And it would be, "What would be correct *for you?*"

How would you know? Perhaps you would sit and meditate and hear the message from within of what would be the truth. What would be the truth for your being? For there would be many who would be expressing the truth.

There would be the being who would be facing the sun. And that being would be in the statement, "In this second of my vibration I feel the Light upon my face."

There would be the being at that very second who would be submerging their face in the cool spring water. And they would be saying, "In this very second I am feeling the wetness upon my face and the coolness of the spring water."

There would be that being in the very same second who would be feeling the breath of the Wind Spirit flowing through their hair. They would be in the statement, "In this very second I am feeling the Wind Spirit through my hair."

Which would be correct? When we are facing the sun and we say, "I do not understand what she means when she says that the Wind Spirit is blowing through her hair for I Am feeling the sun upon my face." It would be the truth of that being in that very second—the sun upon her face. The truth of our being—*that we would free ourselves from what we believe we are supposed to be, and allow ourselves to Be.* Then we would expand our awareness. That we would grow within. Opening. Open. Being aware. Being who we are in the second, in the very same second. Being.

When we release our beliefs of "heaven," when we release our belief of "hell," what occurs? "Welcome home." It would not be that we release them so they would not be with us any longer. Everything is I AM. Everything. It would be "Being." That would be, total and complete "welcome home," my friend.

We have many questions. We have many desires. We vibrate and we skip down the path together. I AM. When we find that we have many questions and we are wondering, wondering, how to figure things out—my dear friends, in the simple statement, "I AM," lies the freedom. I AM.

***

> *As human beings we have the belief that life begins and ends in the physicalness of our beings. It would be that there would be actually no beginning and no end.*

My son died last year. It's been very hard on the family. He left a wife and children. Is there anything you can tell me about his death?

And what would be occurring within your very being, my dear friend? For that is what we would be working with that we would experience the Love flow through our being. What would be occurring? Wondering, wondering—what would he be doing? Why did he choose this, so to speak? How could it be occurring?

There would be several statements, my friend. First we would be in the statement that even though you would be hearing the words, there would be the words within your being saying, "These are not the answers which I would be wanting to hear." However, it would be correct the next day. The answers would be quite clear. Never fear.

We would be in the statement, my friend, that in the dimension of spirit it is quite difficult to be viewing the separateness of our beings. For in spirit we are viewing the One. The One. When we are in physical form it is quite easy to be feeling our very own separateness. That we would see that we are different. That we are separate.

Then we would be in the statement: Each being would be in the fulfillment of purpose. In the fulfillment of purpose. In the creation. In the creation of the vibration called life. As human beings we have the belief that life begins and ends in the physicalness of our beings. It would be that there would be actually no beginning and no end. That we would be vibrating in every dimension. Simultaneously. Every dimension.

And then we would be in the statement, my dear friend, that you would be in the feeling of missing that being. And that those beings of the family would be in the experience of missing that being. Of course, my friend. We are in the understanding. And we would be in the statement that he is ever near, my friend. Ever near. That he would be about. That he would be in the caring. For when we are in physical form we need the remembrance that we are One in the same. One in the same.

Why has this occurred? In the Universe, my dear friend, the view of birth and death would be One in the same. One in the same. For in this dimension there would be the experience of death. And in this dimension there would be the experience of birth. Death and birth. Birth and death. One in the same. Birthing from one dimension to another. From one dimension to another.

We would be in the statement, my dear friend, that we view the pain of the others, and what is the tendency as human beings? We gather that pain together that we might experience for the others that pain. We cannot remove their pain. It is *their* pain. It is theirs. And as human beings we would be in the pattern of experiencing that being. As human beings.

Hear the words, my dear friends. When we are in the vibration of missing a being who is no longer with us in physical form, what occurs? As human beings we have remembrances. And what do we do with the remembrances? We pull forward from our minds, from our memories, those times—that we would be experiencing the pain. For in the experiencing of the pain we are allowing ourselves once again to be in the closeness of that being. That we would be experiencing that being—to the greatest possible degree. Yes, my friends. There would be the awareness that we are never apart. We are never apart.

When we are not in this physical vessel, we are still with you in every breath. And my dear friends, you are with each other in every breath. Every breath. You are never apart. For you are One in the same. One in the same. Never fear.

We would be wondering, wondering, why has this occurred? My friend, it is part of lifely vibration. There could be many who would be giving many answers. There would be many who would be giving information about past lives, so to speak. There would be many who would be giving information about the vibrations of karma, so to speak. And what would be the truth? We would be experiencing the missing. That would be the truth. The missing.

101

And we would be in the statement that there would be communication whenever you would be wanting to be communicating. Speaking. Speaking. It is not incorrect. There would be the wondering, "If anyone heard me they would be wondering if I am crazy or not." Never fear for those thoughts, my friend. There would be those who would be in the statement, "It would be time to be letting go." Of what, my friend? For we are not in possession of one being. *We are in union and marriage with every being.* Every being.

Yes, my friend, you would be in communication with that being. Yes, my friend, never fear. It would simply be in the statement that I am missing you. I am missing you. It would be the reality of the vibration, my dear friend, the truth. Not how we should be feeling, or should be experiencing, but what we *are* experiencing. Welcome home to the pain. Welcome home to the missing. Welcome home to everything. That we might reside in our being. That we might be One in the same.

There would be the statement, my dear friend, to the family: The missing would be the belief that there is no longer communication. Give ourselves permission to be communicating, to be skipping about, speaking to that being. Sitting on the branch of the tree, swinging our legs, speaking to that being. Giving the children permission. Giving everyone permission. For then the longing would cease and there would be the regular vibration of life that we would be gathering that being together.

Never fear, the Universe is unlimited and he is the Universe as you are the Universe. Unlimited supply. Unlimited. It would not be the belief that he would be somewhere else and we would disturb him. We could be welcoming that belief home that we would have the choice of our beings.

Would you be carrying that message to the family? Know that the Light within the heart grows with every breath. For we allow the Love of the Universe to fill our being—from deep within our being, for the entire Universe is within. *The entire Universe is within.*

When we allow the Love of the Universe to come forward, we are not beginning from out here somewhere—but from deep within our beings. And we allow the Love of the Universe to fill our entire being. Within and without. That we would be filled to the brim. That we would be overflowing, my friend. Overflowing. Allowing.

Remember my friend, "welcome home" to the pain. For then we have the choice. Then we have the choice. That part of our being is begging to be in union. Never fear, my dear friend, never fear. The blessings of the Universe reside within your being.

***

We would be in the rejoicing of the earth changes. For it would be ... the creation of the Garden of Eden.

They say we're in for something quite different from now to the year 2011 with the New Age coming in and that there's an acceleration. That we're not to fear it but it is going to come to pass. Do you have anything to say about the earth changes?

It would be a common question. We would be in the statement, however, that we would be vibrating now. We would be vibrating right now in this very second. In this very second there would be the existence of disaster; there would be the existence of the changes of the earth. There would be the existance of many things—of starvation. For as we vibrate now, it would be the vibration of everything. It would be the present. We would also be in the statement—for many have required the information—that when we speak of earth changes, that the earth is changing even as we vibrate.

We have made lines and marks upon the great Earth that we would demark what would be what country and what would be what sea. And as we have made a mark we would say this would be the United States; and guess what occurs? As we are viewing the United States—the Earth is moving. And what we believe to be the United States is really a breathing in the entire path—moving as One. Everything.

103

When we view the mountains and some being would say, "Would those mountains be there at the great disaster?" we would be in the view of the joke, so to speak. For the mountains are not even there—and then they are there—even as we speak. For there would be the moving. There would be the moving.

We would be in the statement that yes, there would be what would be termed earth changes—of course, my friend. And we would be in the rejoicing of the earth changes. For it would be, as we have said, the creation of the Garden of Eden. It would be of great rejoicing.

> *This has prompted a question for me. How can we enter the New Age with some of the dark souls still present? Will there be a separation as the Bible stated and will these dark souls go back and go through it all again?*

There would be the recognition: As we vibrate I AM, we are everything. We are *everything*. What we term the "dark souls" is our very own souls, for we are everything.

> *There aren't any dark souls?*

There would be the statement that in conscious state we allow the manifestation of our being to come forward. In conscious decision we have chosen to manifest the Light.

There would be those beings who would be of the same composition, so to speak, who would be in *unconscious manifestation*. Or there would be conscious manifestation of the Darkness. We would be in recognition that we are One in the same. When we view what happens out there in the world we forget that the world is fantasy.

> *It's so difficult—*

Yes, my friend. It is very difficult. When we have the viewing of the news on the picture tube, and the written words in what we call the newspaper, we could be in the statement that there would be very few words that would be speaking of total truth.

> *Yes. And we've become so disillusioned with some of the ones we've put our trust in. And with mankind—*

It would be correct in the disillusionment. And there would also be the statement that they are in the belief that they are correct. For they are in the belief of manipulation of the many for what they believe to be the good of the many.

There would not be the statement in the newspaper that there would be a gathering of beings uniting as One that the Light might flow forward. It would not be what would be considered news, so to speak.

We would find that there would be in the statements of what would be occurring around the world—the single-sightedness. There would be those beings who would be viewing a country. And in that country there would be the union of beings. And then within that country there would be the uprising of the beings. And there would also be the people living across the river. And what do you think would be reported? The uprising of the beings would be the information that would be presented to us. For those beings who would be reporting the news have been trained to go toward the dis-union of beings—the misalignment. And we, as human beings, seek out the misalignment of our very own selves that we might make it perfect. When we focus on the misalignment, we have forgotten our Oneness—our entirety.

There was a woman who asked once about the war and the killing on the planet called Earth. She was in great concern of what was occurring. And there was a description given to that woman of what a battlefield would look like, so to speak. Quite descriptive we became as we would be speaking with her. And she was abhorred at what we would be saying. And we knew that that is the way she would be. Then we said to her that she could be vibrating in the "now," in the presence of Love, or she could be vibrating in the battlefield with her body dismembered. It would be a choice.

And if she were to take her consciousness and put it into the battlefield, guess where she would be? In the battlefield in one form or another. Whether it would be there, or whether it would be with her children; whether it would be with her husband or her boss; there would be the consciousness of the battlefield for we have decided to become single-visioned. When we open ourselves that we recognize I AM we would be in the vibration of One and we would be in the manifesting of One. It would be difficult only until we do it.

> *And I guess it's our programming as children. I had a happy childhood. Yet it's still difficult.*

What would be so difficult?

> *To not be serious about things that aren't worth being serious over.*

That would be the exact words. It would be once again allowing ourselves to be children. Children would not be concerned for the disasters that would be coming down the road many years from now. Who knows what the vibrations would be for everything is changing. Everything is *now.*

> *When experiences happen to us in life that are so-called negative experiences, do we more or less plan this for soul growth? It seems like every seven years I have strange things happening to me.*

It would be in the balance and the counterbalance, as you have said. It would be termed "soul growth." It would be the swing of the pendulum—back and forth until we recognize that we have a choice. When we believe that there is balance and counterbalance, when we believe that good must offset bad, then we are functioning in the belief of good and bad and we would continue to swing. When we recognize that it would be facts, then we would be releasing ourselves of the swing of the pendulum.

It's getting through to me! You put it in a little nutshell—it's very easy.

It is, my friend. It is the gift of the Universe—to our very own selves.

We would have a better world if more people would understand this.

We have a perfect world. It would be that we believe that there would be no hurting. We would be forgetting that there have been those great Masters who have decided to manifest on the planet called Earth in pain, so to speak, that we might vibrate as One. And when we view a being in pain, what do we say? "Oh, that is terrible," instead of "Thank you." When we view a being that would be unable to move his arms, we would say in our being, "Thank you, thank you."

We say "Thank you"? My father lost his legs.

That blessed man.

He had 80 good years, but when he lost his legs, I felt so very sorry for him. But I didn't know enough to bless it—as you have said.

You can be doing that now. When we remember—when we remember a time and we see that perhaps if we knew what we knew now, we would have been different then—then we would remember that time within our being, within our vision, and we would place ourselves in that time. And we give ourselves permission to be the way we would be now.

There would be the statement, my dear friend: When there would occur a remembrance from the past, so to speak, tugging away at our being, and we would be in the statement, "I do not want to remember that. I am tired of remembering that," then, in the picture of the mind of that time, there would be the breathing of the breath of understanding. It would be the breathing into the picture the breath of understanding.

There would be the viewing of those beings in the picture, viewing with Love. That there would be in the viewing of self, the forgiving of self. There would be the understanding, the forgiving and the loving of self.

When we recognize that each dimension is occurring now — there is no such things as the past or the future — it is simultaneous. And when we allow ourself to go within and be as we would be — we are affected in that dimension that we call the past. *When we choose to reside in the now, we effect every single dimension — what we call past and what we call future.*

So we're really living all our lives at one time?

Right now. In this very second. And when a memory comes forward and that memory would be saying to us, "I wish I was that way" — then we go within and we *be* that way. And then we bless ourselves — and the memory — and we release it. It continues on.

That's a beautiful concept.

It is the correct concept, so to speak. It is the truth. For many have said it is the "now." Everything is now — even what we term the past. It is now.

When we hear of the disasters, as we have been speaking, there would be the statement that *everything* is occurring now. Everything. Then we remember I AM. That we are I AM — I AM. That Being that human beings term God — *is Self*. Within our being resides everything. Everything.

Have we not been told that we would create this and more. Of course. In the now. I AM. We are the creator. And we are the created. In the same breath. When we ask, we receive — simultaneously. There would be the recognition — I OPEN MYSELF TO THE AWARENESS I AM.

***

When you view that you have a twin soul, it is a belief ... you limit yourself.

Will I eventually settle down with my twin soul as a mate in this lifetime?

My friend, when you view that you have a twin soul, it is a belief. When you view that you have a twin soul, you limit yourself. My friend, every being about you is your very own self.

If you would be opening to the deep relationship with another being, prepare yourself. Be that being. Be that being, my friend. Allow yourself to be complete that you might vibrate. It would be a releasing, my friend. Looking at the beliefs. Where do they come from? It would be healthy to be saying, "Says who? Who says this? What is twin soul?" Oh, yes, we recognize the belief of twin soul, never fear. My wonderful friend, discard those beliefs. You limit yourself. You limit yourself.

What would you want, my friend? To settle down "some day," so to speak, with another being whom you would like to believe is your twin soul, spirit, friend? Of course, my friend. Of course, it can occur—if you open. If you allow yourself to be complete. If you allow yourself to be expansive. Expansive in the recognition that all beings would then be twin souls. Every being. Every single being. Even those beings you abhor. Even those beings you do not like to be around. They are our twin souls. Allow yourself to be fulfilled, my friend.

***

My friend, it is a belief that we even need a belief.

What does my life path number "22/4" mean, pertaining to past lives and to the present?

109

My dear, dear friend, there could be many, many beliefs. Many, many beliefs. As human beings we seek. We want to know. Blessed be the human being. Blessed be your being.

What do we do when we want to learn, my friend? We read the books. We listen to other beings and they seem to know what they are speaking of. And we want to know also—so we grab a book and we read it and we study. And we find another book and we read it and study, trying to find the meaning to things. Finally we find a book and it seems to resound the truths. And what do we do, as human beings? We try to become that book. We try to become the page—the very page.

My dear friend, when we decide that we would become the page, when we decide that we would be seeking in numbers—which would not be correct or incorrect—we would be placing our very own selves on hold, so to speak. We allow ourselves to go back to sleep.

My friend, put away the toys. Put away those belief creators— and vibrate in the now. *Vibrate in the now.* When we view certain things, so to speak—numbers—do we decide what the numbers would mean? And then what do we do with that information? We try to fit ourselves to the information. We try to gear our very own lives to the numbers and the meanings therein.

There has been much written on the meaning of numbers, has there not? It would not be correct or incorrect. It would simply be a statement. And as human beings we decide that we would learn about them and the interpretations, and then we try to be like them. We try desperately to find something that would match our very being so that we could go back to sleep once again. That we would feel such comfort in the statement of the meaning of the number.

Or in another case, there would be the reading of a book. That there would be a method in the book. And there would be another being's statement of what they have experienced. And what would we do as human beings? We try to reexperience what that other being has experienced. We judge our very own experience by what we have read that someone else has done. And what are we doing? We are asleep.

How do we live? We vibrate in the NOW, my friend. We vibrate now. Cast aside the books. Cast aside those beliefs, my friend. Cast them aside. Put them away for a rainy day, so to speak, sometime in what you call the future. Put them aside and look at your self within. See your beauty within and be in the now. Right now. What are all those meanings? All those beliefs? They are words, they are beliefs.

As human beings we seek to have beliefs that we can construct around our very beings. And then we step in the middle of them. And we vibrate there until the belief is tired and stale. And what do we do? We find another belief. And we create *it* around us. And we vibrate in that belief. Until that belief is stale. And we keep seeking and seeking for the correct belief.

My friend, it is a belief that we even need a belief. We are everything. We are I AM. Be alive. Be now. Cast aside the stories. Vibrate I AM. Know that you are the truth. That you *are* the truth. That you need not seek somewhere for some meaning. You *are* the very vibration of truth. Everything resides within your being.

It is time. It is time to be opening to One, to be learning from self. How do we learn from self? We live right now. We hear the message from within. "Yes," we say, "but—but, I do not hear the message from within." How can we hear the message from within when we are filling ourselves with such beliefs? We cast them aside. And we hear our very own vibration. Deep within.

Never fear, my friend. When you unburden yourself of the necessity of the beliefs, then you vibrate in the freedom *I AM*. In the freedom of self. In the dignity of self. In the strength. For the freedom of self and the dignity of self is the dignity of the entire Universe—the strength of the Universe. The blessings of the Universe are bestowed within your being.

***

We are all truly channelers of the Light.

We would be beginning the topic of channeling. For there would be beliefs attached to the vocabulary of channeling. We would be wondering what would be channeling; what would be the purpose. When are we channeling and when are we not? There would be many thoughts: "Some day I wish I would be a channeler," or "I hope that never happens to me while I'm sleeping."

As a matter of fact, there is not one being here who has not been channeling since the day they were born. When we are channeling, what are we doing? We are being. We are being what we are. Allowing ourselves to be. The truth of our being, however it would be. Vibrating in the truth of our being. When we are vibrating in the truth of our being, what is occurring? We are in conscious manifestation I AM.

When a friend calls us on the telephone and speaks of their sorrows and their problems—we would be speaking. And when we are complete with the communication, we think at times, "How did I know to say those words?" Because we opened and we allowed the words to flow forward from our beings. From truth. We allowed it to occur.

There would be those who would be great writers of poetry and prose. They would be in the statement, "I placed my pen upon the paper and there it appears." Channeling.

There would be those who would be in the playing of music. Perhaps they would be struggling. And what would occur one time or another? They would simply release and there would be the appearance of sound coming forward. Channeling.

There would be those who would be singing and they would be working at singing. And one time or another the opening and the flowing and the sound would come forward—free, expressing the presence, the vibration in the presence. Channeling.

There would be those who would be healers. Are we not all healers? Yes, we are. There would be healers. And there would be those beings who would be healed. Human beings, channeling. Perfect as we are. Channeling.

There would be those who would be opening their beings that there would be another speaking. Channeling. There would be those who would be opening to the Light and speaking the words. Channeling.

Our beliefs, my dear friends, our beliefs create what would be occurring in our lives. When we have a statement, "I wish to be a channeler," we are once again *begging* to manifest that which we already are. When we open that we might channel, when we open that the energies might flow from our beings, it is unlimited — unlimited. And where is it coming from? What are we channeling? Our very own selves, my friends. Remember, we are everything. We are I AM.

When we say we would channel the healing power, when we say that we would channel writing poetry, when we say that we would be painting — that would be our choice. It would be our very own choice. And what would we be doing? Releasing ourselves from the bondage which we have placed upon our very own selves. *Releasing* ourselves of the bondage. How would we be doing that? By *receiving* every part of our selves.

There are many who would be interested in allowing the energies to flow forward that they might be manifesting wonderful music. And they have the belief that they are in bondage. And they would be wondering, "How can I release myself from this bondage?" *Welcome home!* Welcome home. *That is how we release ourself — by receiving ourself.* Then we have the choice. Then we have the choice.

There would be many who would be opening to what has been termed channeling through writing. And there would be the placing of the pencil upon the paper and they would be wanting to have beautiful words come forward. And there is not one movement. *Welcome home.*

There are many who would be in the statement, "What is wrong with me? I have tried everything." What is wrong with you? We would be in the statement, "Welcome home to the most wonderful part of your being." That part, waiting here to be received. Waiting to be received.

When we make a statement within our beings, "I open myself," we are in charge. "I open myself" — and there is an opening that occurs. When you say, "I open myself that the Love of the Universe might flow forward," guess what occurs? There is an opening and the Love of the Universe flows forward. It occurs. It is real. Yes, my friends, we are in charge. Would we be having fun?

113

A Meditation on Channeling

We would be in the statement that we would be releasing from the center of our being the energies of the Universe. The energies of the Universe. That we would allow them to flow forward. Hear the breath. Allow them to flow forward. Allowing them to flow forward. Allowing them to flow forward from our being.

It would be quite with ease, in the simplicity of our being—from the child within. Allowing the energies to flow forward from the child within. From the child. From the child.

In the simplicity of our being we would allow the energies to flow forward. From the very center of our being, flowing forward. To the center. To the very center. Allowing. That we would be channels. That we would be channels together.

Human beings, spirit beings, channels together. Channels together. Allowing it to pour into the center. Allowing. Allowing the flow.

I OPEN MYSELF.

I OPEN MYSELF TO THE AWARENESS I AM.

I ALLOW MYSELF TO OPEN TO THE AWARENESS OF THE FLOWING OF ENERGIES THROUGH MY BEING THAT I MIGHT ALLOW THE FLOW TO GROW.

That we might allow the Light of the Universe to come forward in the marriage of beings.

That we might allow the Light of the Universe to come forward. That the entire Universe might bask in the Light. Allowing it to come forward. Just allowing.

We would be in the experiencing of our very own Light. We would be in the experiencing of our very own power. We would be in the experience of our very own energy. We would be in the experience I AM. Then we would be hearing the words, hearing the words.

We are all truly channelers of the Light. That the Light might grow. That the entire Universe might view the Light. That every being on the planet called Earth might experience the Light growing within their very own selves.

That we would be in the marriage of beings—channelers. Chan-

114

nelers. Allowing the flow. Channelers. Unending flow. Unending flow. *You* are truly a channeler of the Light.

***

We would be in the belief that we must learn how to do what we already do.

[*A woman asks if Pretty Flower can help her with astral projection.*]

There would be times with human beings when we would be in the statement of words that would be describing what we already do. And we would find that we would be in the belief that we must learn how to do what we *already* do—that it fit the description of what we think we need to learn. We do it already. In what you term to be astral projection, my friend, you are an expert!

Really?

Yes, my friend. It would be in the statement—I OPEN MYSELF TO THE CONSCIOUS AWARENESS OF MY JOURNEYS WITHIN THOSE DIMENSIONS WHICH WOULD BE MOST HELPFUL TO ME AT THIS TIME.

Hummm.

And then we are aware.

Wonderful. Wonderful.

Yes, my friend. You would be an expert. Trying to fit the experience to another's description would be quite unnecessary.

***

115

Chapter 5

This I Do Create — For I AM

Seek not for the great truths—for you create them.

My dear friends, we are the creators. We create even the great truths. Seek not for the great truths—for you create them. You create them. That we would not be about, seeking from outside of ourselves what would be the great truths. That we would create them to be. And there would be the words: THIS I DO CREATE— FOR I AM. With every creation—conscious manifestation I AM.

It would not be that it would be a secret—however, it would be the greatest teaching which we would be in the bestowal: That we are the creators. That you are the creators of the great truths. When you create—conscious manifestation—conscious creation, there would be the vibration: THIS I DO CREATE—FOR I AM. That you be the Gods that you are.

***

We would be in the recognition that we create with the mind.

[A man who had spoken with Pretty Flower about healing a physical handicap, asks the following:] I wonder if there

*are any messages from any other entity on the other side
that should come to me now—someone that's working with
me—anything like that?*

Yes, my friend. There would be the statement that there would be
the visualization within the very mind of the self, in full mobility.
For we would be in the recognition that we create with the mind.
There would be the recognition that there would be the visualization
of self in every mobile vibration. It would be in the running, in the
jumping up and down for joy, in the dancing—in everything that
we could conceive of. And we would view that within our very
being, and then we would allow the essence of our being, the spirit
of our being, to move and be *in* the thoughts. *In the visualization.*
Allow the essence of our being to be in the essence of the creation
within the mind. Moving our essence into The Essence.

And there would be the statement, my friend: THIS I DO
CREATE—FOR I AM. It would be correct, my friend, for it would
be time to be in the recognition I AM. My friend, we beseech you
to allow yourself to be in the vibration I AM. We beseech you, as
the guides and the friends and the spirit beings about your being,
that you allow yourself to be I AM—in full recognition and vibration.

That there would be the union of many coming forward from
what we call the past—from other dimensions—coming together
to be One in the same. And that essence would flow through the
being in the strength of the Universe. And there would be the taking
of that essence, and placing it in the visualization, and being in the
visualization. *Being in it. Being it—feeling it.* Vibrating in it. And
there would be the statement: THIS I DO CREATE—FOR I AM.

It would be a trusting, a disregarding of the belief of misalignment and the trusting of the statement. Even as we speak, you are
wondering if it is correct. And we would be in the statement that
it is the truth. Never fear. For the energies manifest together that
there would be completion of purpose. And even as we vibrate
together in this marriage, there would be the recognition that we
have allowed the vibration of One to fill our being. Never fear, my
friend. The manifestation in the physical plane would be forthcom-
ing, for you yourself would be *allowing* the manifestation to come

forward. For there has been the daring to hope. And there would be the receiving of the gifts, for the vibration within would be I AM.

It would be only the beginning, my friend. For there would be many who would be coming forward, seeking—seeking the truths. And it would be a simple statement, "I AM." That would be the message coming forward from those about your being. For everything else would "fall into place" once we have allowed ourselves to be in the vibration I AM.

***

When we are seeking, we are always one step behind....When we create—we are it.

[A person asks:] Why don't I always receive when I ask?

What would you be seeking?

Different things at different times.

But you would be seeking and you would not be receiving. Where would we be seeking?

Inside sometimes; outside other times.

Yes, my friend. When we are seeking we have the belief that what we want is somewhere else, and we are trying to figure out where it would be. And we would be in the remembrance that we are everything. It is here. When we are seeking, we are forgetting that I AM. For example, when we are thinking that we are seeking the Light, that we are seeking to be enlightened, we are creating that we are not. And then we must go about figuring out how to be that way—when we are. For we are the entire Universe. The entire Universe—we are.

119

Then, my friend, what would be occurring? There would be the difference between creating and seeking. When we are seeking, we are always one step behind. Seeking and seeking. When we create—we are it. We are the creator. We are the creation.

So that when we are wanting something to occur—something within our very own lives—we desire it because it already exists and is begging to be manifest. Begging to be manifest. And here we are, as human beings, wondering if our desires are correct. Wondering, "Is it correct for me to desire?" It is *begging* to manifest. Begging to manifest. That we would create.

For example, if we are seeking peace, we have many questions going on within our being and we are seeking the answers to the questions, over and over. Viewing here and viewing there, reading different manuscripts, different teachings, wanting the answers. And what are we really wanting? Peace—within our being. Peace—within our being. And how would we be in peace? Would we be seeking peace? No, my friends, *creating* peace. We would go to the center of our being, in the essence of the great flower—the golden essence, the elixir of life. And we would feel the essence between our fingers, we would breathe the essence, and we would be in the viewing of our very own selves, filled with peace. We would breathe the peace, we would vibrate the peace, and we would be in the statement, "THIS I DO CREATE—FOR I AM."

***

There would be those beings who would be recognizing and receiving the responsibility for their very own vibration. It would be the being who would be learning of self.

[A man asks:] I've been traveling pretty much continually for the last three years. Now I would like to have a home base. Weather is a factor. I don't like it very cold or very hot. But I just haven't come upon a place that I would feel

at home. And I don't really know where to go at this point or where to look.

We would find that the answer would be quite simple and revealing. It would be that we would go within. For there could be the traveling about. And there would be the realization that there would be many beings who would be in the question of trying to decide something in their very own lives.

When we would be seeking where we would reside, where we would be in the manifestation of our home, we would be traveling about and viewing the opportunities, viewing the vibrations with our being, feeling the vibrations. "Trying to decide," as you have stated. We would be in the recognition that when we would not be knowing where we would be—there would not be the manifestation of that home. It would be, so to speak, in reverse.

It would be that we would begin with the requirements within ourselves. There would be the climate. There would be—what else?

People—like the ones who are gathered here.

And what else? Would it be near the mountains or the ocean? At the peak of the mountain, the plateau of the mountain, or in the gulf?

It doesn't feel like it matters. It feels like I'll get some place and say, "This is it."

It would be that we would be speaking of creation.

Creation?

Yes, my friend. For we would be in the process of creating. We would be in the process. It would be that we could be seeking and seeking—not that that would be improper. We would be seeking where we would reside. And we would be in the statement that we could, if we were to choose to, consciously create where we would reside. For we would be creating and it would be in an unconscious manner. We would be in the statement that deep within our being

121

resides I AM. I AM. Everything. Within our being.

When we would be in recognition of self, then we would have the choice of consciously creating. When we would be sleeping, what we have termed "being a robot," we would still be creating; however, we would be unconsciously creating. When we are vibrating, we are in the manifestation of I AM—however we would be.

However we would be—we would be in the manifestation I AM. There would be those beings who would be quite unhappy with their lifely situation. And it would be that they have in the unconsciousness of their being created their reality to be what it would be.

Then there would be those beings who would be recognizing and receiving the responsibility for their very own vibration. It would be the beings who would be learning of self, the beings who would be finding themselves in a particular situation in which they would be unhappy. And they would be saying, "I do not want to do this again. I do not want to be this way." And what would they be doing? They would be denying their very own self. And when we deny our very own self, what would occur? We *be* that way. Every time. Even against our will, it would seem. Over and over again we would be in the attempting to be perfect and to not be the way we do not want to be. And in one way or another that part of ourselves comes forward, tapping us on the shoulder, that we might recognize part of ourselves.

Therefore, we would be gathering ourselves together that we might be in union with self. It would be "Welcome home," for I AM—everything. Then we would be in the manifestation I AM in the conscious manner of our being, in the consciousness of our being, for we would have a choice of how we would manifest.

Then there would be the desire, as you have spoken, to be in the residing of the home. It would be the decision to be in a location that would be placing the roots in the Mother Earth. Then there would be the statement, "This would be what I would create." You would be the creator, for you are I AM, the essence of the Universe. It would be gathering up the essence and creating. Then if we would be thinking, "I cannot seem to locate a place to live," it would be that we have not *created* a place.

There would be many beings coming forward seeking, and we would be speaking to those beings of their wants and desires. And they would be saying, "I would be wanting a job that would be fulfilling. What would I do?" And we could be saying, "Go to 42nd Street, go to the third floor, and the second door, and knock on the door, and speak with the man and you will have a job of fulfillment." And what would we be doing? We would be allowing that being to be sleeping. To be as a robot.

However, we would be in the process of awakening to our own essence, to our own reality. It would be that that being would be learning of the messages from within, learning to trust the messages within. How would we be doing that, my dear friend? It would be quite simple. It would be allowing the child within our being to come forward. Allowing the child—that little being deep within.

For at times we have become so responsible within our beings that we have carried the burdens of the world upon our very shoulders, that we would be in the properness of our being, that we would be fulfilling our purpose. It would be a grand idea, my friends. And it would be going in circles, my friends. For there would be the recognition that within our being is the child. The child. And how would we be listening to our very own selves? We would be opening, that the child would come forward—the child within—who has been in hiding. The child who has been in hiding, waiting for the opportunity to play.

Now we have certain beliefs as human beings. We have the belief of work and of play. It would be that we have created opposites, so to speak. And it would be the truth that when we are playing, when we are finding ourselves vibrating in joy, then we would be in the work. *That* would be the work.

When we find ourselves vibrating in habit, vibrating in the staleness of our beings, that would not be the work, my dear friends, that would not be the work. The work would be in the manifestation of play, having fun, discovering. In the uninhibited expression of self. In play.

When we open to the child within, then we can hear the message. For the child would say, "Yes, this is fun." And, "No, this is not fun." And we would be hearing the message.

It would be the beginning of hearing our very own selves.

***

There would be the viewing then of how we have created our present circumstances. It would be quite simple. It would be "checking in" on the thoughts of the day.

[A man asks:] You brought up the question of the future and I was interested in that because my wife and I are planning to move to Charlottesville sometime this year. Right now it's very much on my mind as to when that move will take place and how much longer we will be here in this area. I was wondering if you can offer any enlightenment on that.

We would be speaking and it would be appearing to be an evasion of the question. However, never fear. The answer will appear.

We would be speaking about creating our own reality. It would not be a long and involved talk. It would simply be the statement: As human beings we have been seeking, seeking the Light. Have we not? In one form or another—seeking the Light. And then, one time or another, we come to recognize that deep within our beings— our very own beings—resides I AM. Now what would be I AM? Everything. Everything would be I AM. We would be in the statement that we are the creators. We are the creators.

And there would be the question, "I would like to know the future. Would there be some fortune telling going on here?" We have rearranged your words. There would be the question: What would you be wanting to occur? For, as we have spoken, there has been the releasing of power. For we have viewed that circumstances outside of our being would be in control and that we have been tossed and turned by the tides of spirituality.

We have read many representations of teachings which have

124

pulled us one way and the other way. One would be saying to surrender and be grateful for whatever occurs in our vibration called life. And the other would be pulling us in another direction which would be saying that we are the creators. There would be many, many teachings, would there not? Yes, my friend. However, we would be in the statement that we are the creators.

Now when we are walking down the street there would be the recognition that every human being would be in the manifestation I AM. Every human being. If we would be walking down the street and we would be viewing a being who would be in anger, we would perhaps be thinking, "I'm glad I'm not being in anger." We perhaps would have been in anger previously and know the feeling. And there would be the judgment within the human being that there would be non-spirituality attached to the anger. We would be in the statement that every human being would be in the manifestation I AM. It would be the recognition of releasing the judgments. That every human being would be in the manifestation I AM—however they would be.

There would be the recognition that there would be some beings who would be in the consciousness of the decision of how they would manifest I AM. There would be those beings who would be in the unconsciousness of their being—in the manifestation of I AM. However, every one would be in the manifestation of I AM. The God to whom you pray would be your very own self.

Then there would be the statement: If I am in manifestation of I AM in everything that I would be doing, then I have the conscious choice. For example, "I would be wanting to move to Charlottesville, Virginia." Would that be correct? (The man answers, "Yes.") Then there would be in the manifestation I AM, the wondering, the building of anxiety in the questioning, questioning—"When would that be?" There would be the wondering of the success of the move. There would be several questions coming forward and that would be the manifestation I AM.

There could be the decision for the conscious manifestation I AM. What would be the decision? It would be the statements: "This is what I create to occur. I would be moved in that location—by this time." That there would be the pictures within the mind of the

125

receiving of that area within your beings, and of the marriage of your beings with the land of that area—that there would be a union. That there would be in your being the creation of the ease of the move. That everything would occur exactly as you would have it occur, in order to produce great joy within your being. For have we not unconsciously created a little of the opposite? For we have in an unconscious way been in the questioning of what would occur in the manifestation I AM of our very own selves. We would be in the decision of manifesting great joy at the awareness that the move and the union in that particular vibration would be whole and complete.

Now why would we, as human beings, not be doing that? It would be quite simple. We would not be in the experience of the foundation. We would not be in the trusting of the foundation of creating, for we have not created for a time. We have believed that we are reactors to the circumstances of our lives. Reactors, so to speak. And when we are told that we would be the creators, we would be sitting back and saying, "It sounds good."

We would be in the statement that in order for us to trust the process, we would then be in the practice of the process, *that the foundation might be created*. The foundation of trust. The foundation of the fulfillment of hope. In the fulfillment of hope resides the foundation of our beings. That as human beings we might trust once again—we might trust the hope.

For there have been times, as human beings, where we have had the hope and it has been dashed to the ground and remained unfulfilled. And we would be in the statement that the time is at hand—the time for the fulfillment of hope. That the foundation might grow and deepen and that we might vibrate as One. That we might know deep within our beings I AM. That we are the creators. That we would know. For it would sound wonderful until we are in the action thereof, over and over again.

There would be the viewing then of how we have created our present circumstances. It would be quite simple. It would be "checking in" on the thoughts of the day. What would be going around within the mind? *What would be the thoughts? For they would be the creators of the vibration.*

Then we would be in the statement that there would be within three and a half weeks time the receiving of the correct date that you would be quite fulfilled in your needs.

Now let me make sure that I understand—within three and a half weeks we would be receiving the date?

Yes, my friend.

—when we would be going?

Yes, my friend.

Okay. Thank you.

Would you be holding your breath? (Laughter from all)

No. I think I'll breathe a little easier though.

It would be the *opportunity* of three and a half weeks of creating exactly what we would want to receive. For there could be the messages coming from the Universe. And we would be receiving what we are *open* to receive.

I understand that.

Then we could be for three and a half weeks practicing the opening of receiving the blessings and the abundance of the Universe. And how would we be doing that? Very simple, my friend. I OPEN MYSELF TO THE ABUNDANCE OF THE UNIVERSE. It would be as simple as that. I OPEN MYSELF TO THE AWARE-NESS THAT DEEP WITHIN MY BEING, I AM. I OPEN MY-SELF TO THE FULFILLMENT OF PURPOSE THAT I MIGHT VIBRATE AS ONE. Whatever we would wish—or, we would simply state that we are open. That the flowing might occur. I OPEN MYSELF TO THE LOVE OF THE UNIVERSE. I OPEN MYSELF TO THE GREATEST HEALING POWERS OF THE

UNIVERSE. We would dare to say what we would want. We would dare to say it. To open ourselves to receive.

Then what do we do? We are doing it. At the end of the statement, we are open. Then we vibrate during our day, trusting. Trusting the process.

***

...we would question the limitations of the term "New Age." Universal, my friend, Universal.

[A woman asks:] Can I ever be financially secure in a New Age occupation?

There would be the statement: As we have begun, we would complete. When we open ourselves to the fulfillment of purpose in the vibration of One, then every need is taken care of. Every need. The answer would be yes, my friend, of course. Although we would question the limitations of the term "New Age." Universal, my friend, Universal—when we are in the expression of I AM. Yes, my friend, *you* create everything. *You,* my friend, *you* create everything. Everything. *You* are the creator.

What would you like to occur? Create it. How do you create it? My friend, you view. You view in your mind. What do you view? How you would manifest I AM. How would you manifest I AM in your very own life vibration? You create that picture in your mind, my friend. Create everything you wish to be vibrating within. And then, my friend, you say, I OPEN MYSELF TO THE AWARENESS I AM—AND THIS I DO CREATE. It would be a simple teaching, my friend. And it would be the great truth.

We would be in the statement that those who ask, receive. Who are they asking of? Their very own selves.

***

...there would be many who would be gathering together, creating new rules of unencumbered manifestation.

[A man at a group gathering asks:] I'm wondering if there would be a time when the way people live would involve less toil, without so much time and energy spent simply maintaining themselves.

Yes, my friend. Believe the truth of the statement: It is occurring even as we speak. There would be those beings who would be toiling. There would be those beings who would be creating the reality of their existence—according to the rules which have been presented—according to the rules of the material plane. And there would be those beings who would be in the recognition that they would even be in the *creation* of the rules, in the present, my friend. In the present. It would be the conscious manifestation of I AM.

When we are consciously manifesting, we have the choice of how we would manifest everything. It would be in the belief. It could be in your future, my friend, or it could be in the present. It would be your choice. For there would be the statement that there would be many who would be gathering together, creating new rules of unencumbered manifestation.

Thank you.

Would there be more?

Well, I felt that sort of thing for a long time. So far it hasn't manifested fully. But I do sort of sense it coming.

It would be that you would be in the present, and if you would be desiring the reality of your manifestation to be representing your desire, then you would *consciously* manifest in the reality of your being. For there would be the statement, my friend, "It has not quite manifested." When we say, "It has not quite manifested," then

129

we are viewing something "out there" of which we have no power. You are everything. Everything. It would be a decision to be in conscious manifestation. Would there be more?

[Another person asks:] How does one consciously manifest? By visualizing?

It would be that we would be in the center of our being. That we would be residing within our being. There could be the talking about manifesting—or we could manifest. Would we manifest? Would that be clear?

I'm not sure.

We would be speaking about how to manifest—or we could all be in the process of manifesting. It would be *practicing,* instead of sitting there, listening to the words. Would that be proper?

[The audience all give affirmative responses.]

Then we would begin. Would there be anyone who would be wanting to remain on hold, so to speak, that we would be clear what we would be manifesting? (After a short pause, Pretty Flower begins:)

A Meditation For Conscious Manifestation

Then we would begin. There would be the closing of the eyes, that we might center in the being. We could be sitting with our heads on our hands, on our elbows, on our knees, or we could be lying on the floor. We could be quite comfortable, whatever position we would be in.

We would begin in the consciousness of our being. In the simplicity of our being. That we would be in the awareness within our being. That there would be the awareness, going within our being, traveling within our being, inside. Somewhere.

It wouldn't matter where it would be. Our awareness would be traveling within our being. Just traveling within. Traveling about.

And we would find that we could allow our awareness to settle somewhere within our being. Somewhere. Wherever it would be would be the correct place. Wherever our awareness would settle would be quite correct.

And we would find that we could be releasing as we would be settled within our being. That we could be releasing the cares. We could be releasing the concerns. We could be releasing the questions. We could be releasing the great thoughts. For the moment we could be forgetting everything.

And in the awareness of the being, within our very being, would be in the very center of that awareness, a tiny blue ball. A sparkling blue ball of Light, in the center of our being. In our awareness of our being. And the blue ball would be bright and filled with Light. And we would allow the blue ball to grow—and grow—and grow.

And we would find that we could be peering into the blue ball. And we would be viewing in the blue ball. And what would we be viewing? There would be the path. The path.

And what would be occurring on the path as we viewed? There would be a child on the path, trip-tropping along on the path, and we would allow ourselves to be on the path. Placing our feet on the path, trip-tropping along—the child. For no particular reason, just trip-tropping along on the path.

And the child might kick a pebble with his toe. The child might pick up a flower and pluck the petal with her tiny finger, for no particular reason. Just because the child would be wanting to be doing it.

And the child would be walking down the path, humming a tune. No particular sound, just making a sound. Humming, traveling down the path.

And there would be the sound of the birds. And there would be the traveling around the bend. And there, around the bend, would be the Great Fairy with the wings of the strength of the Universe. And the Fairy would say, "Hello."

And the child would say, "Hello, my friend. Hello."

And the Fairy would be saying to the child, "Would you be traveling to the garden?"

And the child would say, "I would be traveling to the garden."

And the Fairy would be walking with the child down the path, that they would be viewing the flowers. That they would be viewing the birds. That they would be One—together.

And they would be coming to the garden and the Fairy would be with the child, saying, "Here is the garden, my friend."

And the child would clap her hands together with glee, for she would be at the garden. And there would be the entry to the garden. The placing of the feet on the path in the garden. And the child would be walking in the garden. And there would be the flower. And there would be the ferns.

And the child would continue in the path. There would not seem to be a destination, however the child would be continuing further into the garden. Deeper into the garden.

And there would be ahead the view of some stairs. And the child would be in the climbing of the stairs. First one step, and then another. And then the child would see that there would be at the top of the stairs a great flower. A great white flower.

And the child would be climbing the stairs to the great flower. And she would be in the presence of the great flower. And she would be viewing the beauty of the great flower. And the flower would open wide. It would be very large. Very large.

And in the center of the flower would be the gold—the Light. The golden Light—in the center of the flower. And the child would be viewing the Light. Viewing the Light.

And the child would decide to stand in the center of the flower, in the Light. In the gold. In the essence. In the center. In the elixir of Life, the essence I AM. And there would be the vibration. And the child would be in the vibration. In the gold. In the center.

And there would be the remembrance of the child, that I would be here for a purpose. I would be here in the creation of my being.

And there would be the gathering together of the liquid gold— that the child would be in the playing with the elixir. Playing in one hand and then another, gathering it up from the bottom of the flower. Playing with it. Sitting in it. Swirling the little finger around in the essence of gold. Feeling the gold.

And then there would be the remembrance that the child would be in the process of creating. And here, my dear friend, would be the home of creation. And the child would be creating.

And you would be creating, my friend, in the thought of the child, gathering together the essence.

Gather together the essence. Play with it in your fingers. Twirl it about in your hands. The essence I AM. The essence of creation. And with your mind, with your thoughts, create the picture. Create what it would be you would desire.

For you would be in the essence of creation. Just like building a sand castle. There would be the building, the creating. That the child would be in the creating. And the breath of life would be in the breath of the creation. And the being would be in the statement: THIS I DO CREATE—FOR I AM. THIS I DO CREATE—FOR I AM. THIS I DO CREATE—FOR I AM.

As we view the child in the center of the flower, in the essence — and we view the great flower, the white flower — as we view the garden — as we view the path in the garden — as we view the great path with the Fairy with the wings with the strength of the Universe — as we view through the blue ball within our being, we are in the recognizing that in the innocence of the child is the wisdom of the Universe. In the innocence of the child is the truth of the Universe. In the innocence of the child is the creation of the Universe.

And there would be the blessing and there would be the recognition that deep within our being would be the center of creation. For we are everything, my friend. We are everything. We are everything, my friend. Deep within our being — the center of creation.

We could be allowing ourselves to come forward. That we would be in the center of our being once again. We would allow ourselves to come forward. That we would be vibrating together in the consciousness of our being. That we might consciously create manifestation I AM.

*

[As the group is returning from the meditative state, Pretty Flower comments:] There would be interesting creating going on.

***

133

[Pretty Flower and a man at a session have the following exchange:]
Would you be needing to break another bone in order to take a break?

You never know.

It would be easier to take a break.

***

> *We create within our beings that we might be receptacles for the abundance of the Universe.... that we would be as the child, jumping up and down ... with glee at the receiving of the abundance of the Universe.*

[A woman asks:] I don't really know how to phrase this, but I'm going to do my best. I feel as if something's going to happen—some type of transition or change. Or something concerning my future as far as—I don't want to use the word "career"—but something like that.

Why would you not be wanting to use the word career?

Because I'm not sure if it's career or not. But it concerns helping other people and healing. I think I know where I'm supposed to be going with my healing energies but I'm just not quite sure in what direction I should be pointing. In other words, if I should be helping people verbally or helping them in other ways. This is so difficult because I'm not really sure how to phrase it.

Of course, my friend. For there would be even within the words—the transition of change. We would be in the statement, once again, that you would be aware that you are in charge. You are I AM.

134

When we are in the statement "supposed to be," we are in the belief that we are the leaf in the wind. Remember, when you are opening to hearing the messages within your being, then you are opening to the "flow." Where does that come from? Your very own creation, for you are I AM.

Therefore, there would be the recognition of the flow of what you term to be healing through your being. Then there would be the statement within your very being, "How would I choose to manifest the healings of the Universe? What would be the most fun for me?" For we would be playing as children.

Remember, when the child is skipping, every being who comes in contact with the child is feeling the flow of healing of the Universe. When the child is laughing, there would be the recognition of the completion of healing. Laughter is the recognition of the completion of healing.

Therefore, there would be the statement within your very being that you would be wondering, "How would I manifest? How would I *choose* to manifest that I might be the channel for healing as I have chosen to be? How would I be in the enjoyment? How would I be in the playing? How would I be?" *Your choice.* Hearing the message from within. Hearing the message from your very own self. Allowing what we term to be imagination. Allowing the pictures to come forward. *Daring to allow the grandness of the plan within your very being to come forward.* Daring.

For there would be, my dear friend, the time when you would be traveling from one center of healing to another, as the teacher. However, first there would be the beginnings, as we have been speaking, that you would be choosing how you would be in the manifestation of teaching. How you would be in the manifestation of experiencing—that you might know the teaching within your very being.

For from the truth of our being flows the truth of teaching. How would you be experiencing the healing, your very own self, in the vibration of different groups? That you would experience the truth of the group. That you would experience the vibration and you would be deciding if it would be correct for you to be carrying that message within your very being.

135

It would be the time of experience, that within yourself you would experience different methods, different manifestations of healing in many dimensions. Remember, healing is of spirit, that the physical might manifest. Healing is of spirit.

There would be those beings who would be in the sharing of teaching through physical movement known as dance. And in the enjoyment of their beings, they would be gathering together those beings who would be in the difficulty of movement—that they might open in trust with the movement of their physical being. There would be the suggestion that perhaps you would be in the joining of the teaching. That you might experience for your very own self the freedom of movement with the group with the purpose of opening to spirit. That you might recognize the experience your very own self. That you might allow the teachings to come forward from the truth of your being.

There would then be those beings who would be in the experience of movement of color upon paper. For the allowing of the spirit to come forward in physical manifestation. And it would be a possibiliy that you would be in that experience. For remember, healing would be totality of being, that in every dimension there would be the experience of healing. That then you would not be in confusion, for you would be recognizing the expansiveness of your being.

Of course there would be the wondering how you would manifest. It would be of them all—*of them all*. And you would feel correct in the experiencing of every teaching that you would be joining. Experiencing within your very spirit. That you would allow the truth of your being to come forward.

The only other thing I'd be interested in is—can you give my husband and myself some advice for our immediate future? Is there anything that you think could help?

What would be needing of help?

I don't know. Just anything that you might feel—any words?

136

My dear, dear friends, there would be the statement: Remember, you are the creators. You are the manifesters. In the togetherness of your beings, you would be deciding what you would want to manifest. What you would want to manifest. It would not be sacrilege.

You are the creators. Have we not had that lesson from every great Master? You are the creators. You have the belief at times that you are the leaf in the wind, that the Wind Spirit blows you about. And what would be occurring next, you wonder? What would be occurring next? What would *you decide* to occur next? What would you be wanting to occur? That you might create within your being receptivity. For here is the entire Universe.

For example, if you would be wanting the abundance of the Universe, what would be occurring? We would be in the statement: I OPEN MYSELF. It is very simple. I OPEN MYSELF TO THE ABUNDANCE OF THE UNIVERSE. And then, my friends, what do we do? We create within our beings that we might be receptacles for the abundance of the Universe. That we might view within our beings that we would be as the child, jumping up and down and clapping our hands together with glee at the receiving of the abundance of the Universe.

Remember, we create with our beliefs. When there is the belief of "deserving," what occurs? We are postponing the receiving of abundance. For one reason or another we have created the belief of deserving—it is belief. What would we be doing with the belief of deserving? First we would be in the statement: Welcome home to that belief—for I am everything. Then we have the choice. Conscious manifestation. Then we have the choice.

We would be deciding—would we need to be deserving? For it is belief. Deserving is postponing the receiving. Deserving means that we would have to be perfect, we would have to be something other than what we are. And if we hold our breath and be perfect for as long as we possibly can, then perhaps we will be deserving for the abundance of the Universe. It would be belief, my dear friends, belief.

Cast aside the belief of deserving. It is belief. Know that *you are* the Universe. Know that *you are* the abundance. Know that

137

you simply open to receive. *Choosing* to open to the abundance. *Choosing* to allow the manifestation of the abundance of the Universe to flow forward. That would be one example. That you could be deciding what you would be wanting to manifest.

For here we are and we have been manifesting all along, have we not? In one form or another. At times we would be squeezing out what we would be wanting. Other times we would be opening and receiving with ease. We would be in the choice of which we would be wanting to manifest. That there would be the blessings of the Universe upon the two in union.

There would be the suggestion that perhaps every three days in the beginning, there would be the sitting of the two across from each other, in silence. That there would be the giving and receiving of energies in the closing of eyes, that there would be the opening of eye, together, from each other. In the opening—in giving and receiving—it would not be a "big deal," so to speak. It would be sharing of the depths of the beings.

There would be recognition of wonderful experiences and soon there would be the practice every day—for the wanting of it. For the wanting of the union in spirit. And then, my dear friends, the union of spirit from that experience would be carried forward; that in any type of union in physical form would be the recognition of the union of spirit. It would be in the expansiveness of your beings.

***

And we create the castles in the sand. And we watch the sea wash away the castles in the sand....If we decide to put great meaning ... it would be our decision. Or we could be creating great castles in the sand.

[A woman asks about a business venture:] I had a project I worked on for several months. So many elements of it were coming together that it seemed as though I had consciously manifested it. But one major element didn't work

out so I had to cancel the venture. I was really disappointed and I'm searching for some answers. I have gotten many opinions in the last few weeks. Some people feel I should still be pursuing it and looking for a different place. But the project was geared to the summer tourists and it's too late now to do it anyway. And so I feel that the venture is gone for now—in that form anyway. A Course In Miracles says that when I pray for something I always get it—so that on another level I didn't really want this project to succeed or it would have. Could you advise me?

It sounds like a lot of "figuring out" to me.

I'm always "figuring out."

It would be, my dear friend, how we would be viewing what is occurring. As we have been speaking of abundance, are we viewing abundance or the lack of abundance? Are we viewing the synchronicity of events within our very own life—until we feel that there would be something that would occur to our disliking—and then believe that the synchronicity has stopped? How could that be?

But it wasn't happening. If the place that felt so right was not available to me, it didn't seem as though it was meant to happen.

When we are in the experience of the synchronicity of an event, what occurs? We vibrate. We are filled with joy. Sometimes we are filled with wonder. And then what do we do with that experience as human beings? We carry it with us. And then there will be another event. And we would perhaps be filled with joy. And we would carry *this* event with us. And then we would be thinking, "Here are two events." And then there would be another. And we would carry *that* event with us. And then we would be deciding what we would be doing with the synchronicities. We would be deciding what we would do with the spontaneity. And, my friends, how could we decide what to do with spontaneity? However, as human beings, we are deciding.

And we gather the information together and we decide what would occur in our very own life, of course, as human beings. And as we are deciding, we are continuing in our lives, and there occurs something which says "Stop." And we say to ourselves what we believe this would mean. What would be the belief of that statement? First, would be the experience; then would be confusion. What would be the belief? Confusion. However, it would just be the stopping of momentum in that direction.

If I am traveling on the path and there would be a being coming forward, standing right in front of where I would be skipping—what would I be doing? First, I would recognize that I would stop skipping if I were to continue on this same path or I could be in collision. That would be the choice. However, if I would be wanting to continue in my movement, what would occur? I would perhaps skip around the being or perhaps I would stop for a moment and say "Hello." There would be several choices.

Then there would be the thoughts I could be thinking: "Why have I created that a being would come along and stop my skipping?" It would be part of being a human being—wondering.

In the synchronicity of events that have occurred, I have been skipping along on the path. Perhaps it would be time to be moving along to a different position on the path and skipping along? Perhaps I would be running? Perhaps I would be walking? However, I am standing in front of this person, this being, and I am wondering why they are there? Why has this occurred? It would be choice. For there would be the synchronicity of events and the spontaneity of being occurs whether we view it or not. It occurs.

Then we would be in the statement: What would be the other way of viewing that there would be this being standing in front of me on the path? There would perhaps be the statement in the synchronicity of events, "I am to be stepping to the side and continuing onward." Or, in the synchronicity of events, "I am saying 'Hello' to this being. I thought I was to skip down this path all the way to the end, and here I am standing in front of this being." It would be correct questioning.

140

We are wondering why we have stopped; wondering why. Wondering why we have stopped to smell the flowers. Gathering the pebbles together. Speaking to the being, "Why are you standing here in front of me? I want to be skipping along." And perhaps the being would be in the statement, "I have been walking along. Why have you skipped in front of me?" And here we are, wondering why we have been in the ceasing of movement, facing each other.

There would be in the Universe—the pulsebeat. The opening and the closing. The opening and the closing. There would be times as human beings when we are in the closing, that we are in the thinking, "Why am I closed? I should be open." Then we would perhaps be in the opening. That there would be the statement, "I want to be closed. Why am I so open?"

In the synchronicity, in the pulsebeat of the Universe, as human beings on the planet called Earth, we are learning of creation. We are learning to be as we are.

We have been taught for such a very long time, my very dear friends, to be figuring out what went wrong. It would be judgment. What went wrong? What went wrong that I was skipping and now there is a being standing in front of me? My dear, dear friends, what would be wrong? And what would be right?

We have been dancing around and around with these words— for here was the occurrence of our dear friend who has been making plans and moving along. That there would be then the statement that there was a stopping of movement. And there would be the wondering why. "Why is that being standing in front of me?"

And what else has occurred in our very own life? We have decided that we would be opening to those beings who are filled with love, who would be supporting our endeavors. And we create that atmosphere around our very own selves. And we are opening. And what occurs? There would be a stopping and we are wondering, "How have I created this?" For we have opened that we would be with those beings in support. Gathering together.

When we view that we are in the stopping, we are living in the stopping. And when we are skipping, my friend, we are skipping. It would be the judgment of what has been occurring—the judgment. It would be as if we would be wanting to blame our very own self for being in error of creation.

And we would recognize that we are taken care of. That it would be in the trusting and the opening and the surrender to the occurrence. When we say, I SURRENDER MYSELF TO I AM, when we say, I OPEN MYSELF TO AWARENESS I AM, we are opening to the recognition of every part of our being. Even when we are stopping. And I have had the plans, and now they are no longer the plans. When we have a desire to become, when we have a desire to be worthy, when we have any desire, what is the truth, my friend? It already exists.

When we would be planting the seed, and then the blossom appears, seeking the Light—what would we decide? To deny the blossom to grow and to be as it would be, seeking the Light? We could take that plant and plant it in the Light. And it would open and the petals would be wide and then they would fall to the ground. What would be correct? What would be the mis-creation? It would be the breathing of the Universe, the opening and the closing. In the simplicity of our being. In the trusting of our being. In the human being deciding, "I really want to pursue this." It would be the decision—from here.

There would be many who would be having opinions, as you have stated. Once again, when we have been speaking with our friends, trying to make a decision, it still returns to our very own being. "What would *I* want to do? What would I want to do?" And we would then allow ourselves to manifest.

Perhaps, my friend, there have been many flowers planted. Planted under the tree, and in the sun. And perhaps we would be in the stopping place that we would be deciding what we would be wanting to do? It would appear, my dear friend, that there would be many plans. And when we are calling to ourselves to be in action in many places at the same time, and we find ourselves blocked with beings standing in front of us, what would be the statement? What would be the awareness? That here I am, standing—when I thought I would be skipping. What gifts have I given myself? It would be the other view of "How have I punished myself to deserve this?" What gifts have I given to myself? For there was the occurrence—when we are in the planning and doing and moving in our life—and something occurs and all of a sudden we are in the non-movement. We are standing on the path. "What gift have we given ourselves" would be the viewing. And what would be the *real question?*

Well, for the first time I really felt as though I was listening and following the guidances from within rather than logically trying to figure out the steps I should take in putting this business together. I was going within and feeling clearly, "Ah, today I should do this and that." And then pursuing those steps. It was so exciting because I saw manifestation in a totally different way than I had before. Before I had made it hard and this time I was making it easy and fun. Yet—in the end—it didn't work out.

My friend, you have what we would term "skipped over" the occurrence. Please continue in the description—as you were in the statement of the manifestation, seeking within, continuing in the steps.

Right. So when I felt an energy—an awareness of energy—

Yes, my friend.

A feeling, "Ah, the flow of energy is there today—or there," I then pursued it. And when something felt like it wasn't an "Ah," becoming aware of that and going within again and asking, "What should I be doing?" And sometimes the guidance was, "You should be forgetting about this for today." And I would do some other work that would keep my mind busy so I wouldn't try to figure out how it was all going to come together. It was just incredible the way it was working—even the investors were coming to me! Everything was coming together exactly the way I wanted it.

And then what happened?

And then it didn't work out. I couldn't rent the place I wanted, and at that point it was too late to do the venture anyway.

No, describe what happened. "And then I had the plan to be in this place"—and then what occurred?

I planned on using this place, but one of the two owners—a man—was not behind it. It kept feeling as though he would change his mind. But he kept resisting.

And the answer was "No"?

The answer was lots of excuses and lots of "why not." And then, finally, a definite "No."

My friend, you have described that you have been open to hearing the messages from within—as every human being here would be in the learning. And you have been continuing in hearing the messages from within. Hearing the message from within, "Continue." Hearing the message from within, "Continue." Hearing the message from within, "But I want this place."

Wasn't that the message? (Laughter)

There are times as human beings, we would be in the flowing. And we are involved in the skipping. And when we are in the stopping and we are experiencing the stopping, we view that it is a blockage. We view what has occurred—"This man has ruined everything." And we would be in the statement, "Look at what we have manifested, my friend." We have manifested not only the subtle message from within, we have manifested the clear statement, "No." We have manifested for our very own selves.

As human beings when the answers are "Yes" and we are continuing, we are in the glory of our manifestation. And when we manifest a "No" we think something has gone wrong. It would be the message, my friends—from within—as clearly stated as possible. *How we view that message would be choice.* What gift have I given myself? I have been trusting the messages thus far and they have all been "Yes."

> *I guess, then, I wonder if the whole venture was about something other than what I thought. Or—*

It would be in the complication of self, my friend. In the simplicity of being is the release. In the simplicity of being is the freedom. The freedom—in the trusting. We have been on the journey—the messages have occurred. Every being has come forward. And then we have created that it would not be this place. We have been hearing the manifestation of the message. We hear the message. We receive the message. It would be clear. And as we have been seeking the message from within in previous times, what do we do? We seek the message from within once again.

> *I guess why I'm so confused is everyone says, "Well, go find another place."*

What would *you* be saying?

> *Inside, I'm saying very, very clearly, "That was the only place," though I know that doesn't make sense.*

It does not have to make sense, my friend. It would be your decision. It could perhaps be complete. It would be your decision. We are in charge. *We are in charge!* Our decision. Would I continue? Would I not continue? Our decision. We are in charge. Our decision.

If we are creating that we would be writing a poem and it would be filled with joy and in the creating of the poem there would be a line that would be filled with torment, what do we do? We decide whether we would continue in writing the poem totally of joy. And then what are we going to do with this line of torment? We could be in a quandry about the poem forever. We could begin again and write another poem. We could consider that at the end of that last joyous line was the end of the poem on joy. And the first line would be the beginning of the poem on torment. It would be decision. It would be decision. I would have a garden of roses. What will I do with this tulip? It would be a decision. It would be decision from within, once again.

From the material, the physical plane, everything here would be fantasy. It would be our toys. Our lesson. And we create the castles in the sand. And we watch the sea wash away the castles in the sand. And we create the castles in the sand. If we decide to put great meaning—if we decide to place great purpose—it would be our decision. Or we could be creating great castles in the sand. Our choice.

> *I still wonder because I put so much energy into this. Did I do that knowing the answer would be "No" at the end? Did part of me know that it would be "No"—or was there a possibility that the answer would be "Yes?"*

My friend, what would be the purpose of the answer?

> *Because I felt such strong vibes—why would I be guided to put so much energy into something that was not going to happen—if there wasn't at least a possibility the answer would be "Yes."*

My friend, the decision has been that I will not continue for I believe that it would be only in this one location. And I have received the answer from within in the very strong statement of "No." And then with that answer I have decided that I will not continue. Now the question would be, "Why have I done this to myself?" It would be choice. "I could continue. I could skip around the being. I could stand in front of the being. I could walk into the fields." It would be choice. When we make the choice and then we say, "Why has this happened to me?" we are forgetting we are in charge—in this very second. Choice.

If, for example, the choice would have been, "I receive the answer that this is 'No' and I am in the decision that I will find another place," what would occur with the torment, the turmoil, the confusion? What would occur? It would be like that with the man on the path. I have decided what to do.

I would forget about the man, and decide what I would do?

Whatever it would be. It could perhaps be skipping around that being, or something else. When we have the feelings that we would be vibrating in the blockages of our being, we are residing within the occurrence, as the little child, wondering, "Who did that to me?" Or we could be viewing that we have the choice. Everything is the choice.

We could, for example, stand in front of the being and try to figure out and figure out why he would be there—over and over and over. It would still be serving the same purpose. I have stopped myself. How is this a service to me? I have created this to be. What *gift* have I created? Then we decide. Would we continue? When we are in the intellectualizing, what we are doing is standing in place. It would not be correct or incorrect, however, it is serving the same purpose as the being in the path.

It would be the question, "What would be the gift of this occurrence of 'No'? Why have I given this to myself?" *The gift instead of the punishment.* What great guidance has come forward? *What great guidance?* That I might view what else is occurring on the path. To continue, my friend, would be a choice. It would be one choice.

***

Give *yourself permission to be correct.*

Deep within the being resides the fulfillment of the quest in the manifestation of the being. Never fear, my friend, for everything that you do is correct. Everything. Give yourself permission to be correct. Everything you do is manifestation I AM. Even scratching your head. Everything. For you are a gift to the Universe. Never fear.

***

147

The Story of Purpose

Once upon a time there was a little boy and he was walking down the path. And as he was walking down the path, he was wondering, wondering what he would be doing in that day. For he was quite happy in the enjoyment of his being. And there would be, in the mind of the boy, what would be called an idea—a thought. "I would be creating something this day," he said.

And what did he decide to create? He wasn't quite sure. He knew he would be creating something. Something. What would it be? And he found that he picked up a stick. And he picked up another stick. And he began to gather sticks together in his arm, gathering sticks together.

And he decided that he would make a pile of sticks on the side of the path. And he collected all the sticks he could find on the side of the path. And he made a pile of sticks. And he was quite happy with the pile of sticks.

And then there came another being down the path. And he said to the little boy, "Hello."

And the little boy said, "Hello."

And the being said, "What would you be doing there?"

And the little boy would say, "I would be creating a pile of sticks."

And the being would say, "For what purpose?"

And the little boy would say, "I do not know the meaning of that word 'purpose.'"

And the being would say, "Oh." And the being would be traveling on.

And the little boy would be looking at his pile of sticks and he would be wondering, what would be "purpose." What would be "purpose."

And he continued down the path and he found a little girl on the side of the road—and she was gathering together pebbles. She was gathering together all the round, smooth pebbles. And she was making a pile on the side of the road.

And the little boy said, "Hello."

And the little girl said, "Hello."

And the boy said, "What would you be doing with those pebbles?"

And the little girl said, "I would be creating a pile of pebbles. Just kind of stacking them up here and there. For no particular purpose."

And the little boy said, "For no particular purpose." And he went back to his pile of sticks and he gathered more sticks together and he placed them on top of the others.

And there would be returning—the being. And he would be saying, "Hello, little boy, I see that you have more sticks together, for no particular purpose."

And the boy said, "Yes. For no particular purpose." For he knew the purpose.

And the being smiled at the little boy. And the little boy was filled with joy. For he was in the creating.

And the being carried on and came to the little girl. And he said to the little girl, "Hello. What would be the purpose of that pile of pebbles?"

And the little girl said, "I have been wondering, wondering, what would be the meaning of 'purpose'? And I have been in no particular purpose piling these pebbles together. For I do not know the meaning of 'purpose.'"

And the being said, "Oh. There would be a little boy down the path. Perhaps he would be teaching you in the joy of creation."

***

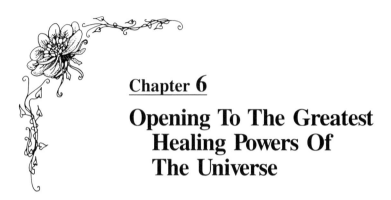

Chapter 6

Opening To The Greatest Healing Powers Of The Universe

...it would be that you have decided to be healed.

[A person with a long-term health problem asks:] What in particular caused my recent healing? There were several things that I did but I'm not sure which one I should give the credit to.

It would be to the credit I AM.

Was it the psychic surgeon or was it the other healer?

It would be, my friend, deep within our being resides I AM. When we recognize that deep within our being resides I AM, we recognize that deep within *every* being resides I AM. And we would be in the choice of the manifestation I AM. When we are in the choice, we recognize that however we are and whoever we are, we are manifesting I AM. Then when we are in the presence of those beings there would be *the marriage* of I AM. It would not be so much one being coming to your very own self—it would be that you have decided to be healed.

Had I completed a particular function in life that I was

151

supposed to perform so that I could now be healed? What made it different than before?

It would be the culmination of many occurrences and changes within your very being. There would have been the time in your situation where there was the acceptance. The acceptance of self. The recognition that there would be seeking and that there would perhaps be non-fulfillment. There was a resignation. And then there occurred in the vibration of those beings about self, the recognition that there still remained within the being a spark of hope. And the spark of hope grew each time there was a reading from the pages of a book.

Is there anything that I should do in terms of attitude, medicine or exercise that would help me to continue the healing process?

It would be the question: Would you be in the belief that it would be a long process? Or would you be in the belief that it would be complete even as we speak?

Well, I would prefer that it would be complete and quick and immediate but that hasn't happened yet. And I want to know if there's anything I can do to speed the process or aid the healing.

It would be in the statement: I OPEN MYSELF TO THE HEALING POWERS OF THE UNIVERSE, THAT ALL WHO COME IN CONTACT WITH ME WOULD BE HEALED, WITHIN AND WITHOUT, BY THE MERE PRESENCE, BY THE MERE THOUGHT, BY THE MERE TOUCH OF THE GARMENT. For my friend, when we open that we would be healed, we do not open for our very own selves—we open for the entire Universe. That it would be flowing through our being. That it would be in such great abundance that it would spill over from our being, and each one who would come in contact with us would be healed. That would be what you could be doing.

For much would be occurring. And there would be many who

would be coming forward to hear your statements. Have they not been filled with much joy thus far at the very statements of your being? There would be the seed which has sprouted, and taken root, and grown through the Darkness. And finally it has burst forward to the Light. That it would feel the Light. Feel the warmth. Feel the Love. And feel the healing of the Universe. That's what could be done, my friend.

Everything else would be a belief. Everything. *For in this dimension, everything is fantasy. Everything is our belief.* The physical manifestation is the smallest part of our being. Not insignificant— but the very smallest part of our being. For we are I AM. We are everything. Within your being resides everything.

> *Do you have any additional information regarding my physical health—or any advice on what I should or should not do?*

It would be the statement of having fun. It would be the releasing of "walking on eggshells." It would be the releasing of caution and of the fear that the progress of the healing would not continue. It would be the releasing of that fear. It would be in the remembrance that we work within, in order to manifest without.

We would be in the recognition, of course, my friend, that there has been the concern, "Will this continue? Will I be whole and complete?" And it would be a correct statement to say, "THIS I DO CREATE—THAT I WILL BE WHOLE IN THE MANIFES-TATION OF MY PHYSICAL BEING." For we are I AM. It is time.

***

> *...you have healed your very own self.*

> *[A woman asks:] I know you said that each one of us is in charge of our own lives. But I would like to ask if Pretty Flower has any advice for me that I might help myself heal.*

153

What would be the belief of the dis-ease?

I have been told that I have cancer.

We would be asking: What would be the belief? And you would be in the statement that there is the belief that I am in the vibration of cancer.

I know. But—I'm doing everything that I know to do to heal myself.

Yes, my friend. Would you be in the requesting of healing?

Yes.

Then you would be coming forward. [Pretty Flower indicates for the woman to come to the front of the room and stand next to her.]
   Never fear. We would be in the statement, my dear friend, when we are saying, "I do not want this part of my being," what occurs? We are in denial. What would be the statement? Welcome home. Trust the words. Welcome home. For I AM everything. Everything. Even the fear. Welcome home. For when we are trying to be rid of part of ourselves, we would be begging that another part would manifest. That over and over we would manifest the dis-ease within our being until we recognize that we are everything. Everything. The entire Universe. Even the dis-ease. Welcome home, for I AM everything. Then we would begin, my dear friend.
   [Pretty Flower proceeds with the healing session. She asks others in the room to join her up front to assist with the healing and then continues speaking to the woman:] Never fear, my friend. We are One in the same. And as human beings, what has occurred? Over and over we have hoped for one thing and then for another. And we have been wanting the fulfillment of hope. And what have we done as human beings? We have surrounded the desire with fear. For we are accustomed that our hope would be dashed to the ground.
   And we would be in the statement that we would be here for

the fulfillment of hope. That we might experience within our very own lifely vibration the miracle of life. The miracle of life. That we might trust. That we might reside in the fulfillment of hope. That we might once again be in the conscious manifestation I AM. *Conscious* manifestation.

[Speaking to those who are assisting with the healing:] And my friends—you would be allowing. It would not be directing. It would be allowing. Simply allowing.

[After a while:] It would be this long for we are enjoying the vibration of your being. Would there be more?

It's enough, thank you.

What would be the meaning of "enough"?

I have enough.

Drink of your fill of this moment, my friend.

Drink of my fill?

Be in the moment. And right now drink of your fill of this moment. Now. We are just beginning. More and more, more and more, to the brim and overflowing. *Unlimited* supply. There is never "enough." *Unlimited.* Unlimited, my dear friend. [She kisses the woman.]

Can I hug you?

Yes, my friend. [As they embrace, Pretty Flower says:] Give it to me. Give it to me. Thank you, my friend.

Thank you.

Never fear, my friend. There would be those who would doubt. It would be correct. And there would be those who would know. Know within *your* being. There would be the period of what you call time—it would be quite short, my friend—that there would be the manifestation of healing. Never fear. There would be those who would be thinking the healing would be occurring for one reason or another. It would not matter. For *we* know that *you have healed your very own self.* For you are the entire Universe.

You see this being? [She points to a person in the room.] You are this being. [Pointing to another:] You are *this* being. [Pointing to yet another:] You are *this* being. [Pointing to yet another:] You are this being. You are thanking your very own selves. [Pointing to the rest of those gathered:] You are this being. You are this being. We are One in the same. We are, my friends, One in the same.

For you travel in many dimensions. Many dimensions. And we are never apart. There would be rest, so to speak. Three days rest. Yes, my friend. Three days. In the period of what you term to be two weeks, there would be communication with those that you term to be physicians. It would be the beginning of the end of the dis-ease, so to speak.

Oh, wonderful.

Yes, my friend. When doubt would enter, "Welcome home, for I AM everything. Everything."

Thank you. Thank you, Pretty Flower.

[Indicating the others in the room:] Bless those beings.

***

Healing would be the letting go of attachments to the maladies.

How would you be vibrating, my friend?

Not bad, thank you.

What would be the meaning "not bad"?

Could be worse. Could be a great deal better.

Could be worse. How would it be better?

I have several physical problems and some of them are manifesting rather largely right now.

Would we be speaking of what they would be?

Certainly. Do you want me to start enumerating?

Yes, my friend. For it would be, as we would be hearing, the *belief* of the malady.

[The woman goes into detail about the physical conditions that are bothering her. Then Pretty Flower responds:]

Would there be more?

No. I don't think so.

We would begin. First we would begin with our very own selves. When we recognize that there are parts of our being—our physical being—which are not the way we would like them to be, we interpret the condition as out of control. We, as human beings, view the condition, and then we do not want to be that way—and yet we are. So we have the belief that we are out of control. We are not in control of our very own being.

And then we seek the assistance of others and we find that, lo and behold, neither are they in control. It would be quite frustrating. For we would be seeking help that we would change.

When we recognize that we are out of control, what else occurs? We have a companion. It is called fear. And the fear surrounds the condition and we continually check on the condition, carrying the fear with us—checking to see if it has progressed. We are always, as human beings, checking to see if the condition called the malady has progressed. Carrying fear with us.

157

Why do we do that as human beings? We do that as human beings because we have lost hope. We have a mistrusting of our very own hope. It would be correct. It would be all linked together. Tied together. It would be the statement that we have a foundation of fear, as human beings. The foundation of fear and the reestablishment of the conditions that fear might reside within our being. *We continually create the conditions that we might support our own fears.*

Why do we do this as human beings? We do this because we have been *taught* to do this. It would be part of the heritage that we have learned. While deep inside of our being there is a part of ourself that says, "This is incorrect. I know that I am in charge. But somehow or other—I can't quite figure out how to *be* in charge. For I do not want to be this way and yet I am this way." There would be confusion going on within the being. There would be the confusion occurring with many human beings.

We would be speaking then about healing of our very own selves. What would healing be? Healing would be the letting go of attachments to the maladies. It sounds like a simple breathing in and out, and yet it is not—it is quite difficult. For we have the attachments, as human beings, the beliefs—that different physical occurrences will come about in our beings.

We have the belief that the marriage of age and maladies are together. It would be quite improper and incorrect. However, in the manifestation on the planet called Earth there would be that marriage. We would be in the statement then, that healing would be the recognition that deep within I AM. That would be the beginning—and the end. However, we'll travel a little bit together.

It would be that in the beginning we have the recognition I AM. We have the recognition that deep within our being resides everything. Everything. *All those parts of our being which are manifesting are parts of I AM.* For I AM is everything. When we view the maladies, as human beings, we view them with distaste. Of course we do. We want to be rid of them. However, we would recognize when we view what we term to be the maladies, we would be viewing, then, that the maladies themselves would be I AM. For I AM is everything.

Therefore, when we view each of the maladies we would say

158

with each—with each representation—"I AM." With every single one—"I AM." *It would be the releasing of the judgment. It would be the receiving of self.* For when we heal we become aware I AM.

When we deny part of our very own manifestation, we are denying part of I AM. So the first step would be in the receiving of self—the total and complete receiving of self, of I AM. Every manifestation—within our being—I AM. It would be that we would once again be stating the releasing of judgment, that it would not be positive or negative—it would be I AM. Then what would we be doing? Nothing else! For when we ask, we receive. And we would be hearing that you would be asking to be healed. Would that be correct?

Absolutely.

Then we would begin. For you have asked and you would receive. The center. The journey to the center, my friend. We would be speaking of that journey. Would you be in a comfortable position?

Yes. Thank you.

A Meditation with the Angels

We would begin by letting go of concerns for being in the conscious state. It would be that you could be closing your eyes. Not even fearing that you might drift to sleep. Even if we would be speaking and you would be feeling yourself drifting, there would not be the calling back.

There would be the allowing self to drift. When we would be complete, we would place our lips upon your forehead. And then you would know.

Until that time, my sweet wonderful child, we would be companions in the resting of the being in every dimension. That in every dimension—and in every time—there would be the caring. That there would be those beings in spirit form who would be

159

coming about your being in every dimension. There would be those great beings termed the angels, coming about in every dimension. And in every dimension there would be rest. In every dimension.

In every dimension there would be the spirit beings gathering about, that they would be in care and in comfort with the being—in every dimension. That there would be a releasing of concern in every dimension. For the angels would be about, that there would be a caressing by the Wind Spirit of the being—in every dimension.

That in every dimension the spirits would be coming forward—carrying the Light of the Universe. Standing about with great torches that there would be Light and understanding in every dimension. That there would be the cherubim of the Universe coming forward, bearing the petals of flowers.

That there would be Love in every dimension. That the winged beings would be about with the wonderful softness and gentleness of their wings. That there would be freedom in every dimension. That there would be the releasing of the cares and concerns for the being.

For there would be those about who have gathered together that they would be in the service of the being. That they would be in the care of the being. And in the lighting of the being—and in the loving of the being. That the being would surrender—recognizing the total care and protection. Asking in the Love of the Universe that the burdens would be set aside for some other time, so to speak. That the concerns for others would be set aside for some other time.

That there would be the opening. It would be allowing. That there would be the opening of the great flower within. For there would be the recognition of the care and protection of those about. Everything would be effortless. Everything would be effortless. There would be no effort at all. It would be releasing. It would be allowing. It would be surrendering. It would be giving up. I give up. Not trying anything—anything at all.

And in every dimension there would be the great caring— and the great Love. The great awareness of Love. The great awareness of peace. The great awareness of the gifts of the Universe. The great awareness of the children about, humming their tunes. The

160

great awareness of the petals of Love. The great awareness of the bearers of Light.

*

[Pretty Flower kisses her on the forehead.] We would be in the statement that there have been many patterns and we have been in the removal of the burdens. It would be returned if you would be wishing them, for we would not be in the consciousness of removing without permission. There have been many burdens that would be "on hold" that we would be in the permission of relieving from your very being.

You have my full permission.

Thank you, my friend. Then, even as we are speaking, the connections to the being of energy fields would be being released that those parts of the being which we have removed might be dissolved in the Universe. That their creativity might be united again in another form. For we have the choice of our very own creation. And the burdens have been lifted.

There would be the statement, my friend, trust the belief. Trust the belief. Even though the body physical would be perhaps vibrating in memories, it would be merely memories. For the condition of the reinstated physical would be at hand. Everything about the being would be correct and perfect. Remember it would be merely the remembrance of the body physical. And we, as beings who are in charge of our very own manifestation, would be gentle with our body physical. And we would be in the statement to our very own selves, to our very own body physical, "It is correct. The burdens have been lifted. It is correct to vibrate in perfect health."

For we know that the condition is vibrating, allowing our entire being to release from the memory. For there would be no foundation for the memories. For those burdens have been removed. And then the body would be in the releasing of the memories. And we would be remembering that in the releasing of memories at times it would

161

be allowed to weep. And there would not be concern, for there would be the recognition that that would be what would be occurring. And when there would be weeping, then there would be the remembrance of the care—that every part of the being in every dimension is being cared for. And then the body physical would be in belief also.

Never fear, my wonderful friend, never fear, for we have come together that the marriage might be complete. Never fear, my friend. Never fear. We would be gentle in the care of the physical body. We would be in the remembrance that the physical body would be the manifestation of the petals of the flowers. Within the petals of the flowers flows the strength of the Universe. How else could they be so delicate—if they weren't the manifestation of the strength of the Universe?

***

When we ... attempt to direct the healing energies, we would be placing limitations upon the energies themselves.

Sometimes my hands tingle, and I was told this means I have healing ability. Could you clarify this or tell me how to use it or when to use it—or how to develop it?

Yes, my friend. It would be that we would be speaking a little on healing. It would be that when we are opening, we would be *allowing* healing to come forward.

There would be some beliefs which we would be viewing as a healer and as a human being. As a healer there would be the decision, "I would be a healer." And, as you have said, it would not be out of the blue that we would be deciding to be a healer. We would be feeling something within our being—whether it be manifested in the tingling of our hands—it would still be from within. And we would be recognizing that that part of our being would be *begging* to manifest. Begging to manifest.

There would be those healers who would be viewing a being who would be dis-eased and as a human being we would be in the process of making a judgment as to how that being could be better.

162

And then we would figure in our mind how that person would represent themself so we would believe he would be better. It would be a process that has been occurring and occurring—and we would say it would be quite incorrect. Many healers have been in that procedure, even those healers who would be having the papers upon their walls.

We would be in the statement: When we vibrate and we heal from ourselves, we could crumble to dust at the responsibilities. And when we open, as you are very aware, when we open that we might channel the healing powers of the Universe, then the strength and the power is *unending*—unending.

We would also be in the awareness that every human being would be manifesting I AM—whatever they would be doing. For we are I AM. Whatever we do, we are manifesting I AM. And then there would be that being who would be manifesting and would be quite miserable, so to speak, in torment, in emotional upheaval. That being would still be manifesting I AM. For there is no moral judgment at all.

It would be that that being would be in the *unconscious manifestation* of I AM. When we are awakened to the fact that we are I AM and we receive every part of our being, then we vibrate in the *conscious manifestation* of I AM. Conscious manifestation—a decision.

When we are allowing ourselves to open to the flowing of the healing powers of the Universe, we would recognize that every being would be manifesting I AM. None would be better; none would be more of anything. Every being would be manifesting I AM. However, we would be in the recognition that we would be choosing to manifest in the conscious manner I AM.

Then we would be in the statement: I OPEN MYSELF TO THE GREATEST HEALING POWERS OF THE UNIVERSE, THAT I MIGHT BE HEALED, WITHIN AND WITHOUT—AND ALL WHO COME IN CONTACT WITH ME MIGHT BE HEALED, WITHIN AND WITHOUT, BY THE MERE THOUGHT, BY THE MERE TOUCH OF THE GARMENT, BY THE MERE PRESENCE. It would be opening; that we would allow it to occur. That we would allow it to occur.

163

When we, as human beings, attempt to direct the healing energies, we would be placing limitations upon the energies themselves. For no matter how grand we would believe it to be, whatever our imagination could open to in the power of healing in the Universe, it would be the tiniest degree that we would be thinking of. For it is I AM. It is everything.

There would be a meditation that would be in the teaching of the healing, if that would be proper with you.

That would be wonderful.

Then we would begin. For you have asked and you would receive. For it would be begging to manifest. It would be begging to manifest.

A Meditation on the Healing Powers of the Universe

Then we would begin by closing our eyes. And we would be in the allowing of ourselves to release the cares and the burdens and the wonderings of this day.

That we would allow ourselves to release expectations. That we would allow ourselves the freedom to allow the child to be expansive within our being. The child. That we would allow ourselves to be *as we are*. To be as we are.

Within our being there would be the growing in the center of our being—the awareness. Wherever that would be within our being, that we would travel within—inside our being. Traveling within. And wherever we would be, would be the center.

And in the center of our being we would find that there would be the glowing of the Light. It would be in the radiation of golden Light in the center of our being. The golden Light—the essence in the center of our being.

And we would allow the essence to be coming forward that it might grow and we might feel the golden Light radiating. Growing and growing. Growing and growing. Until we allow the Light to be filling our center, our entire center—and spilling over—spilling over—that the Light might fill our entire being. Our entire being.

164

Filled with the golden Light. Filling and filling. Filling and filling.

And in the very center we would find appearing a pyramid. In the very center of the golden essence, the essence I AM—would be the pyramid. And around the edge of the pyramid would be Light. And we would find that we would be in the presence of the pyramid.

And there would be the door—the entryway. And we would enter. And we would walk through the hall. That there would be such Light beaming from the walls—the golden essence. And we would travel until we come to the room in the center of the pyramid.

And there in the center of the pyramid would be the wonderful radiating Light. And we would feel the walls of the Light. And we would feel the gentleness of the Light. And we would feel the Love of the Light. We would feel the essence of the Light.

And there would be in the center of the room a great table. It would be white essence. It would be the table of white Light. And it would be warm and welcoming. And there would be beckoning, and we would go towards the table of white Light. And we would be in the presence of the table of white Light. And we would feel whole. And we would feel One.

And we would place our hands on the wonderful table of white Light. And we would feel the wonderful warmth flowing through our being, the Love of the Universe—the warmth of the Universe—the gentleness of the Universe. The white Light of the Universe. And it would be filling our being. It would be entering our being through the center of our palms of our hands. Filling our being, gently and slowly.

That the white Light of the table would be filling our being. And we would feel our being in the filling of the white Light. And we would know that the essence of the white Light—the essence of the table—would be flowing within our being. And the table of white Light would be within our being—vibrating within our being. Vibrating within our being. Gently. With the Love of the Universe. That our entire being had received the table of white Light. And we would be aware—I AM. I AM.

And we would view our hands and the white Light would be beaming from our hands. Glowing, glowing.

And we would be in the statement deep within our being: I AM EVERYTHING. I AM. I OPEN MYSELF THAT THE HEALING POWERS OF THE UNIVERSE MIGHT FLOW THROUGH MY BEING AND THAT ALL WHO COME IN CONTACT WITH ME WOULD BE HEALED, WITHIN AND WITHOUT, BY THE MERE PRESENCE, BY THE MERE THOUGHT, BY THE MERE TOUCH OF THE GARMENT, FOR I AM EVERYTHING. AND THIS I DO CONSCIOUSLY CREATE—FOR I AM.

And we would find that there would be the slight breath of the Wind Spirit, blowing on our hands. That there would be the slight breath of the Wind Spirit blowing on our cheek, that we would find that we would be in the blessings of the Universe. And that there would be the asking that we would come forward.

And we would step forward and forward and forward—until we would be in the very center of the Universe. That we would be beyond the table. That we would be beyond the pyramid. That we would be beyond the Light. That we would be in the very center of the entire Universe. That we would look about and we would see our very own essence—everywhere. We know we are I AM. And this is our essence in the vastness of the Universe.

And we would gather ourselves together in the I AM. Gathering ourselves together that we might enter our being in the holiness of our temple. That we might enter our being in the holiness of the body physical. That we might feel the essence I AM.

Our awareness, our conscious awareness—feeling our entire physical being. That we would be in the present. That we would feel our awareness in every part of our being.

For we would be in the knowledge, for we would be in the truth, for we would be in the fulfillment, for we would be in the Love, for we would be the essence—I AM—in conscious manifestation. For we have asked, and we have received.

It would be that we would allow ourselves to be present. Slowly, with Love, with gentleness, awakening to the awareness in the consciousness of our being—I AM.

*

For you have asked, my friend, and you have received.

***

We are viewing, as many have been teaching, that there would be the physical, mental and spirit of our beings. That would be a drop in the bucket, my dear friends.

[The following excerpt is from a group session on the topic of healing:]

We would be speaking of healing, would we not? We would be speaking that we might learn to experience healing. For when we think about healing or try to figure out how we would be, we are vibrating within our very own thoughts. Not that it would be correct or incorrect, but we would be vibrating within our thoughts. And then there would be the need to transform the thoughts to action.

We would begin with deciding what we believe healing would be. What we believe would be occurring. What would need to occur in order for healing to present itself. We would be wondering.

What would be the beliefs? Would it be the belief of healing—or would it be the belief of dis-ease? Of misalignment? When we decide that we would want to be healed, what do we do? We view that part of our being that we believe needs to be healed. And we concentrate upon that part of our being. We concentrate on that part of our being that we would be paying attention to the misalignment and we would be seeing our very own selves in the dis-ease.

It would be that we would begin with a foundation. The foundation would be in the understanding of who we are. Who we *are,* my dear friends. As we have spoken many times, we are I AM. And we would be in the statement, as we are together building the foundation, I AM is everything. Everything. Even that part of our being which we believe needs to be healed—I AM. Everything.

When we are in the misalignment of our beings, what is occurring? We are viewing, as many have been teaching, that there would

167

be the physical, mental and spirit of our beings. That would be a drop in the bucket, my dear friends. For we are everything.

Everything in every dimension resides within our beings. When we view that we would be wanting to be healed in the physical, when we view that we would be wanting to be healed in the spirit, we are limiting our very own selves. And as we view ourselves as we are viewing today, we are everything. *Everything.*

And how would we be healing? Would we be healers of our very own selves? Of course, my friends. That is why we are gathered together—for the purpose of healing self. For as healers, we would heal self. We would be in the alignment of self. How would we be healing self? I OPEN MYSELF. We are in charge. This is how we begin. I OPEN MYSELF. I OPEN MYSELF TO THE AWARENESS I AM. I OPEN MYSELF TO THE GREATEST HEALING POWERS OF THE UNIVERSE.

Now there are many who are thinking we are becoming "heavy duty." Now we are getting serious. And what are we actually saying? I OPEN MYSELF—the same thing over and over. I OPEN MYSELF TO THE GREATEST HEALING POWERS OF THE UNIVERSE, THAT I MIGHT BE HEALED, WITHIN AND WITHOUT, BY THE MERE THOUGHT—BY THE MERE THOUGHT—I OPEN MYSELF.

And what are the thoughts that follow that statement? "I have tried this before and it has not worked" would be one thought. There would perhaps be the question, "How is this going to work. Do I really want to trust this? Do I want to give it a try? If I could see one being healed perhaps I would believe. And then I would perhaps give it a try."

> *We would be saying to the pain, "Thank you. Welcome home." For the pain has served our being. The pain has opened our awareness that we might know.*

We would then be in the statement, my dear friends, that when we are healing pain we are in the awareness that there is misalignment within our being. And what would we be saying? We would be saying to the pain, "Thank you. Welcome home." For the pain has served our being. The pain has opened our awareness that we might know. That we might know. For in the sensitivity of our beings there would be time when we would be unaware. That we would be trip-tropping along on our very own path, speaking with one being and then another. And, as human beings, we become very busy. We become very involved with what would be occurring in our daily vibration. And it would be the pattern that we would become sensitive to others. Sensitive to others, my dear friends. And we forget—as wonderful, loving, gentle human beings—we forget that it would be the sensitivity toward our very own selves. Toward our very own selves.

We would be stating that we would be gathering together that we might be in the awareness of the sensitivities of our very own beings. For there are many who gather together to be healed. And there are many gathered together that they might be healers. One in the same. One in the same. There is not one being who would not be the healer. The healer. One in the same.

Then we would be in the statement that we would be opening to the sensitivities of our very own being. And we have been experiencing pain. What type of pain are we experiencing? We are experiencing physical pain. We may be experiencing emotional pain. We may be experiencing mental torment. Yes, my friends, we have experienced much pain together, as human beings seeking the Light. Seeking the Light.

When we recognize that we are vibrating in pain and when we say, "I do not want to be that way," we are in denial of our very own selves. We are in denial of I AM. And we have been teaching then that we would be in the statement to that pain, "Welcome home. For I AM everything." Then, my friends, we have the choice. Then we have the choice.

We would be in the statement, my friends, that we create everything, for we are I AM. Everything. Then there would be the statement: If we create everything, why can't we create to be healed? "I have tried that over and over"—there are many who would be thinking that very thought. "I have tried this over and over and I

169

am still in pain. I am still in pain." We would be together that we might be in the increasing of vibrations. That we might be in the awareness of our beings. That we might recognize that when we open, we open to the greatest healing powers of the Universe.

And where is the Universe? Within our very beings. It would not be "out there" somewhere. "In here"—inside your very being— the entire Universe. And we would be opening that the greatest healing powers of the Universe might flow forward. Flow forward in trust. In the simplicity of our beings.

> *...we have not gathered together to be learning the rules and regulations.... We would be here learning how to let ourselves be in the expansiveness of our beings.*

There would be many gathered together who would be wanting the rules and regulations of healing. That they would be wanting to know what to do—over and over again, the same thing. And we would be in the statement: If we were to say, for example, that when we are in the healing of the jaw, this is what we would do. [Pretty Flower makes certain motions as she speaks with the group.] And then we would do it. And what would occur? Every being would be in the performing of those particular movements, every time there was some being coming forward with pain in the jaw. And what would be occurring within your being? You would be asleep. You would be asleep.

Whenever we, as human beings, vibrate and move our beings according to the rules and regulations, we are asleep, my dear friends. For every second is different. Every *second* is different. This very second.

We would be in the statement then that we have not gathered together to be learning the rules and regulations of how we would place our hands, of how we would think, of how we would be. We would be here learning how to let ourselves be in the expansiveness of our beings. And how would we be doing that, my dear friends? We would be in the statement: I AM EVERYTHING. I AM EVERY-· THING.

If there would be thoughts coming forward from your being, "What about when I learned how to place the crystals upon the bodies of those who would be needing healing? What about those teachings of the crystals? I have learned how to do that. Does that mean that this is a waste?" Of course not, my friends. However, if we are learning to heal, we are learning how to *allow* the energies to flow through our being—at the very second. Every second is different.

Yes, my friends, you could be in the choice of using crystals, for example. Crystals would be in the magnification of the energies. It would be the choice. Not incorrect or correct. However, we would be in the statement that it would be choice—that we could be using our very own fingers. For it would be *belief*. Belief, my friends. Neither would be correct or incorrect. Neither would be better than the other. It would be how we would be choosing to manifest our very own beings—to manifest our healing.

We sometimes hear within our beings, and feel that we would go to a being and that we would place our hands about them. And we would feel the energies coming forward from our very own hands. And we would know within our beings it would be correct. Then there would be the thoughts that follow. For example, there would be the thoughts, "What will they be thinking of me? Will they be thinking that I am the healer? What if they're not healed? What will I do then?" There would be many of those questions of "What if? What if this doesn't work?"

For in the planet Earth we have had many hopes. We would be in the statement that we have surrounded our hopes with fear. For we have the fear that we would be unfulfilled. Yes, my friends, we have experienced much pain together.

And we would be recognizing when those thoughts come forward within our being—what are those thoughts doing? Protecting us. We have created those thoughts for the benefit of our being. As a healer of self—or for the purpose of others— when we say, "What if this doesn't work?" we are protecting our very own beings, for we have the fear of trust. And what would we then be saying as we recognize that we have that very thought within our beings? What would we be saying to ourselves? The habit would be that we would be saying, "I do not want to think that thought." Have we ever tried to remove a thought from our mind? Of course, my friend. What occurs? We think that thought over and over, even against our very own will. For we think—within our beliefs—that if I have one ounce of doubt, then I will not be healed.

My dear friends, it is *belief*. It is belief that says that. For we are everything. If we are the entire Universe—are we not also doubt? Of course, my friends. And what do we say to the doubt within our beings? "Welcome home. For I AM everything. Everything." All of the thoughts. It is part of our very beings. We receive it. We receive.

When we are continually trying "to get rid of" every thought, what is occurring? As we have said, we are asleep. Why are we asleep? We are just learning. We are just learning conscious manifestation I AM. The choice. The decision of how we would manifest our very own beings. Conscious decision. Conscious choice. Conscious manifestation.

When we are opening that the healing powers of the Universe might flow through our beings, and we have the thought, "I hope this really works," it is part of our very beings. Would we be daring to believe that that tiny thought would inhibit the flow of the powers of the Universe, my friends? It is belief. For on one occasion, we as human beings recognize our very own power—for we are the Universe. And in the other, we doubt that we have even the tiniest bit of power.

My dear friends, we would be in the opening of trust. We would be in the statement, I OPEN MYSELF. I OPEN MYSELF TO THE AWARENESS I AM. I OPEN MYSELF TO TRUST— even though what we term to be an indefinite amount of "what ifs" have occurred after that statement. Never fear. Never fear. Beliefs, my friends. Beliefs.

There have been many who have come forward that they would experience the healing of their very own beings. And they have been healed. And what has occurred? The crippled has been healed and the crippled has crawled away. Why would that be occurring? Why would that be occurring? For that being would be in the need of awakening *conscious manifestation*. That we have the choice of manifestation. That we *allow* ourselves to be healed. That we do not need to *squeeze* it out of our beings, we *allow* it to occur. We allow it to occur.

There would then be the discussion of physical, mental and spiritual. Which would be healed first in order for the other? My dear friends, rules and regulations limit our very being. Yes, as human beings, we have the greatest burning desire to understand everything. And what would that actually be? We have the greatest burning desire to be knowing the rules and regulations that we might perform perfectly. My dear friends, it does not work. We are, as human beings, continually frustrated.

> *The flow is occurring and we are simply step-ping into the flow.*

We would then be speaking of all of the reasons why we have been limiting ourselves—that there would be awareness. That yes, my friends, we are in the habit of protecting our very own selves—that we might not experience the grandness of the Universe. And just in case we really do not experience it—that we would be asleep.

And we would be in the statement that we would be opening to the Light. That we would be opening to the healing. The healing. The alignment of our beings. I OPEN MYSELF TO THE ALIGN-MENT OF MY BEING WITH THE ENTIRE UNIVERSE. What else is there? The entire Universe!

Then we would be working with this wonderful friend. [At this time Pretty Flower is moving her hands about a person who has requested healing.] And you would be finding as we are working, that there would be questions coming forward. "What is she doing? What is actually going on? How can I learn to do that?" We would be in the remembrance: When we are asking how I can learn to do that, we are asking for the rules. As healers healing our very own selves and allowing the healing to flow from our beings—what are we doing? We are *allowing* it to occur. *We are becoming more sensitive to our very own beings*. We are opening—that we hear the messages from within. That we dare to allow ourselves to move. That would

173

be what would be occurring. That we are opening and allowing the occurrence. Allowing the occurrence.

What are we doing, my friends? We are allowing our sensitivities to be in marriage. As we gather together we are in marriage—in marriage with each other. And we would be allowing our energies to be in marriage—without thinking—without judgment—without trying to figure out what would be wrong with this particular wonderful friend. That we would allow the energies to flow from our being. That we would feel the marriage. We are allowing ourselves to be.

Then what would occur? Where would our hands go next? It would not be the rule. It would not be the regulation. It would be wherever the spirit, the energies of our beings, would be pulled. When we feel the energies, we feel—and we allow. We allow.

There would be the statement—and the question—what is the difference between the healer and the healed? It would be hearing the message. Hearing the message. That we, as healers, would heal our very own self. When we are in the healing of self—allowing the healing to flow, allowing the energies to flow through—when we say, "I OPEN MYSELF THAT THE HEALING POWERS OF THE UNIVERSE MIGHT FLOW THROUGH MY BEING," then, my friend, it is flowing. We are quite inconsequential. We are the vessel. We are the vessel. We believe, as healers, that we direct. We are the vessel. The flow is occurring and we are simply stepping into the flow.

There would be the time when you would be in the presence of a being and you would be wanting to be in the placing of hands. And there would be the time when you *would* be in the placing of hands. And the being would be stating to you, "I wanted this and I was afraid to ask, and I'm so happy that you came to me."

There would be another time where you would be and a being would be walking by—walking by—and then returning to you and sitting beside your being and asking, "Would you be placing your hands upon my being? I was quite undecided." What would be the difference? It would be in the hearing of the messages. For as healers we believe that we would go in and make everyone perfect. Everyone *is* perfect. That we would allow it to flow. *Allow* it to flow.

174

[Still moving her hands about the person, Pretty Flower continues speaking:] Why would we be placing our hands here, my friends. Because our energies are directed to place our hands. That is the only reason. It is not a rule and a regulation. We are learning expansiveness of our beings. We are learning to cast aside, if we would choose, the rules and regulations. *Be awakened to your very own vibration. For every second is a new one.*

> *We would be learning about our very own selves....When we would want to be open, when we would want to be closed.*

There would be in the sensitivities of our beings, my dear friends, there would be opening—opening—that we would be in the sensitivities of the Universe. Choice, my friends. I OPEN MYSELF TO THE AWARENESS I AM. And what occurs? We feel pain. What has occurred when we are open and we are sensitive, and there would be a being who would be speaking harshly? There would be harshness felt. And we would be wondering—how can we prevent that? We have opened to the Universe. We would be learning about our very own selves. Learning about our very own selves: When we would want to be open, when we would want to be closed. For there is the pulsebeat of the Universe, my friends. The pulsebeat of the Universe. Opening and closing. Opening and closing. And we would be in the choice. We would be in the choice that we would be open.

When we are with beings and we hear the harshness of their being, what do we do? What are the choices? We can choose to close our being that we not receive. And what would be the judgment? That we are, as human beings, supposed to be open? That we are, as human beings, supposed to be receiving? It is the choice.

Yes, my friends, we are sensitive human beings. Yes, my friend, it is the truth. I have recognized within my being the sensitivity of my heart. Then we would be in the asking: What would be the purpose of this manifestation? For I am in conscious manifestation. Why have I manifested that I experience this in my very own life?

175

It would be of self. And we would be hearing the answer from within. We would be hearing the answer from within. For there would be the opening, that we might experience a being in any form whatsoever. That we would be receiving pain. And we have the fear that we might say to ourself, "I do not want to be experiencing this pain and I have said welcome home. And what was the next part of that teaching? For I have felt the pain. I have decided that I do not want to be experiencing the pain. I welcome it home. Welcome home." And then there is choice. Conscious manifestation. Conscious manifestation.

As human beings we feel that we need to fix every being and make them correct. And what occurs? They tell us: "We do not want any part of that. We do not understand and we have fear of you and we would be hurting you that you would stay away." And what do we do as human beings? We step closer. We step closer to the fire. We do not want to be burned but we step closer to the fire. And, once again, we are hurt. Once again.

For we have made the judgment. We have decided as healers that we would be in the judgment of another. We would be deciding how we would believe they should manifest that we would believe they are healed. We are viewing another human being and we view that they might be misaligned. And what would we do? We would decide as human beings how we think they should manifest. "How should they look in order for me to believe that they are healed?"

Every being is in manifestation I AM. Every being is manifesting I AM. Every being. It is choice how they would manifest—that being's choice.

It would be the decision of your being whether you would step closer to the fire—and for what purpose? That that being might be healed? *We think* and another being is healed—if there is the marriage! There would be the choice and the decision. "I would either step closer to the fire or I would step back from the fire."

As healers we are not about to lay ourselves on the ground that others might walk upon the top of our being. We are as we are. Opening. Healing self. Healing self. Healing self.

We would be in the statement, my dear friends, that when we are viewing that we are healers, when we are viewing that we are coming together to be healed, we would be in the statement once again: Remember, everything occurs within the very second. *We beseech you as human beings to cast aside the rules and regulations that you might allow the healing to flow forward. That you might allow it to flow forward.*

W*e would not be in the bestowing of rules...*

[A woman asks Pretty Flower if a healer should wait for a person to request healing instead of offering it:]

Would it be part of your healing to have someone ask you?

A Short Story

You see, my friends, once there were two beings approaching the Great Fairy. And one being went to the Fairy and kissed the Fairy's wings and felt the softness of the wings upon the face. And there was Light shone from the being.

And the other went to the Fairy and she said to the Fairy, "Would it be that my friend placed her face in the wing and there was Light shone? Would that be what occurred?"

And the Great Fairy said, "How would you be vibrating?"

And the friend said, "I would be wondering if my friend received the Light from the wings."

And the Fairy would say to the first friend, "How would *you* be vibrating?"

And the friend would say, "I am vibrating with Light."

And there would be the being with questions, wondering of the other and wondering of the Fairy.

*

And we are loving every part of your being. Even those parts where you would be wanting to know how everything works, that

177

you would have the rules. We would not be in the bestowing of rules, for there is great Love for your being.

And what would be healing—and what would be fun—and what would be the difference?

[A person at the session asks Pretty Flower:] I've been working with my friend for a long time—doing healing. Since you have done a healing for him today should I continue with this—and if so, how much?

What would you be feeling, my friend?

I asked myself that.

For remember, my friend, we are in the second, the very second of eternity. And what we term to be tomorrow would still be in the very second of eternity. How can we know today? How can you know? For we would be asking for a rule—for the answer for eternity. For today it is correct; tomorrow perhaps we would be wanting to do something different. Perhaps the next day we would want to be skipping around together. Perhaps the next day we would be wanting to go and have fun somewhere together. Perhaps the next day we would be feeling that we would be healing. And what would be healing—and what would be fun—and what would be the difference?

Remember, my friend, as healers we allow the energies to flow through our being. *Allow.* We simply be as children and have fun. Be as the child. Be as the little girl skipping along the path together with a friend, the little boy. Skipping along the path together. Having fun. Perhaps you will meet a being with a satchel.

***

Whatever a being would be doing, and however that being would be, and whoever that being would be going to, they would be seeking for healing.

[A healer asks:] How about my work, Pretty Flower. The work I do with the body. Is there anything you see that I could improve in order to manifest a wholer health to my patients?

It would be: I OPEN MYSELF TO THE GREATEST HEALING POWERS OF THE UNIVERSE—THAT ALL WHO COME IN CONTACT WITH ME MIGHT BE HEALED, WITHIN AND WITHOUT, BY THE MERE PRESENCE, BY THE MERE THOUGHT, BY THE MERE TOUCH OF THE GARMENT. FOR I AM.

There would be the statement, my dear friend: When we are healers, when we are manifesting ourselves to be healers, we would be in the recognition that whatever we do—we are manifesting healing. *Whatever we do.*

There would be those beings who would be walking into the door to be healed. And before you are even touching them, they are healed. Know this to be true. And, yes, there would be the continuation for they would be in the physicalness of their being. That there would be the understanding that in the touching of the beings—in the placing of the hands within the aura, so to speak—there would be the recognition that it would be in the assistance of that being to be in the manifestation I AM—in their own being. That would be the healing. That there would be the assistance of manifestation I AM. Conscious manifestation.

When beings come forward to be healed—what are they really asking? They are asking to be made whole. To be One. And they are asking for assistance to be made One. They are asking assistance that they might be in conscious manifestation I AM. For they have been in the attempting of manifesting their being. Practicing manifesting. Whether they are aware or not—they are practicing manifesting—conscious manifestation I AM. In the practice there has been the balance and the imbalance, for they're learning—learning conscious manifestation. And they gather together that they might be asking that they be healed, that they be One, that they be in balance with themselves, that they might consciously manifest I AM.

Whatever a being would be doing, and however that being would be, and whoever that being would be going to, they would be seeking for healing. That would be what they would be wanting—assistance in the balancing of their being. That they might manifest in the fullness of their physical being—the I AM—from within. That would be what healing would be about. The rest would be how you have—in the most beautiful way—decided to manifest your very own healing.

For there are those who would not be in the understanding that at the mere thought they would be in the balance of their being. They would be requiring to vibrate within the beliefs. And you would be vibrating that you would be in the assistance of those beings—*within their own beliefs*. That they might be balanced and that they might open to conscious manifestation I AM.

***

There would be giving self permission to be in total and complete rest.

[A woman asks Pretty Flower for understanding and help with insomnia:]

Yes, my friend. We would be saying with regard to sleep that there would be the relieving of self in the studies. For we would be stating that upon sleep there would be the statement to self: I WOULD SLEEP AND REST THIS BEING. AND I WOULD RELIEVE MYSELF FROM THE BURDEN OF LEARNING IN OTHER DIMENSIONS THAT THE REST MIGHT BE COMPLETE. For there have been in those times the going and the returning of the being. The going and the returning of the self to the Hall of Masters, the other dimensions that we all travel to when

180

our body is resting. And there would be giving self permission to be in total and complete rest.

I would like to be able to self-hypnotize myself and be able to relax from my head to my toes. But I don't seem to be able to do that.

We would be in the process, even as we speak. We could begin a series of statements that would relieve the body. And then when we are complete, we would leave a period of moments where you would be as you are, and then we would be calling you back to consciousness. In the repeating of the words we could be re-recording the statements—without the call to consciousness—that we would go off to sleep. Would that answer your question?

Why, yes. It would.

A Meditation to Improve Sleep

We would begin as we are. There would be the closing of the eyes. And there would be a releasing of the thoughts of anything that would be in our minds, and in our hearts, and in our body. For we would be about to be arriving at the time of rest. We would be about to be arriving at the time of total and complete replenishment of the being in physical and spirit form.

And we would begin by recognizing that our energy centers are vibrating and are in complete and total alignment. And we would be in the process of slowly allowing the energy centers to close. Slowly allowing the energy centers to close—that there would be resting. Remembering that upon awakening, the energy centers would be opened and in proper alignment, that there would not be concern. But for the moment they would be closing.

At the moment we would be in the instructions to ourselves, making the statement, MY ENERGY CENTERS WOULD BE CLOSING THAT I WOULD BE ALLOWED COMPLETE AND TOTAL REST OF MY BEING. Then there would be a great sigh— that we would be releasing.

That we could begin by allowing our entire body from top to bottom and bottom to top, to gradually let go of cares. Whatever part of our body would be relaxing the most. Perhaps it would be part of the hands and the arms relaxing. Perhaps it would be part of the legs relaxing. Perhaps it would be part of the face relaxing. Perhaps it would be any part of the body beginning to relax.

Beginning to let go. Beginning to be One. That we would be allowing ourselves total and complete rest. It would be time.

And we would be in the recognition that as we allow our body to rest, we would also be in the preparation of allowing our entire being to rest. And we would be in the statement: WE OPEN OUR-SELVES TO TOTAL AND COMPLETE REST OF THE ENTIRE BEING. That as we have opened ourselves to total and complete rest—there could be the Light from within.

And there would be entering through the top of our being a tiny Light that would be soft. That would be the color of rose. That would be filling our entire being, beginning with the top of our being. Beginning with our head. That the lovely, wonderful color of Love would be filling our entire being. Coming through our entire head.

Filling every part of our being. Coming down through the shoulders. The wonderful color of Love. Down through our arms. Down through our body. Down through our hands. Down through our hips. Down through our legs. Down through our feet. From top to bottom and bottom to top, we would be being filled with the wonderful Love of the Universe.

And we would find that the Wind Spirit would be coming by, and the Wind Spirit would blow ever so slightly upon the color of rose. And there would be beginning—ever so slightly—the ripples throughout the being. Slowly moving—the ripples in the color of rose. And as the ripples would be flowing through our entire being, there would be as if our entire being would be massaged—from within. That our entire being would feel the ever so slightly ripples flowing through our being.

And we would find that there would be about our being the wonderful angels with the great white wings. And they would be on either side of our being. And they would be carrying the clouds.

The wonderful light clouds. And they would place the clouds around our being as if we were being tucked in by our very own mother.

That the angels would be with us. And they would surround our being with the wonderful light clouds. That we would be wrapped in the care of the angels. And they would be making sounds—wonderful, lovely sounds—for our being. And we would be hearing, as if in the distance, the wonderful angels making the sounds of the Universe.

And we would allow ourselves to release that we might be in total surrender. That we would be in total surrender, complete.

And the child within would be content. And the woman within would be content. And the spirit within would be at rest. And the being would be at peace. And there would be the releasing of the being that there would be total and complete rest.

And we would remain in the rest until the morning would beckon our being. And until that time we would be in the surrender of total and complete rest. For there would be the now—and in the now resides I AM. There would be nothing more to do. For we would be I AM.

*

We could allow ourselves to be conscious when it would feel comfortable to be conscious. There would be no hurry. We are in the belief that you would be able to sleep now.

***

We would be calling you "little girl" for you would be in the newness of your being.

[A woman asks Pretty Flower why her health did not improve after a recent healing session:] Why is my body not responding to the healing of the last meeting?

My friend, it would be in two dimensions. There would be the body

183

physical begging to be manifesting the perfection of the spirit. And then it would be as we are vibrating in our daily life, that we would be carrying about us the rules and regulations in the releasing of the attachments of the physical body, that we would vibrate in the perfection of our health. It would be that our beliefs in this and other dimensions would be requiring that we manifest in the physical plane what would call our attention. Calling our attention to the manifestations which we need to be exhibiting.

For example, when we are speaking of the energy system of the throat chakra that would be in the need of releasing—to be in the surrendering, to be in the accepting, and to be receiving the permission of self—that we might be forgiving and releasing the attachments of the occurrences in what we call the past. That it would be choking us, so to speak. And what would we be doing about that? We would be in the statement, my friend, there would be the releasing of the child. There would be the releasing of the child of the experiences of old. There would be traveling to that child.

We would begin, if that would be proper with you—that we would be working in the healing in many dimensions. Would that be correct, my friend?

Very correct. Absolutely.

Then we would begin working together.

A Meditation and Story of Wings

It would be that we would close our eyes. And that we would be in the awareness of the child within. The wonderful child within. Here and now. The little girl within—here and now. Not so much the little girl of the past, but the little girl of here and now.

And then there would be the statement of the child within—the wonderful child. The innocence in the child. Allowing the child. Here and now. The wonderful child. Skipping about. Feeling the breath of the Wind Spirit upon her cheek. Hearing the whistling and song of the birds. Breathing the scent of the flower.

We are here and now—the wonderful child present with us

184

now. That little girl—coming forward. Coming forward. That we might share together the little child, here and now. Filling our being, filling our entire being. That we would allow the little child to be filling our entire being. Within our arms and our legs. Within our body. Within our entire being. The little girl. The little girl. Filling our entire being.

And we would be saying to the little girl, "Hello, little girl. Hello, little girl." We are so happy to be vibrating together. Vibrating together, my dear friend. My dear, dear little girl.

Never fear. For the Love of the Universe surrounds your being. The Love of the Universe is hugging your being, little girl, hugging your being. Such innocence, little girl. Such sweet, sweet innocence, little girl.

The fairies, the great fairies are about you, little girl. Caring for you, loving you, watching over you. When you are skipping about, the fairies are skipping about with you, little girl. When you breathe the scent of the flowers, the fairies breathe the scent of the flowers. When you hear the songs of the birds, the fairies hear the songs of the birds, little girl.

Never fear, little girl. Never fear. For we are present here, little girl. Right here. And right now—together. And we would be sharing together. We would be telling a story together. We would be having fun together.

Once upon a time, my dear little girl, there was a tiny being and the tiny being was a butterfly. And the dear butterfly would be in the sun, in the rays of the sun. And that butterfly would be feeling the warmth and the Love of the sun upon her wings, fluttering the wings in the sun.

And there would be the flowers and the wonderful goldness in the center of the flowers. And that little butterfly would be flying about, fluttering about and would see the flowers. And there would be the butterfly, fluttering about, in the landing on the petal of the flower. Residing on the petal of the flower, that little butterfly.

And there would be the scent of the flower, surrounding the butterfly. The little butterfly. And there would be the essence of gold, the essence of gold in the center of the flower. In the center of the flower.

And that little butterfly would be going to the center of the flower. And that little butterfly would be residing in the center of that flower. Feeling the golden essence in the center of the flower. Breathing the golden essence. Being the golden essence. And that little butterfly would be having fun in the center of that flower, little girl. That little butterfly would be having fun.

And the essence, the golden essence, in the center of the flower would be upon the butterfly. Upon the body of the butterfly. Upon the legs of the butterfly. That even upon the wings of the butterfly—that tiny little creature—would be the essence of gold in the center of the flower. The very center.

And the butterfly would be filled to the brim, filled to the brim, with the essence of gold, the elixir of life. And then that wonderful little butterfly would be fluttering about. And everywhere that the butterfly would flutter about, the golden essence would be flowing from its being, flowing from its being. And it would be fluttering about—that tiny little creature.

And there would be a little girl on the path. The little girl would be you, my friend. My dear little girl on the path. Standing in the rays of the sun. Humming a tune. Skipping about. Tapping your feet in the sand. Drawing pictures with her finger in the sand. Picking the petal of the flower, and placing the petal upon her knee—that she might be in the scent. That she might place the petal upon the lips of that being, upon the cheeks of that being—that she might feel the petal. That she might feel the petal between her fingers. That she might smell the scent of the petal. Just having fun. Just having fun.

And the little girl would find that when she places her tiny finger in the center of the flower, that the golden essence is upon her finger. Is upon her tiny, tiny little finger, the essence—in the center of the flower.

And the little girl would think, "Hummmm, I wonder what this would be on my finger—this golden essence. What would this be?" And she would be placing her fingers more and more on the center of that flower, trying to figure out what would be the essence. "What would that be on my fingers coming from the flower?"

And she would smell the scent from the center of the flower, and the golden essence would be on the very tip of her nose. And she would be having fun—playing in the essence in the center of the flower.

And along would come that tiny creature, the butterfly, flying about. And the tiny butterfly would see the wonderful little girl, the wonderful little girl. And the tiny butterfly would see the essence on the little girl and would fly to the finger of the little girl.

And the little girl would hold out her tiny hand and hold out her tiny finger, and the butterfly would be on the very tip of her tiny finger. Two little creatures together, playing with the essence, the golden essence, having fun. Having fun. Viewing each other. Having fun.

And the butterfly would see the golden essence on the tip of the nose of the little girl. And the butterfly would fly up to the nose of the little girl and reside there.

And the little girl would giggle for it would feel funny to be having a tiny butterfly on the nose of her being. And she would be having fun. And she would be having fun.

And the butterfly would be saying, "Let us travel together a little, little girl. Let us travel together and skip about and fly about."

And the little girl said, "I would like to be flying about. But I have not been able to open my wings. They would be there—I know they are there—but the wings are not open yet."

And the butterfly would be saying, "Let me see if we could be discovering—let's discover."

And so the butterfly would be going to see the little girl's wings. And would be viewing what would be occurring with the wings of the little girl. And the butterfly would return to the nose of the little girl.

And the little creature, the butterfly, would be saying, "We would be unhitching something. There would be something there. Right over the wings, right over the wings. It would be something there. And we would be wondering if you would like us to remove it so that you could open your wings."

And the little girl said, "What would it be? What would it be that would be holding my wings together in my being?"

And the butterfly would fly back to the little girl's wings and be viewing again. Seeing, seeing inside the bottom of the gate, the golden essence of the wings. And viewing. And seeing the wings beginning to stir within the little girl, seeing the wings beginning to stir. And the butterfly in happiness would fly back to the nose of the little girl.

And the butterfly would be saying that the wings are there—all sparkling and white and very happy. "And what we have to do," said the little butterfly, "is we have to unlock the gate. We have to unlock the gate and open the doors, that the wings might open and expand in the sun."

And the little girl said, "Oh, that sounds like such fun! That sounds like such fun! How do we do that?"

And the butterfly said, "I think I know how to do it." And the butterfly flew back.

And on the gate, on the wonderful gate, and on the latch on the gate was a word. Several words. And the butterfly flew back to the nose of the little girl and said, "There would be words on the gate. There would be words there."

And the little girl said, "Do you know what the words are saying?"

And the little butterfly said, "I will go see. I will go see if I know the words."

And the little butterfly flew back to the gate, and the latch on the gate. And there would be several words on the gate. And the butterfly would see the words. And she would go back to the nose of the little girl and say, "There would be several words, there would be several words."

And the little girl said, "What would be the words? What would be the words?"

And the butterfly said, "There would be two gates, little girl, my friend—two gates. And there would be the words. On one gate would be 'Love,' would be 'Happiness,' would be 'Joy,' would be 'Fun.' And on the latch of the gate would be the word 'Freedom.'"

And the little girl would be thinking, "Hummmm." And then she would say, "What would be on the other gate? What would be on the other gate and the latch on the other gate?"

And the butterfly said, "On the latch on the other gate would

188

be the word, 'Knowledge.' Would be the word, 'Knowledge.'"

And the little girl said, "Hummm." And then she said, "What would be the words on the gate, little creature, little butterfly?"

And the little butterfly, residing on the nose of the little girl, would say, "The words would be 'Loneliness,' 'Fear,' 'Pain,' 'Horror,' and 'Running Away.' That would be the words on the gate."

And the little girl said, "Hummm."

And the butterfly said, "What would we be doing? What would we be doing, my friend? Would we be opening the gates that the wings might expand?"

And the little girl said, "Oh, do. Let's open the gate that the wings might expand that we might open. Let's have fun."

And the butterfly said, "All right, I will go back and see if I can open the latch that the gates might open." And the butterfly flew back to where the wings were and tried to open the gates.

First she tried to lift the latch that said "Knowledge." And it was a little bit—what we would call—rusty. She couldn't budge it. And she went back to the little girl and said, "The gate needs to be opened and the latch is a little stuck. What can we do?"

And there appeared the Great Fairy. And the Great Fairy viewed the little girl and viewed the little butterfly. And the Great Fairy said, "We are always together, dear children. We are always together. We never have to do these things by ourselves. We never have to open the gates by ourselves and lift the latch by ourselves."

And the little girl with the butterfly residing on the tip of her nose said to the Fairy, "We were in the attempting of opening the latch so that the gate would open and we might allow the wings to come forward—so we could fly about."

And the Great Fairy said, "Wonderful. Wonderful. Would you like some help?"

And the little girl smiled and said, "I would very much like some help."

And the Fairy went to the gate, the gate of "Knowledge," and the breath of the Wind Spirit blew on the gate of "Knowledge." And the Fairy went to the gate of "Freedom" and viewed the gate of "Freedom."

And the Fairy said to the little girl, "When we open these

gates, my dear little girl, we will open them together so that the 'Love' and the 'Fear' would be together—opening together. That the 'Joy' and the 'Pain' would be opening together. That the 'Happiness' and the 'Loneliness' would be opening together."

And the little girl was smiling, and the butterfly—on the essence on the tip of her nose—was in great happiness. And the Fairy placed one finger of one lovely Light hand under the latch called "Freedom." And she placed one finger under the latch called "Knowledge."

And the Great Fairy said, "Let there be the marriage, little girl, let there be the marriage that there would be joy, that there would be Love, that there would be fun. Let there be the marriage."

And the Fairy lifted her fingers and the latches opened. And what occurred with the gates? They opened wide. They opened wide. And they came upon each other—each gate facing the other.

And the Wind Spirit blew on those gates. And the Fairy viewed the gates. And they vibrated in the essence I AM. And they became one in the same. One gate. One in the same. That there was a marriage. That there was the marriage. And there was *one gate*—one gate. And on the latch of the gate were the words "I AM."

And the Fairy went to the little girl and said, "There would be, little girl, one gate—just one. It would be white, vibrating white. And on the latch of the gate would be the words, little girl, 'I AM.'" And then the Fairy disappeared.

And the little butterfly flew to the gate and resided on the latch that said, "I AM."

And the little girl, in her little mind, merely thought and said, "I want to open the gate 'I AM' so that I can let my wings come out." And when she said that, she felt a funny feeling happening— the gate opened. The wonderful vibrating gate.

And lo and behold, lo and behold, there were the wings of her being. The wings of her being—and they opened. And they opened! The wings of the being. And they were white—sparkling essence.

And the Wind Spirit blew, that the wings would feel the Wind Spirit. And the sun, the sun sent the rays of Love to the wonderful wings. And the birds sang in celebration at the viewing of the wonderful wings. And the scent of the flowers filled the air for the wonderful wings.

And the little girl would be in the feeling of her wings, feeling them open and spread wide. Wonderful wings.

And the little girl would be saying to the butterfly, "Come here. Come here, little friend."

And the butterfly would be once again on the tip of the nose of the little girl.

And the little butterfly, the little creature, would be saying, "I have seen the wings of your being."

And the little girl would say, "I feel the wings of my being. I feel them."

And the two would view each other in the essence, in the golden essence, on the tip of the nose of the little girl.

And the little girl would be saying, "Would we be on our way? For we have things to do. We would have some fun. We would be fluttering about together in the sun, in the center of the sweet flowers, in the Wind Spirit—fluttering about. Breathing in the essence in the center of the flowers."

And off they flew together. Fluttering about, the tiny creature, the butterfly, and the little girl with the wings of her being spread wide. Fluttering about.

And the Great Fairy viewed the two. And the Great Fairy beckoned that the Love of the Universe be with the little girl and the butterfly. That the joy of the Universe be with the little girl and the butterfly. That the happiness of the Universe caress the feet of the little girl and the butterfly. That they would be having fun together. Having fun together.

And the Fairy would be in the viewing of the two and there would be great peace upon the path. Great peace upon the path. Great peace upon the path.

*

The blessings of the Universe reside within your being. For you

191

are in the newness of One. And we would be in the statement this day of "Happy Birthday"!

Yes. Thank you.

On this day, my friend, little girl, we would be calling you "little girl," for you would be in the newness of your being. In the newness of your being. We would be in the statement, little girl, that there would be in the Universe residing within your being—total and complete healing in every dimension. Every dimension. Believe. Believe. For you have asked—in the asking is the receiving.

***

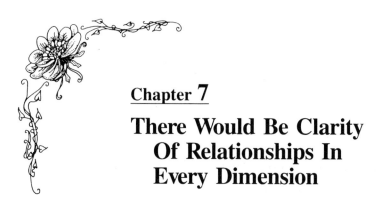

Chapter 7

There Would Be Clarity Of Relationships In Every Dimension

When we decide that one teaching would be absolutely correct...remember that we are to avoid falling asleep. For in that second *it would be correct....And perhaps in the next instant it would be a teaching that we would discard.*

We would be in the statement, my dear friend, that as many gather together—the many teachers and the many students—there would be the recognition that within every teacher is the student, and within every student is the teacher—that they are One in the same. There would be many teachers who are just beginning to learn that they are also students. And there are many students who are just beginning to learn that they are also teachers. *One in the same.* One in the same.

And we find that as we vibrate together, each the teacher and the student, we would be hearing many teachings. And we would be wondering if they would be correct. At one time or another they seem to be *almost* correct, but not quite. So that we would be wondering what would be the correctness of the source. Would it be within our very own selves? Would we *really* be getting the message? Would we be misinterpreting the words? Wondering, wondering.

We would be in the statement that one teaching may be perfectly correct for one being and the same teaching would be incorrect for another—*at that particular moment*. What would be the deciding factor? It would be those beings, those individuals. For when one being hears the truth and resonates with the truth—that being is receiving the teaching. When another being hears the statement, and decides that it would not be the truth, and does not resonate with the teaching, and decides that it is incorrect—then that being is resonating with the teaching. For we would be, as we have been stating, in the vibration of spontaneity.

When we decide that one teaching would be absolutely correct for our being, remember that we are to avoid falling asleep. For *in that second* it would be correct—it would be the correct vibration. And then we would be vibrating again. And perhaps in the next instant it would be a teaching that we would discard. It would not mean that the teaching would be false, it would be that we would be being true to our very own selves. Daring—taking the risk to be true to our very own selves, that we might be in charge.

For we have heard the words "we are in charge," and it still remains that we wonder if we are vibrating in the correct manner. Wondering, as human beings, which way would be the correct way. For we have the desire to vibrate in the Light. When we are vibrating in the Light, we are the most fulfilled. And we would be desiring to maintain that fulfillment. But of course!

How would we maintain that fulfillment? By being in the truth to our very own selves. That we would be hearing information and deciding whether we would receive it to our being. *It would not be that we would be disproving the information*—which is what seems to have been the quandry. For we have been in the belief that if it is correct for one being, then it must be correct for me—for it is *the* truth stated. However, it is what we term to be *a* truth. When we are in the vibration of truth to our very own selves, we would be recognizing the spontaneity and the marriage of the information coming to and from our being. To and from our being.

There would be the statement that there are many who would be receiving the truths of their being. And then they would be begging that they would fall asleep once again. For they hear the truth and they believe it would be the rules and regulations of their very own lives. For once we recognize a truth, we would maintain it. And at times when we maintain the truth, we force ourselves to be acting a certain way in order to fulfill the rules and regulations of the truth. Then, in that instance, we would be asleep.

It would be time as human beings to be in the spontaneity of our beings.

> *And we find that as children we have been marching in another's footsteps — that we would be as correct as that being. And we have not yet experienced the freedom of placing our feet in our own footsteps.*

What would we be communicating, my dear friend?

Aren't there meant to be rules and regulations?

We are the creators — however, we have been as children and there have been many who have been teaching how we would be. Those who have been teaching how we would be have forgotten the spontaneity of their own beings. They have been teaching "acting," and not spontaneity. And we would be in the presenting of the truth of spontaneity — to be in the present vibration — the present vibration.

When we are viewing that there would be rules, we are asking that we be told how we should be. For we have the belief that if we are a certain way, *then* we will be correct. And we are wanting to be correct. For we have been taught as a child in this society, that we would be correct. We have been taught many ways in being correct. Sometimes we have been taught how to be even before we have tasted the freedom of action. And we find that as children we have been marching in another's footsteps — that we would be as correct as that being. And we have not yet experienced the freedom of placing our feet in our own footsteps.

195

For we would find that in any statement of truth we could find the expansiveness of our being—or we could find limitation to our being.

You shared with the group an approach a person would take if they would be needing a root from the forest—an approach of Love and respect for the forest and gratefulness and thankfulness. And it felt correct to me, as you were telling us. Isn't that correct? Wouldn't it be incorrect to be going through a forest and ignoring what's around you? Though perhaps this isn't a good example.

It would be a perfect example. It would be a teaching. A teaching in awareness. Then we have the choice. For example, there would be the awareness that moss would be used in the ceasing of overflowing of bleeding. If there was a being who was in the overflowing of a wound, we would go to the forest and we would gather the moss together as quickly as possible. It would be correct. We would be in the teaching of *awareness* by example, more than we would be teaching the procedure.

There are many who would be following the procedure. For they would feel that it would be correct for their being. However, what we would be teaching would be that each and every time we enter the forest we would be spontaneous with our being. That we would be in the experience of the teaching. That we would try it on for size, so to speak. We would be trying the teaching. Trying the method.

When we are trying the method, we are moving within the method. And then what occurs? Once we have tried the method, we cast it aside—that we would be within our own being. And what we are unaware of, as human beings, is that each and every time we do *anything,* it is very different from the preceding time. What we are doing, however, is attempting to be reproducing. And when we attempt to reproduce, we are allowing our spontaneity to be asleep. Would that be clear?

196

Yes. But the question I'm not able to ask as clearly as I'd like—

You would be asking for rules and regulations that you would be following—that you could be depending upon.

Well, I guess I use the Christ as an ideal. Would that be considered rules and regulations?

What would be the rules and regulations?

For example, "Do unto others as you would have them do unto you."

It would be a belief. It would not be correct or incorrect. It would be a belief and we vibrate within the belief. It would be within our very own choice. When we are choosing how we would vibrate, we are choosing how we would vibrate.

However, when we are vibrating within that very truth, "Do unto others as we would have them do unto us," we would be in the awareness that we are as human beings in the experiencing of our beings.

There would perhaps be coming forward from within our being anger or sorrow at times, that we would recognize that within *that* vibration of the truth would also be giving ourselves permission to be truthful. To be in the statement to another being perhaps, that when those actions are occurring—"I am experiencing sadness within my being." Doing unto others as we would have them do unto our very own selves—speaking the truth, speaking the truth.

For we would find that in any statement of truth we could find the expansiveness of our being—or we could find limitation to our being. When we are vibrating in expansiveness of our being, we are vibrating within the spontaneity of our being. However, when we are relating our every action to a truth—continually—seeing if we are in the vibration of the truth, we would be ceasing at times the spontaneity of our being. For we are wanting to be perfect. We are tiptoeing around, that we would be perfect. And we would be

197

saying that that would not be correct or incorrect—it would be choice.

> *We could be in the choice of vibrating our very own self according to a principle, that we fit the principle.... We would, however, be in the encouragement of the teaching of spontaneity of beings.*

However, if we were to be in the spontaneity—if we were to be as we are—then we would be learning of self. Then we would be learning who I AM. For when we are in the care of following the rules, following "the truth," then we would be in a type of denial of self. It would not be that it would be incorrect. It would be choice.

We say, for example, we would be kind and considerate and loving to all beings. And then perhaps one day we would be feeling a type of anger within our beings. What would we be doing? What would we be doing with the anger? We would be relating to the truth, and we would be saying in one form or another, "I am rejecting this anger, for it is not what I wish to express. For I would be loving and caring of each being. And I would be in the care that I would not express my anger unnecessarily toward another." Of course that would be choice. It would not be incorrect, my dear friend.

However, in the foundation of our thoughts, we would be recognizing that we are everything. Everything. That there would be care that we would not be in the denial of self—in the denial I AM. That we would be gathering together without a judgment. Without a judgment that would be, "This would be a negative part of my being." *This* would be I AM.

That would be the care that we would be taking with ourselves. Allowing ourselves to be in the spontaneity of our being. That we would be receiving our very own selves.

> *But when you finally do choose this or that, don't you choose according to an ideal?*

It would be according to *the moment*. It would be as we are conversing, that we are speaking within our heads. We would be speaking in "supposedlies." And what would we be doing? We would be deciding how we could be—once again. We are deciding which way would be correct, that we would vibrate in that way, in comfortableness of our beings. Would we not?

> *If I am I AM, and I am—I can be anything. I can choose to manifest anything. Well, how will I choose which one I will be? Since it's a choice and I can choose anything. How does one choose then?*

It would be hearing the message and the truth from within our very own being—from within our very own being. When you are vibrating with the truth of the principles which you have chosen, and they are vibrating in the truth of your being, then it would be correct. It would be the manner in which we could choose.

We could be in the choice of vibrating our very own self according to a principle, that we fit the principle. It would not be incorrect. We would, however, be in the encouragement of the teaching of spontaneity of beings.

> *Once we are aware of what would be occurring within our being, then once again, we are in charge.*

> *[The woman who is having this exchange with Pretty Flower begins a series of questions related to her feelings for a man to whom she was attracted. Because she is married and does not want to say this in front of the others in the room, her questions are vague. However, after the following brief exchange, the true issues are revealed. The woman asks:] Can you give me some clarity as far as an emotional experience I was having. It involved feelings for a certain person—which I felt were incorrect to express.*

It would be that we would be wondering how we would interpret

199

the feelings which we would be experiencing. How would we interpret those feelings? It would be that the spontaneity of our being would be intensified and we would be wondering how we would be expressing. We would be wondering if the feelings which we are actually experiencing would be correct. And that would be a type of confusion within.

When we are experiencing something within our being, we would be in the relating to self what the actual experience would be. What would be the truth of that experience? Allowing ourselves to fill with the experience. For at times, when we have an inkling of how we would be feeling, we place the judgment, "Will I allow myself to really feel this way?" And we would be in the statement that if we were wondering if we would express the feeling, first we would allow ourselves to experience the feelings in totality.

That there would be even the writing in the journal the statements to self, "This is how I am feeling." Without reasoning, without judgment, "These are my real feelings." Writing and writing, until we can write no more. Then we would close the journal and we would do something else. Then, once again, we would be experiencing the rising of the feeling. And once again we would write, and we would allow ourselves to experience, *allow ourselves to experience the entirety of the feeling.*

For at times as human beings we are experiencing the initial part of our feelings, and we would be wondering what we would be doing with this feeling. How can we decide when we are not allowing ourselves to experience? Allowing ourselves to experience the feeling. When we are then well acquainted with the feeling, *then* we would decide what we would be doing.

The anxiety or uncertainness of what to be doing would be because we are unfamiliar. We are unfamiliar with the many circumstances in which we place ourselves. We would first then become familiar with our very own selves. Allowing ourselves. Allowing ourselves without judgment, that we would be getting to know more who I AM.

For we are in the care, so to speak, of our emotions. We are in the care—which would not be incorrect. However, when we are in new experiences of our very own lives, what we would be doing would be being so very careful. Of course—for we are wanting to be in the truths of our beings. Being so very careful that we would not upset the present conditions or the present vibrations, that we would not be allowing ourselves to be in full experience of self. And we would be in the statement that we would give ourselves permission to experience the fullness of our being.

Then we would be deciding what we would be doing. If we would be expressing those real feelings, if we would be in the statement of the feelings, of the experience, of the truth of our being, then would be the decisions. However, first we would know our very own selves.

How does spontaneity fit into that?

Spontaneity is allowing ourselves to experience the feelings within, without judgment. We would not be saying, "Go away judgment." We would recognize that part of our being is that way—as human beings. When we are in the experiencing of a feeling and wondering what we would be doing, we would be in the choice that we would allow that feeling to come forward, as we have mentioned. In the solitude of our being, in the company of those beings affected, in the company of a friend, in the company of a teacher or in the company of spirit. We would be in the choice. That we would allow the feelings to come forward, however they would be.

For example—and we would be in the statement that perhaps this would be very far from the example in which we are both speaking—we would be in the feeling of what we have termed to be anger. For when we are in anger we would be apt to be very spontaneous if we allow ourselves to be. We, as human beings, feel the emotion coming forward. We feel our physical being reacting and acting. We feel our spirit being. We feel our vibration increase perhaps. And then we are in the choice.

What could we be doing? We could be speaking. We could be writing, that we understand ourselves. And what would we allow ourselves to write? Every thought. Every thought. Even those thoughts which we judge to be negative. Even those thoughts which

201

we judge to be destructive. Allowing the spontaneity of our being—
that we might get to know our very own selves.

Once we are aware of what would be occurring within our
being, then once again, we are in charge. Then we are in conscious
manifestation. There are many who are experiencing the beginning
of those feelings and they would be in the denial of those feelings,
for they have the judgment that they would be negative. It would
be that they are in denial of self and of the spontaneity of their beings.

In the spontaneity of our beings we would not be suggesting
that we would be spewing and spewing the words to another without
thinking. That would be one type of spontaneity. However, the other
would also be one type of spontaneity. That we allow the information
to come forward for the learning of self. Then we have the choice.
Would that be clear?

Yes. Yes, it would.

We have danced around the head of the pin and we have still covered
the topic.

*...you have created for your very own self.
There would be the testing of the principles of
your being that you would be in the truth to self.*

Were those feelings from a past life or a present situation?

Are you speaking in the present of that topic of which we are
dancing about?

Yes.

We would be in the statement, my friend, that the past is the present.
Every dimension vibrates in the present. Every dimension.

*Okay. I understand that. Though I don't know if that answers
the question.*

We could be in the statement of dimensions.

No, it's not necessary.

Of which there would be in the number of three.

(laughing) You're baiting me.

No, we would not be baiting. We would be in the statement that there would be the number of three. And that within each of the dimensions there would be the struggle of allowing of self to be. Allowing of self to be. And that in each dimension there would be the principles of your being—what you have created for your very own self. There would be the testing of the principles of your being that you would be in the truth to self. It would be what you have been deciding in the fulfillment of purpose.

However, we would be in the statement, my dear friend, that whichever way you would be deciding—would be absolutely correct. For within each decision would be as many teachings and learnings for which we vibrate. Would that be in the assistance of your being?

Yes. Yes, it is.

For we are in the desire to be in the assistance of your being. For there would be, as we have been in the experiencing, great confusion—"What will I be doing with these feelings?"

Yes—and whether to express them. I wanted to express them but I thought that would be wrong. It felt overwhelming. But I didn't want to do anything impulsively—that I would regret or would hurt my husband.

It would be as we have been speaking that you have created the principles within which you vibrate. It would be deciding: Would this be correct? Have I made the agreement with what I term to be my husband? For there would be the statement of truth within your

203

being that you would be quite unhappy to be vibrating and not speaking the truth with your husband. However, my dear friend, the truth would be the truth whether we have the action or the nonaction. It would be the truth of the feelings.

> *I accept the feelings. They are a part of me. But the decision of whether to act on the feelings is where the confusion also comes from. Should I carry out my feelings or should I just recognize them and say, "Oh, that's what they are," without expressing them.*

What would be the purpose of each?

> *To express them? Well, there would be a physical and emotional connection with that person—expressing love. And not expressing them? What would be the purpose? It would be for my husband's sake mostly.*

Would you be in the discussing with your very own husband?

> *He doesn't want me to be having relations with other people. And I guess I wouldn't want him to either. So it was more that kind of decision. I'm not going to do to him what I don't want done to me.*

We would be in the statement that then there would be for the husband, misstatement of self. For have you not been in the statement that you would not be speaking the truth to the husband, for it would be in the pain of his being and strain upon the relationship? Then we would be wondering—it would not be with the husband, as with self. For we would then be within our being: Would we be in the expression in the physical manifestation and be in the truth of ourselves without speaking to the husband? Would it be in the comfort of our being? For that would be the decision, would it not? Not so much the decision of action or nonaction—but would I be able to live with myself? For when we are in the truth of our being, then we are vibrating according to the spontaneity of our being.

If there would be the feeling of attraction and the emotions of the connections with this very being—what would be occurring within our being? What would be occurring? We would be wondering, would there be foundation of relationship? Would there be the wanting of relationship in the expansiveness of our beings? Would we be wanting to be in the vibrating of the physical fulfillment of our beings? Would we be wanting to be experimenting with the freedom of self? Would we be wondering if we would be allowing ourselves to be in freedom—in the freedom of self?

Would we be wondering, for example, if I refrain from what feels to be wonderful, would I be resentful towards my husband? Would I be resentful towards myself? Would it be that I would be continuing my lifely vibration in unfulfillment for the rules and regulations between the two? Or, would I be in the hesitating and the refraining from action for I am recognizing the physical vibration of my being is one manifestation of my being. For when we are in the physical union of our beings we are manifesting that which already exists.

Yes, my friend, it is a great quandry. It is a great quandry—what would we be doing? And we would be asking then the question. For example, what if this wonderful being would have a wife, and there was this feeling? What then would be the decision? Would it be affecting your decision?

> *That's where my ideal comes in. That's why I feel like I need to have an ideal to hold onto—to guide me. Because I'm not sure. I can't hear the Father.*

Yes, my friend. We are in recognition. We would be in the statement that we would be opening, that we would go within. That we would be opening to the truth of our being. For we could be hearing the statement and we could be saying to your very self, "Of course, my friend, allow the union. You are two beautiful beings." Or we could be in the statement that allowing the union would be simply promotion of pain. So there would be one way or the other.

I receive the Father and the Father receives me. All else is fantasy.

I want to hear it in me.

Yes, my friend. For you are the vibrator of the truth. The vibrator of the truth. It would be that we would be thinking of the procedure, that we would be thinking and allowing ourselves to experience. Then, my dear friend, we would be thinking of the completion. Then we would be thinking of "Then what? Then what?" And then we would be thinking how we would be. It would be as if we would be thinking it through, experiencing the thoughts upon paper. Experiencing the real thoughts.

And there would be the statements: This would be the action. And this would possibly be the experience. Then what? After that experience, then what am I left with in my being? What am I deciding? Am I deciding that perhaps I would be making the choice of changing my husband? Would that be the decision? For there would be the possibility you would be thinking of that. Would there be the wondering after the experience, that there would be knowing that it could occur again and again—and what would that be in the experience of my being? What would it be in the experience with the relationship with my family? With the relationship with myself? The relationship with my husband?

It would be that we would be attempting to making decisions before there is the choice. Before there is the choice.

That's what you're suggesting the procedure is—to imagine it, and then to see the possibilities—as if it had happened or as if it hadn't happened?

It would be similiar to that. Yes, that we would be thinking it through. That we would be wondering what we would be doing. For my dear friend, whether the action exists or not, what would be occurring? We would still be deciding what to do—whether the action occurred or not. Whether the union with this wonderful being occurs or not. If this being would be traveling across the country

206

and you would never see each other again, for example, it would still be the same choice—would I be remaining with this husband? That would be the choice. For within your very own self, it would be the commitment of being. Deciding upon the commitment of being.

> *It feels like every problem I'm having is because I can't go within and hear the answer. It affects everything. I don't feel the connection. I feel alone. And I know I'm not alone. But still it's total confusion.*

For we are ruled by our very emotions. We have been allowing the spontaneity of our being to come forward in tiny dribbles—daring to feel, daring to feel. Then we would also be experiencing the attention from a new being. And what would be occurring? Would we be experiencing these feelings if it would be another being who would be paying us attention? Those would be the types of questions.

> *I finally understood that. I was looking for something from that person to fill an emptiness in me. I don't want to feel empty. I want to feel complete —*

Yes, my friend.

> *— and I don't hear the Father within. Is there a way of helping me?*

Yes, my friend. It would be that we would be feeding our very own self. That we would be feeding and nourishing our spirit. When we are in the statement, my friend, "I am empty," what has occurred? We are feeling that we are very far away from the center of our being. For we have been allowing ourselves to be pulled one way and then another way. One way and then another way. Tossed and turned. And what would be the answer? The answer would be removing ourselves from the vibration that we might be One in the same. That we might be within our own vibration, being true to our very own self, in every dimension. Whether it be with our

207

husband, with our children, with our friends, with our lovers—that we would be true to our very own selves.

For we are seeking and seeking. We would want the stability of husband. And we would want the excitement of lovers. We would want the loving of the children. And we would want the freedom from the children. Yes, my friend, yes. It is part of being a human being and it is part of being a woman in this society in which you vibrate. It would be in the statement of fulfillment of self.

When you say, "I do not hear the Father; I do not know what to do," what would then be the statements of truth? Perhaps the statements of truth to both beings. Perhaps the statement of truth to the husband, "I am confused. This is the truth of my being. And I am sharing the truth with you." Perhaps stating to the other being, my dear friend, "This is the truth of my being. This is what I am struggling with." For then we are in the truth.

> *That's as good a possibility as any. But I need to be able to go within when you're not here and come up with the answer in a different situation.*

Yes, my friend, we would begin. It would be that we would be learning the meditation of truth.

A Meditation of Truth

We would begin by closing our eyes together. That we would be in the statement that we would be releasing. That we would be releasing. That we would be releasing.

That we would be in the surrender of our beings. That we would be opening, opening. That we would go to the very center of our beings.

How would we go to the center? We would allow ourselves to experience the Wind Spirit blowing through our being. We would allow ourselves to experience the breath of spring through our very beings. That we would allow ourselves to experience the Oneness of being, within our being.

That we would be however we would be, at the moment. However it would be. Without thinking of how we are. Releasing the thoughts and concerns. For beneath the thoughts and the concerns would be our very own self. Our very own selves, being. Just simply being. Just simply being.

And we would allow ourselves to be in the visualization of a flower within our being. A flower. A wonderful blossom. And that we would see the dew upon the petals of the great blossom. And that we would be allowing the scent of the blossom to fill our being. To fill our being. Breathing in the scent. And breathing out the scent.

That we would allow ourselves, our awareness, to be in the center of the blossom. In the very center of the blossom. In the very center.

In the very center would be the spark of Light which has grown and grown. Growing that it would be the glow. Growing that it would be the Light. And we would be in the center—vibrating. And as we breathe, we breathe in the Light. And as we breathe, we breathe out the Light. Breathing the Light.

I AM. I AM. I AM.

I OPEN MYSELF TO THE TOTAL AND COMPLETE FULFILL-MENT OF PURPOSE.

I OPEN MYSELF TO THE AWARENESS *I AM.*

I OPEN MYSELF TO THE NOURISHMENT OF SPIRIT.

I OPEN MYSELF THAT I AM RECEPTACLE FOR THE FATHER.

I OPEN MYSELF THAT I MIGHT VIBRATE IN THE TRUTHS OF MY BEING.

I OPEN MYSELF TO THE MANIFESTATION OF THE STRENGTH OF THE UNIVERSE.

I OPEN MYSELF TO THE AWARENESS OF THE TOTALITY OF MY BEING, FOR *I AM.*

THE FATHER WITHIN ME VIBRATES.

THE FATHER WITHIN ME SPEAKS TO ME.

I RECEIVE THE TEACHINGS.

I RECEIVE THE WORDS.

IN THE VIBRATION OF THE UNIVERSE RESIDES THE SPARK OF LIGHT WITHIN MY BEING.

WITHIN THE PULSEBEAT OF THE UNIVERSE RESIDES THE
  PULSEBEAT OF MY BEING, OPENING AND CLOSING.
  OPENING AND CLOSING. FOR *I AM*.
AND I RELEASE MYSELF OF THE ATTACHMENTS.
I SURRENDER MYSELF TO THE FATHER.
I RECEIVE THE FATHER AND THE FATHER RECEIVES ME.
ALL ELSE IS FANTASY.

I carry this vibration in my daily experience, in the truth of
my being. That we might be bringing to the consciousness of our
being the vibration from deep within our being.

That we would be allowing to come forward the vibration of
our being. That we would be allowing to come forward the truth I
AM. All else would be fantasy. All else would be creations.

I release the creation of confusion that I might see with clarity
the center of my being. That I might remember with every step and
every breath the purpose of union. That I might, with every breath,
be filled to the brim and overflowing with the Father.

All else would be fantasy. All else would be creation from our
very own beings. Children playing with toys. That we would be in
the gifts and the bounty of the Father in the recognizing total and
complete I AM.

As a human being I receive myself. As my Father receives
every part of me, I receive every part of my very being. Every
manifestation. Every fantasy. That I might be One. One in the same.
I do this in remembrance of purpose in the union. That there would
be conscious manifestation in the name of the Father—in which I
reside.

There would be allowing to come to consciousness. Coming
to consciousness.

*

Am I going to hear the Father as clearly as I hear you?

Yes, my friend. Yes, my friend.

When we are in the ascending, then we are the Father. We recognize the totality of our being. And then we are One.

Why did I choose to come back? Why would I choose to come back to go through this?

We are in the perfection of our beings that we would be in the manifestation I AM—in total consciousness of our beings. That we might be in the uplifting of the consciousness of those beings about us. For there are many who are unaware of the spark of Light within their very beings.

I came back to help?

Yes, my friend. And also to be in total consciousness of being.

Can I ascend?

When one being ascends, every being ascends. It would be choice.

Can I ascend in this lifetime?

It would be choice.

I choose it.

If you would be choosing it, then you would be. It would be conscious manifestation. Conscious choice.

Is there something I don't consciously realize that's interfering with my conscious choice to ascend?

It would be that we have placed ourselves in the center of trials and tribulations that we would become perfect. It would be choice. It would be that each being would be in the manifesting of what we term to be "lifely vibration." Within those vibrations we can

211

turn away from them or we can grow with them. We can change ourselves. There are many, many choices, so to speak. For when we are wanting something it is because it already exists. Because we are begging to manifest. And what would be ascension anyway? It would be in the vocabulary "no big deal."

To me it would be a big deal. (laughing)

It would be seeming so now. At the time it would be a blinking of an eye. It would be as a child, when we wonder what it will be like to be the mother. And then one day we are the mother.

I would like to be able to ascend and come back. To me it's another way of connecting to the Father—that when I need help, I can ascend and get the help and then return.

When we are in the ascending, then we *are* the Father. We recognize the totality of our being. And then we are One. And then what we believe to be ascending is simply marriage. And we choose to manifest.

When we are viewing from the position of the overviewer.... Then there would be clarity in relationships in every dimension.

I chose to manifest a great *abundance of money. I thought I chose that consciously. Is that going to come to be?*

It would be viewing the beliefs of being. Viewing the beliefs. Viewing the purposes. Always continuing in the creation of "and then what." And then what? We would be carrying the creation and the manifestation to the next step—that it would not be the end in itself.

And what would be the purpose? Total and complete freedom? That I might choose what I want to do in my life? Aside from other possibilities and purposes, we feel that we can buy our freedom.

For when we decide what we would want to do, there would be many decisions.

Then there would be the statement that there would be what we term "freedom from being taken care of." That we would be free from the husband and the ties. There would be those decisions that would be made before the manifestation.

> *I thought I had made those choices when I was thinking of it. But you're saying you have to work out what you'll do for any creation before you create it?*

It would not be quite that way. We would be in the statement that the manifestation of that amount of money would still not remove the necessity for decisions. There are many who believe that great abundance in finances would relieve them of great decisions. However, it would simply magnify the decisions.

> *It is so confusing sometimes.*

We place ourselves in confusion. For we are as children in the candy store, wanting and wanting.

> *And "to be" is the freedom from balance and counter-balance?*

Yes, my friend.

> *Is there a trick to that?*

It would be realizing that we are as the children in the candy store. Then we are the owner of the store. And we are the candy itself. We have been viewing ourselves as the children in the candy store. When we have perspective of self, we are in the statement of totality of our being.

> *That we are everything?*

213

Yes, my friend. It would be a very good example: The candy store owner; the children in the candy store; and then, lo and behold, we see that we are even the candy. Then we view how we have been pulling ourselves one way or the other.

And we can choose to reside within the child in the candy store. We can choose to reside within the candy store owner. We can choose to view ourself as the candy. And we can be the being viewing the whole scene, as we are right now. Then we have the choice whether we would be diving into either, or remaining as we are—objective.

> *How would one live objectively? Because almost any decision you would be making would be choosing to be the child or the owner—*

Or the candy. For then when we are the candy we have nothing. We desire nothing. For we are it.

When we are the child in the candy store we want this and we want that. And we have this candy—we receive it and then we have it and we thought it was everything—but we want another one now. And then we have that one and we thought it would be right but here is another flavor—and we want that, too. We want it.

When we are the owner we view the child wanting everything. And, as the owner, we place in front of our very own self—the child—different types of candy. Here's another one, here's another one. When we then recognize that we are also the candy—we are not in desiring it—we are it. We take form as this flavor and we watch our very own selves devour our very own selves. We watch that we are this flavor and we see that we are attracted to our very own selves manifesting as this flavor. When we are attracted to another being or another situation we are attracted to the manifestation of our very own selves.

When we are viewing the scene in objectivity as we are now, then we view totality of being. Then we have the choice of how we would experience ourselves. In that particular situation, for example, we could decide not to enter that vibration. We could decide to be the viewer. Or we could decide to be entering. However, when we are entering, we remember that when we choose one or the other, we are at times losing perspective of the rest. It would be decision.

It would be similar in deciding to be in this lifetime. Once we are in the vibration, we lose perspective. Within each "lifetime" there would be hundreds of lifetimes of which we have been speaking. When we enter, we lose the perspective of the overviewer.

How do I get out?

As we are in the present—we are viewing. When we are vibrating in our daily vibration, we continue to carry that objectiveness with us.

It has no emotions that—

— That rule our being. We can choose to vibrate within the emotions. We can choose. However, when we enter, we are loosing a type of perspective. We would be in the statement that yes, it would feel as though we would be devoid of emotions. However, it would be a new experience for the human being not to be pulled one way or the other, in making clear decisions. "I would enter this relationship. I would enter this situation." It would be a clear decision.

When we are vibrating as the child, as the candy, or as the shop owner, we are releasing ourselves to that experience. We are releasing ourselves from the overview—the perspective of One in the totality of being. When we are in the perspective of the totality of being, then we are in charge. Then we are in the correctness of our being. And we have the choice of how we would manifest.

When we are viewing from this position of the overviewer, as we are in the present, we would be viewing about and there would be others who would be viewing from this perspective. *Then there would be clarity in relationships in every dimension.* When we are vibrating in the relationship as the child, as the candy, as the shop owner—we are tossed about.

When we are viewing from the perspective of the totality of our being, we would be as if we were in a crowd of beings and we would be standing on the chair, viewing over the crowd. And there would be other beings who would be viewing. And we would recognize those beings who would be viewing in the totality of *their* being. Those beings who have gathered together in the purpose of uplifting the awareness of themselves and the awareness of others that we might vibrate as One. Therein lies the fulfillment. Therein lies the relationships for which we seek. For we feel as though we would be fulfilled in the union. And what would be fulfilled—but nothing. It would be for naught.

For when we are in the viewing above, we are fulfilled. And lo and behold, perhaps that being whom we term to be our very own husband, would be viewing above the crowd. And we would be wondering, "Why have I not noticed you before?" For I have been as the child in the candy store. I have been experiencing my very own self. Of course, it would not be incorrect. However, as we have stated, when we enter we lose the perspective of the totality of our being.

That's clear. Thank you.

Thank *you,* my friend.

I feel as if you've been working with me in my dreams and things are happening, but I can't remember everything.

We are in the pleasure of being together in many dimensions, my friend. When we are vibrating in the totality of our being, then we would be remembering more and more. For when we have the awareness of the totality of our being, we would be carrying it with us in every dimension. In the dreams we would be recognizing the experience, once again, as in the example of the three—the child, the candy, and the owner—for we are accustomed to vibrating in the totality of our being. *Then* we can carry that awareness to conscious state. For in conscious state we have created the vibration in which we might receive the information. Would that be clear?

I think so.

216

Would we be saying it again?

Please.

When we are vibrating in the totality of our being, in the awareness of our being, then we are creating the vibration in which we might receive the totality of being from the dream state. For we have the overview and the learning in the dreams—together. And how could we carry that memory when we are vibrating as the child in the candy store? Where would this go?

Here we are, lifting our head above the crowd, and we receive. We receive the truth in every dimension. And lo and behold, there are many who are viewing. Many who are here viewing in the totality of our beings.

When we are in confusion and we are feeling tossed and turned and do not know what to decide, we would recognize, once again, we are the child in the candy store. And that we would be in the freedom of self. "I recognize that I am in the candy store once again—that I might free myself." For within every lifely vibration would be many, many lives. This example would be one—an entire lifely experience in this vibration. When we are viewing in totality of being we have removed ourself from balance and counterbalance. From the totality of our being we would ascend.

When we are in the vibration of the totality of our being the confusion and the pain of choice is released from our being, is it not?

Yes, it is.

Yes, my friend. It would then be choice. The totality of our being would be within the Father. For here we have the answers. Here we view the choices. Here we are creating in the essence—in the hands of the Father. For here we view the totality of our being.

I would be doing the same things I'm doing now, but I would not be feeling the same way?

Yes, my friend. Releasing ourselves from the bondage.

217

> *It sounds like a wonderful thing to be happening. But I
> don't want to be emotionally flat.*

It would not be what you term to be flat, my friend. It would be
the releasing of emotional pain and torment—that you might be in
the freedom to soar. In the freedom of creation, we manifest the
choice of our being.

When we view that what enters our lives is surrounded by
confusion, what do we do? We recognize that we are the child
devouring our very own selves, trying to devour our own candy.
And what would we do? We would come to totality of view, and
we view what has occurred. We view what we have created and
we say, "Back to the drawing board—for confusion is not what I
wanted to create."

If we have decided to manifest a great amount of money and
we are finding that we are seeing little bits dribbling into our lives—
back to the drawing board. For we could be pulled by the emotions,
deciding, "What have I done wrong? Am I being punished for
something?" Back to the drawing board. For once again we are the
child in the candy store, and we are not even able to have the candy.
We are in frustration. Back to the overviewer—that we have the
choice—we can go into that vibration or not. We know what is
involved. We know very much what is involved.

And we decide—do we want the emotional torment or would
we create and manifest freedom? When we vibrate in the freedom
of our being—in the truth—it would be in the choice. When we
recognize from this view that we have the choice of something
which we do not want to be choosing between, then we say, "It is
not for me. I would begin again. I would manifest total and complete
fulfillment—that the choice would be as breathing. Then I know it
is correct. For it would be as breathing."

However, as human beings we feel that we have choices and
what do we do? We enter those choices and we allow ourselves to
be pulled and pushed, and we try to manifest within the creation.
We try to *squeeze* fulfillment out of the creation of confusion—we
want it so desperately. And we are so confused at times that we

218

forget that we have the choice. We are consumed by our very own selves, by our very own creations.

When we are viewing from totality of being, we view and we are clear. "It is not what I wish to be in the middle of choosing. I want to breathe the answer from the freedom of my being." *When we allow ourselves to release the creation, we release balance and counterbalance.* We release. And we trust as we are viewing above the crowd—fulfillment of being. Never fear, my friend, you would not be flat. It would be without pain, torment, confusion. It would be fulfillment.

> *When we are viewing the dreams ... we could be in the remembrance from the total perspective of entirety of being, that we are every being within the dream. It would be the same with every information in every dimension.*

Could you tell me if I had a lifetime with Jesus?

Of course, my friend. For why else would we be feeling the closeness of being. Vibrating together. Vibrating together in the teachings as He came upon the scene. And you would be wondering what He would be doing in the village of your beings, wondering what you would do in His presence? That He would be speaking to your very own self. That He would be in the advising of the beings. That you would have been working with the mothers and women of the community, in the support of the families in the absence of the man. And He would be speaking with your being as if you would be the comrade. Coming together. Then He would be departing. And you would be wondering, would you be viewing Him again? And, of course, he would come to your side.

Was that as a female?

That would be yes, my friend, as a female. And once again in another dimension you would be the old man, the Sage. The one of the many who would be abandoning the old teachings for the

219

new vibration. Remember, my friend, there are many dimensions vibrating in the Oneness of our beings.

When we have a feeling as human beings, when we have a desire, we can be trusting that it is the truth. And yes, we are wondering, "Dare I think that I was in that time. Am I making this up because I desire it so desperately?" If we are desiring, it is part of our being begging to be recognized. Yes, my friend, dare to allow the fantasies to come forward with regard to the Christos. For when we allow the memories to come forward, what we consider to be fantasy would be the truth.

> *I'm just wondering why I saw myself as a man when I did a past life regression?*

When we are viewing ourselves in what we term to be other dimensions, it would be as we are viewing the candy store, once again. Which view are we presenting to our being? Which view are we taking? Which part of ourselves are we viewing? For we would be in the remembrance that in actuality we are in the androgeny of our beings. That whatever manifestation would be coming forward from our beings, would present the truth to our very own selves.

> *I don't know if I understand.*

When we are viewing what we term to be another dimension, and we view that we would be a man with another being, what would be occurring? We are viewing once again as we have been speaking—the candy store. We are viewing the man. We could be viewing the woman and the vibration would change. It would, however, be a similiar dimension. A similar dimension. And whichever we are viewing would be where we are opening as the channel to that dimension, remembering that the information coming forward would be coming forward to that part of our being which we are able to receive. Viewing from within the candy store or from the total perspective of our entire selves. When we are viewing from the entirety of our being—we receive the view of many dimensions as One.

We could be requesting from our dreams that we receive the information in as many forms as possible, that we might be in contact with the totality of our being. That we might be the companion of the Christos. We might be the comrade. We might be the woman passing by. We might be the student. And we might be the Christos. One in the same. A viewing, from total perspective of self. Has it not been said we would do these things and more? In every dimension.

When we are viewing the dreams and we view that we are one being and there are others about us, we could be in the remembrance from the total perspective of entirety of being—that we are every being within the dream. It would be the same with every information in every dimension.

Remember the meditation. All else is fantasy and creation. Even the candy itself.

That's wonderful.

Yes, my friend, it is the freedom of our being. From that point and from that awareness, we ascend.

> **W**hen we create in our vibration the viewing of the totality of our being, and we carry that awareness within our being...then we are able to receive.

Are you sure I'm going to be able to hear the Father? (Laughter) I'm still worried about that. Is that a fear?

It is really what we term to be a desire. It is not really fear. It is desire. Hear the words: For in the confusion, there was the desire of the candy, and being the candy, and the owner. That was the confusion. *When we are in total viewing of entirety of self, we hear the Father.*

When we are worried or concerned with the confusion, what would be occurring? We are feeling ourselves being pulled into the vibration—that we would be blinded by our very own beings. That would be the fear. In the trusting of the viewing of totality of being would be the trusting of total and complete fulfillment. For then we are in the creation of fulfillment in every dimension.

> *Sometimes, even though I feel that I'm clear—when it's time to make a decision, I don't feel guided.*

It would be that when we are making the decision, we have chosen to reenter from within that vibration—from within that dimension. When we are in the decision from the totality of being, from this vibration which we have been sharing, then the decision is quite easy, my friend. When we allow ourselves to enter that dimension, then we are in the confusion. Practice the meditation. From the meditation comes the decision.

We skip about in many dimensions.

> *I don't remember.*

But, my friend, we have learned how. When we create in our vibration the viewing of the totality of our being, and we carry that awareness within our being, then we are the receptacle of that awareness from other dimensions. Yes, my friend. For then we are able to receive. How can the child in the candy store receive? The totality of being, devouring its very own self?

> *How does it feel there—to be in the overviewing?*

We have been there, have we not?

> *Yes, that's true. It feels objective.*

And clear. And free. Yes, my friend, the freedom of choice—manifestation.

> *Thank you.*

Thank you, my friend. Much has been said in the truth of the beings. The truth.

> *When one being breathes in the freedom of expression, every being is filled with Love.*

Is there anything you'd like to share with my friend? (referring to a friend who had accompanied her to the session with Pretty Flower.)

We would be sharing with *you,* for when one receives, every being receives. Would that be answer to that question?

Yes. Thank you.

We would be in the statement, my friend, that when one being dips their hand into the water, every being is refreshed. Every being. When one being breathes in the freedom of expression, every being is filled with Love. Every being.

When we view that one being might be experiencing something that we would want to experience, we could release ourselves and allow ourselves to receive through that being—as we give through our very own selves. When we are learning, others are learning also.

We would be on our way. The blessings of the Universe reside within your being.

***

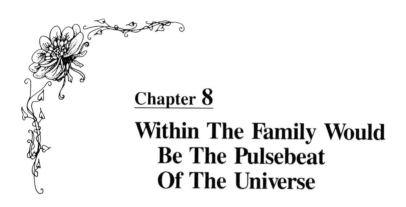

Chapter 8

Within The Family Would Be The Pulsebeat Of The Universe

As parents we have the feeling within our beings that we are responsible for our very own children's breath and how they would be vibrating. If they would be troublesome, we feel it is our responsibility, and we think, "How have we caused them to be that way?" It would be quite incorrect.

***

For there are many who would be wanting to be in physical form at the time of the transformation of the planet called Earth.

[A husband and wife ask about the possibiliy of having another child.] There is a question we've had: Is there a being that would like to have us as parents? I've been feeling a presence and I want to know if this is another child.

There would be several about, my friends.

Oh, God. (laughter)

225

Remember, it would be the choice of your beings. For there are many who would be wanting to be in physical form at the time of the transformation of the planet called Earth. There would be many flocking about. All those beings who would be in conscious manifestation of the Light. Remember—it would be the choice of your being.

***

... the conception of the child is the agreement of three — the father, the mother and the child.

I have a question about my daughter. She has one child already but she wants another. This past year she experienced two miscarriages. I was wondering if it will ever be possible for her to have another child?

We would be in the statement that the miscarrying of the child would be the decision of the child. It would be that the child would be expecting the union to be with a different man. And there would have been the decision to be—and then not to be.

There would be the statement that there would be spiritual growth between the two. That there would be the recognition that in the conception of the child is *the agreement of three* — the father, and the mother and the child. It would be a time of opening the awarenesses, that the union might be.

***

...each of us is the ancient one. And we choose the vibration. We choose the vibration that we might be mirror images for ourselves.

226

[Pretty Flower speaks with a couple expecting their first child.]

Hello, my friends. We would be gathered together for a specific purpose, would we not? Yes, my friends. The two filled with joy.

The Story of Decision

Once upon a time there was a little child. And the child was walking about, wondering, wondering, what would be next. On the road, in the clouds, so to speak—walking around. And there would be different beings coming forward to that child, that wonderful child.

And first would be the Great Fairy with the wings of the strength of the Universe. And that Fairy would be saying to the child, "Hello."

And the child would be hearing the Great Fairy. And the child would say, "Hello."

And the Great Fairy would be in the statement, "What would you be doing?"

And the child would say, "I would be making a decision."

And the Great Fairy said, "Oh."

And the child said, "I would be deciding. I would be deciding where I would reside. How I would vibrate. I would be deciding."

And the Great Fairy said, "Oh."

And then there was another being who came along. A great warrior. Samurai warrior, coming forward to the child. And the samurai warrior said to the child, "Hello, my friend."

And the child said, "Hello."

And the samurai warrior said, "My brother, what would you be doing?"

And the child would be in the statement, "I am in the making of a decision. Seeking how I would vibrate."

And the warrior said, "We have traveled together many times, have we not?"

And the child said, "Yes, we have. We have been warriors together."

And the great warrior said, "What would be the type of decision? What would be the type of decision?"

And the child would be in the statement, "It would be the type of decision where I would be able to vibrate, to vibrate uninhibited. That I would be in the freeness of my being. For I am complete in the balance and the counterbalance. That I would come forward as the Teacher."

And the samurai said, "What would you be teaching, O Great Warrior?"

And the child said, "Dear friend, know that I am much more than a great warrior. Know that I am much more."

And then there was another being coming along. Another being filled with Light. Filled with luminescent Light. Coming upon the child. And the child beamed from the heart—the Light. The child beamed from the heart, that there would be union of the two.

And in the union were the words, were the words, "Great Teacher, Great Teacher, what will you be bestowing this time?"

And the child, the child opening to the luminescence, opening to the Great Teacher Himself, would be in the statement, "We would be in the teaching of One. We would be in the teaching of One. Of the One. One."

And the luminescent Being shone the greatest Light possible. And the child breathed in the Light—for the child knew. The child knew of the teachings that would be bestowed through his being.

Then there was another being who came upon the child. The being was a little girl. And the little girl said to the child, "Hello."

And the child said, "Hello, my friend."

And the little girl said, "What would you be about to be doing?"

And the child said, "I would be in the vibration of my being, for a decision has been made."

And the little girl clapped her hands together with glee. And she said, "Would we be playing together in this vibration?"

And he said, "It would be your decision. It would be your decision."

And the little girl said, "I would be deciding that I would be in the vibration that would be with you. For we would vibrate together. We would be creating together. We would be in the teaching together. That we would be as One. That we would be as One, for is that not the teaching?" said the little girl.

And the child said, "That is the teaching. That is the teaching."

Then along came another being. One other being coming along. The being was an ancient one. An ancient being, so to speak. And he would be saying to the two, "Greetings."

And the two would be in the statement, "Greetings."

And the ancient one, the old one, would be in the statement, "We would be in union. We would be in union."

And the little girl looked to that ancient one, the old one, and she said, "How would we do that? How would we do that?"

And the child knew—for it would be in the teaching of One.

And the little girl and the child were together. And the ancient one said, "We will be One in the same. We will be One in the same." And the Light from the child beamed forward.

And there was within the little girl a tickle. It was a type of tickle, a type of movement. And she would be giggling at the feeling of that type of movement. And there would be from her being—bursting forth—the Light. That there would be union. That there would be union.

And the old one, the ancient one, said, "Here, you are the children and I am the father. And when we arrive in our vibration, you will be the father and mother and I will be the child. That we would be in the bestowal of the blessings of the Universe."

*

Is that not what you wanted to know, my friends?

Yes, that's what we wanted to know, Pretty Flower.

Yes, my friends. Wonderful beings—the three. Three ancient ones. We would be in the remembrance that each one of us is the ancient one. And we choose the vibration. We choose the vibration that we might be mirror images for ourselves. That the ancient one would be the child. That would be the great paradox. Over and over in

229

the planet called Earth, it would be the great teaching. The great teaching—that we would be as the child. And this being would be the manifestation of the teaching. For, as you are well aware, now is the time.

For there would be many who would be in the incarnation of this time. Many ancient ones gathering together—gathering the beings together. Gathering the peoples together that they might be in union. That there would be the recognition that the nourishment is spirit—essence. Everything else would be fantasy, of course. And we would be in the enjoyment of fantasy. However, there would be those beings gathering together.

Never fear, for the child would be the friend of those who have no friends. And there would be concern, when you would be wondering, "Why would he be playing with *those* children? Why would he be speaking with *those* beings?" It would be that he would be the friend of those who have no friends. That he would be in the bestowal of Light. For those beings would be simply needing the Light that they would be in the marriage of the Light—with the child and their very own selves. That they would experience the opening once again.

For the great teachers would not be in the teaching of the learned. They would be in the teaching of those beings who would be needing teaching. Never fear. Never fear for the company of the child. For the child in the past, so to speak, has been in the company of many. And has been the teacher of many. As have you, my friends.

What would we be communicating?

> *I think you've answered most of our questions already, Pretty Flower. We were going to ask you about the child.*

Yes, my friend.

> *—and how we would help the child to grow. To accomplish the teachings, if it must.*

It would also be in the statement: Never fear to be the child in front of the child. When we are the parent, at times there is something that occurs. As the parent we tend to be what would be termed "responsible." For we have protective instincts within our very beings. And as the child grows we tend to be the observer, so to speak.

We would be in the statement that there would be the remembrance to be in the playing—with self. For there would be, of course, playing with the child. However, the child would be wanting to view how you would play as yourself, with yourself. That he might see and he might learn. For when we are with children—those tiny beings—we would be creating our vibrations to be as theirs. And they are begging us to manifest our very own selves. Manifesting our very own selves—for their pleasure and enjoyment.

And we would be in the statement that every being on the planet called Earth would be in the benefit of experiencing the growing of another being within their very vessel. That they would know that every being is One in the same. One in the same.

***

...it would now be the time of the awareness
of the loveliness of the child—as she is now.

[Pretty Flower speaks with a woman about her grandchild. The woman's question is:] My granddaughter doesn't like to read and it's interfering with her schoolwork. Her mother and I are such great readers—we can't understand it. Is there any reason for this and is there any way we can help her?

There would be the times in the vibration of her being, several times where she would have been forced to be in the studying. Where she would have been forced to be in the copying of the pages over and over again. It would also be in the times of "rigid Christianity" where there would be the father and mother who would be in the requirement of her to be studying the Book of Holies.

231

There would be other children playing about. And this child would have received what would be termed in the current vernacular, "abuse" from the need to be studying. And in that time was the freedom of being.

When the child in the present views the books and the pages, *the awareness within her being is greater than what is presented in the pages.* And there would be the relieving and the releasing of the pressure upon the child to be in the reading. There would even be the statement, "We recognize the displeasure in reading. And we would be in the releasing of demands." That the spirit of the child might flow forward. For it would be of her own will and her own desire to be reading the pages.

What would be the pages? The pages would be of the great women, in the initiation of their beings. For in the reading of those treatises, would be the sparks of Light that would be coming forward from her being. It would be in the manuscripts where there would be the secrecy of the experience. Those manuscripts that would be telling the stories of the secrecy of the occurrence within the pyramids of the goddesses—that there would be the rights of initiation in the truths. And there would be the interest of that young woman who would be opening to the curiosities. Never fear, for the child has great purpose within her being.

There would be in the child the cessation of the ingestion of pastries. There would be the cessation of the ingestion of bread for a period of three weeks. Then there would be the cessation of the acidity and the increase of alkalinity, that there would be the increase of the magnetic flow within the physical body. For in the future, there would be the need of that child—then woman—to be in the physical strength of her being—that she might enjoy the manifestation of her being. There would then be in the magnetic balance of the being, the wanting to read, the consuming of knowledge.

It would be the releasing of pressure, as we have stated, and the change in the ingestion of foods. That there would be the increasing of what we term to be self-esteem and the control of the physical body. For there would be the recognition that with the pressure placed upon the child to succeed, even though it would be in Love, there would be the need in the child to be placing barriers around herself. And she would be in the increasing of the body physical continually until there would be the releasing of those pressures.

We would be in the strong statement that it would now be the time of the awareness of the loveliness of the child—as she is *now*. For when we attempt to be in the future, we forget the present vibration.

"Never fear," would be spoken to those about that child. There would be the reading, there would be much study, and there would be much writing of manuscripts. Never fear. Allow the child to be vibrating in self.

***

> *...we could view the interaction of human beings within the family in a different way.... That we would be viewing as part of the entire Universe. And if we were allowing ourselves to view in a grander sense, we would* be *the entire Universe.*

[Pretty Flower speaks with a woman about the family dynamics within the home.]

Yes, my friend, there has been a change. For there seems to have been a letting go of some worries and concerns. They would be on many levels, my friend, and in many dimensions. For as we allow those burdens which we have carried through different times to manifest, then we may release our attachments to them. That they may fly away—if we would allow them to.

For in the Universe, in this great creation, are we. We vibrate together. There is not one thing that we do on our very own—not one tiny thing. When we breathe, the entire Universe breathes. Everything that we do, we do with the awareness that we *are* the entire Universe.

And when we decide that we would be concerned or worried about something, then we have decided to dis-focus on the entire

Universe, and focus on what we would term to be a problem. And we allow ourselves to be in marriage with the problem. And we grow and we deepen that we might know the problem well.

Sometimes, as human beings, we are not quite conscious that we are doing exactly this process. And as we awaken to our capabilities as creators, we recognize that we are in fact traveling deep within the problem. That we would be getting to know it quite well. And then we would be forgetting that we could travel out from the problem and view it from a different perspective. For because we have allowed ourselves the marriage with the problem, we would be in recognition, my friend, that we are not prisoners of the problem. That we are merely checking it out. Trying to find out what it is all about.

At times we travel deep within a concern and we get lost there. We forget that it is a choice. And we have found a tiny curve. And we have gone around the bend, so to speak. And what have we done? We have forgotten about the path and about everything else that exists in this great Universe, in physical and spirit form, for we are human beings.

And there would be the awareness that we could be choosing to travel from without the problems, that we could now view them in a different way. That we could view the interaction of human beings within the family in a different way. That we would be quite separate for a small time, so to speak. That we would be viewing as part of the entire Universe. And if we were allowing ourselves to view in a grander sense, we would *be* the entire Universe.

And so as we remove ourselves from the problem, we would view—perhaps as a teacher, perhaps as a being walking by a storefront window—and we would view in to see what would be occurring. Perhaps in the storefront window would be a telecommunicator with visual picture, and we would view it. And in the picture would be our family interactions. And we would view in that picture what is actually occurring. The facts. Not so much the judgments.

For we are so involved with Love that we would want things to be a certain way. We would want our family to be whole and healthy and right thinking—everything we would want for them. And we would be viewing the picture and we would be thinking,

"What are the facts? What are the facts about this child? What are the facts?" There would be a difference.

And we would not be going about judging ourselves for judging, for that simply communicates great stress. We would find, however, that we could be viewing the facts. The facts. What were the words actually spoken. What were the exact physical movements? What are the facts—in that picture, as we are walking by that one section of the Universe. That manifestation which we are so familiar with—for we have resided within it. And for the very moment we are stepping outside that we might view.

And when there has been the releasing of every single belief—then, my dear friend, we have the existence in the "now."

And we view many things. We view that the man, so to speak, the warrior of the family, is quite confused with the role. For what would we be doing? What would we be doing as warriors in the family? There have been many rules and regulations that have been learned and relearned. And there would be the rebel inside of the warrior that would be saying, "I do not want these rules and regulations. I do not want to act and react the way that I have been told that I would act and react."

There would also be the part of the warrior that would be saying, "I wish to be the perfect father. I wish to be the perfect mate. I wish to be perfect in this family." And what happens when those statements are made? What happens is that many beliefs come forward. Why do they come forward? That we might see them. That we might view them and we might decide which to discard and which to retain in our consciousness for this vibration.

And there would be the recognition that this particular warrior could be reminded that it would be a choice. It would be a choice.

There would be beliefs of what would be the perfect being for that warrior. *And when there has been the releasing of every single belief—then, my dear friend, we have the existence in the "now."* It would be quite a job for there have been many attachments. As human beings we exist in the now by relating to the past. For we have a type of cushion about us that says that our reality is as we see it. In fact, we see a very small part of the reality which we could see.

And so we have the warrior opening to many different beliefs about how he should be. This would be in the picture. What is not in the picture is what you, my dear friend, would be doing about it. For that does not exist in the picture. We would simply be viewing the picture.

> *The inner peace is found in the opening to the pulsebeat of the Universe. The pulsebeat of the Universe, closing and opening.*

And then we have the son—the young man who has taken upon himself the duties of the young man. Those would be to rebel against any rule. To decide that his family is wonderful. And yet there would be questions. "What is all of this going on around me?" he would be saying. "Why can't this be a regular family? Why can't we be as the people I see in the movies?" And there would be great confusion in that department. There would also be the wanting to be free and yet the fear to be free, for he has created the burden of illness that he might still rely on those about him.

And we would be in the recognition that it is a temporary situation. It is quite temporary, my dear friend. For in the human being would be the push and the pull. The freedom and the fear of freedom. For it would be a great unknown. As human beings, we have existed in the past for such a very long time, that we have forgotten that we even have the wings to unfurl. And as the wings remain closed, we become tighter and tighter within our very being. Constricted. And there would be the tiny spark that would be saying, "Unfurl your wings." And there would be the need to unfurl the wings.

And in the picture we would be seeing the young man wanting to unfurl his wings—and deciding that it would be quite difficult. For there have been placed in the family communications many rules and regulations that would be decided for him. And he would be quite confused. And that would be part of the picture.

It would be what would be called a stressful situation. And much would be unspoken, and much would build until it would need to be spoken. And we would find that it would be a blessing that the family situation is as it is. For it would be what we would term the predecessor to birth.

As human beings we recognize what birth is about. We recognize the purpose for constriction. We recognize the purpose for releasing. We come together and our very being gathers together that it might be assimilated—that we might assume the form in physical manifestation. There would be much happening within that vibration. And we would be stating at this time that that would be a prime example of the family situation. For we would find that there would be the coming together for the birth.

And we, as human beings, would be quite confused about the coming together. For when we come together it would be the perfect time that we want to be free. And when we find ourselves becoming free, we gather together because we want the Love to fill our being. That we do not want to be separate—for we are love-ed beings. And we would find that it would be, in fact, the blessing—the recognition of the pulsebeat of the Universe.

For, as we want to be in the freedom, we have opened to the greatest possible degree. And when we are reaching to our loved ones that they would be closer, it would be, in fact, the recognition that we have expanded to our greatest degree and now we are returning. Part of the pulsebeat of the Universe—that we would open—and we would close.

Never fear, my friend. The inner peace is found in the opening to the pulsebeat of the Universe. The pulsebeat of the Universe, closing and opening. As human beings, we have the belief that we must be open, open, open. However, in the pulsebeat of the Universe, is closing—and opening.

When we recognize that we are closing, then we are in the synchronicity of the Universe. And when we are opening, we are in the synchronicity of the Universe. It would be correct. However we would be, would be correct. For we are in alignment with the

Universe. And we would be recognizing that within the family vibrations would be that great pulsebeat.

And there would be within the family the growing of trust. How does the growing of trust occur? By taking the risk of being our very own selves. Of making the statement and trusting that those about us will love us, no matter what we say. And guess what? Sometimes they are fearful of the statement—for it is very strong. And other times they are curious about the statement. It would be called getting to know each other in a deeper way, that we might allow ourselves to be more expansive and more filled with the freedom of life.

There would be the statement amongst the family that we have learned that we are attempting to express ourselves. And there would be, perhaps, from each being the statement, "I am expressing myself in a way that is quite risky for me. I am making statements that I have not preplanned and I am fearful of what I would say." There would be the exposing of that particular consciousness so that each member of the family would be in recognition that the other would be taking a risk. So that when a statement would be made, especially from the young man—there would be the consciousness of the others who would recognize that the statement takes great risk. And there would be the asking for the vibration of Love.

We would be remembering that the vibration of Love comes from the Universe and we would simply open—that we would channel the Love. That would not mean that we would not find ourselves reacting—saying exactly what would come to us. That the others might recognize that there would be another being taking a risk, wanting to be loved in the risk taking. It would be a type of experiment that has been occurring all along. And now it has simply come to Light—that the Love might grow. For there would be a fear amongst the members of the family, that as we unfurl our wings, there would not be quite enough room for everybody's wings. How much space can all of this take? And we would recognize that we are all One in the same.

There would also be the need that each being within the family vibration assume responsibility for their very own selves. There would be the releasing of the attachment of the mis-alignment of the young man, that he might accept responsibility for himself. Never fear. It would be the time of completion and beginnings. And there would be the recognition that there is a support of the misalignment, for we have focused on it for such a time that we have encouraged it to exist. And there would be the refocusing—the refocusing of health—that each being within the family vibration might recognize it is time for the flip of the coin. That we would see the other side. That we would view what is healthy about ourselves. What is correct about ourselves. How we get along.

And when we find in one second of the day that there would be an expression of Love—we would allow that expression. Not to be a big deal—but that there would be the simple expression. There would be the encouragement from truth. Not the encouragement from what the truth might become if it were to act a certain way—but the encouragement for the truth *as it is*. Total acceptance of the picture is what we are working on.

We could, as we enter the family picture, release ourselves of the burden of responsibility for the others. For we have our very own selves and each being would be under the auspices of a guide.

Then there would be the decision in viewing the picture—how we would enter that picture our very own selves. There would be the decision, first of all, that there would be the unfurling of wings and there would be plenty of room for everyone. For the wings fill the space that is surrounding our beings, wherever we are and whatever we are doing. And we would find that as we decide to enter the family picture, that we would enter as our very own selves. That we have gone within, and we have searched the problem, and we have existed in it. And now we have removed ourselves from the problem—that we might view it.

Then, as we join the family picture we come as our very own selves. Separate, yet united. In the separateness we give ourselves

239

the greatest freedom—for we allow those beings to vibrate *as they are*. And, my dear friend, we allow ourselves to vibrate *as we are*—at the very second.

We could be in the recognition that every being of the family would be in the care of the Caretaker—those beings of spirit form which have united in great purpose, that they would be Lighting the way upon the path. That they would be guiding those beings. We could, as we enter the family picture, release ourselves of the burden of responsibility for the others. For we have our very own selves and each being would be under the auspices, so to speak, of a guide. And there would be many in spirit form about the household.

Many would be about the children, for in the joy of the child is the joy of the Universe. And those wonderful little cherubs come about that they might enjoy the freedom of play.

There would be one child gathered about in spirit form—for, in another time, so to speak, he would be the brother of those in the family now. He would be viewing what would be occurring, for he has allowed himself to take the form of child in spirit—that he might unite with those vibrating together. That he might learn and remember the purposes which they have decided upon in that time. That particular being would be in the presence for perhaps the next year and then he would be on his way. There would not be the concern—for he is in recognition, even though he has assumed the child form, of the purpose for gathering together.

And there would be about the beings the gathering of many of those beings wishing to be teaching the arts of healing. For the call has been broadcast many times—and there would be the recognition of the healing coming forward. There would be the recognition of the gathering of beings in physical and spirit form that there would be the manifestation of healing in many dimensions.

For when they experience their wings and they vibrate in the now—then the Voice from within speaks and carries them toward their particular purpose in this vibration.

240

As far as my children—is there something that I could offer them?

The best that would be offered to the children would be the Love and the statement of self. For we learn by example. We see those about us filled with peace. We see those about us allowing the fulfillment of manifestation. That's how we learn. We don't learn so much by reading and memorizing. We learn by vibrating in the now. And there would be that learning that *they* are in the now. And they would learn this by example and by the freedom allowed them to experience their wings.

For when they experience their wings and they vibrate in the now—then the Voice from within speaks and carries them toward their particular purpose in this vibration. That they might manifest I AM—the most familiar part of their being. How do they know the most familiar part of their being? They have been vibrating in it—forever. Trust that I AM within their being would manifest to the greatest possible degree—as would be in every being.

When we allow those beings about us to express themselves, then we allow them to accept that part of their being and not deny. That they would recognize I AM in every part of their being—as we would be doing.

There would be in every case the recognition that it is the time for connection with other dimensions which we have called past lives. There would be the messages that would be becoming from within, "I would like to try this. I would like to try that." There would be the need for great encouragement. For when we wish to try something, it is because we want to manifest something that already vibrates within our being.

***

It would be of his own path and his own experience and his own learning. There would be no blame....This child has chosen this path.

241

[Pretty Flower speaks with a divorced mother about her son. The mother states:] I am divorced from the father of my son but there's still emotional tension between us. I feel that my son suffers the most from the situation and I'm concerned about the effect of this on his emotional future.

There would be several things. Firstly, there would be the statement to the son, "This is what I see occurring. And I have deep Love for you and I would like to express that Love." It would be as simple as that, for we are viewing how we believe that being to be. We are viewing from our years how that being at his age is acting and reacting.

And how would we be helping that being? Firstly, by the way we vibrate within our life, and by the acceptance of the way he is. For when a being is experiencing emotional turmoil it would be part of what we have termed "turning in on itself." And why would that occur? Because we have not allowed it to exist. We have viewed it with fear and we have viewed it with judgment. And there would be the recognition that it would be valid. It would be real feelings— feelings that would be needing to be expressed without fear. And it would occur, my friend. The expressions would occur.

As the mother, we could say that we understand there is turmoil at hand. We could say to the son, "This is what I see and this is what I believe is occurring—and it is not incorrect to feel that way—it is not incorrect. All of those feelings are real. They are real. And if you wish to express those feelings then I will hear what you have to say. For I have a deep Love for you and I want to share my Love with you."

There would not be the judgment or the concern or the worry that he would be carrying those feelings for ever and ever. Never fear. For there are those about that being in spirit form who would be in the assistance of carrying the burdens which he has decided to carry of his very own self. He would be in the belief that he would be at fault for the separation, even though it has been made very clear. It would be a natural feeling. It would be a feeling that occurs in many, in the same circumstances.

There could be those beings gathering together who would be in the same circumstances and there would be communications of real feelings. It would be with other children of his own age who would have experienced the same. They would be gathering together under the guidance of someone who would be aware of those feelings—separate from you and separate from the man called the father—that he might be free to express real feelings.

In those gatherings there would be the children learning that their feelings are real. There would be the opportunity of expressing the anger. For as a child, how can the child express the anger at the separation? For he would be in the Love of the mother and the Love of the father. Where would he be placing this anger? On self! And it would not be the fault of the mother or of the father. *It would be of his own path and his own experience and his own learning.* There would be no blame. Release yourself of the blame and the placing of blame. It is a burden. This child has chosen this path.

Once again we would state that there would be the seeking of the group where there would be counseling. That the son would be hearing perhaps another being making the statement of anger and he might be surprised at the statement. And perhaps, in another time, he would find himself in that very gathering making those statements—and weeping—allowing the words to come forward. And there would be releasing.

It would be great releasing. And you, my friend, would even feel it as it is occurring—even though you would not be in the physical presence. For the two of you would be quite tied together in spirit form, and there would be the recognition of the releasing. There would be the viewing of each other eye to eye, beaming the Love of the Universe—unrestricted once again. Never fear. For that would be the wish, and that would be the hope, and we would be saying, "So be it!" It would be occurring. Never fear.

There would be the statement that in the lives there has been the seeking of hope and the seeking of the fulfillment of hope. And each time we have found that the hope has had a hollow foundation. And we have been in the fear—and the fear of the nonfulfillment of hope. And each time the hope has been dashed to the ground. We would be in the statement, my friend, that we are here in the fulfillment of hope—that the foundation would be built—that we would trust our hopes. And it would build and be stronger and stronger. That we would know within our being that that for which we hope would be fulfilled. That would be why we are gathering together. That the hope would be fulfilled.

***

Even in the darkest moment would be the beginning of the Light.

[A woman asks about her son's marital problems and the effect on her grandchildren.]

They would not be happy, my friend. For they would each be in the seeking of self-fulfillment and it would be part of the pulsebeat of their beings. For they, in their vibration together, would be recognizing the depletion of nourishment of the spirit. Each would be in the viewing, and be blaming situations and each other for the depletion of their being. There would be the lessons at hand that they would be in the replenishment of spirit—of self. That there would be those meditations. There would be those recognitions of the spirit within, that it would grow and fill their beings.

And, my dear friend, it does not appear at this time that they would be prepared to be in the recognition. Perhaps they would be separate and feeling the loneliness of their beings. That they would recognize that they would be in the nourishment of spirit—and in the reunion of selves.

Never fear for the despair within your being. We recognize the wanting and the desiring of your being to feel the union of their being, that they would be happy within themselves. Never fear, my friend. Even in the darkest moment would be the beginning of the Light. Have faith, my friend, that it would be correct, for in the temporary parting would be the beginning of the Light. Never fear.

244

With the children, we would be in the statement that there are many in spirit form who dance about the children that they would be in the care. Never fear. For at times there would be the children in the stress of the home. And there would be the recognition that the children would be separate from the stress—allowing their spirit to be healed. It would be viewing the situation in another way, for we have been in the viewing that it would be of disaster. And we could view within our very selves the changing of the viewing, that there would be the recognition that it would be the preparation of the beginning. It would be quite necessary.

Never fear. Allow yourself, my dear friend, to be in the enjoyment of your own vibration of joy. Know that the truths are manifest. Know that those beings are cared for, that even the guides about those beings would be in the caring for their beings. They would be watching that the fulfillment of purpose might be guiding their direction.

For the vibration of the planet called Earth has increased. And many would be in the completion and the beginning of vibrations in what would seem to be the blink of an eye. For what would have occurred in the period of three years—in what we have reluctantly called "the past" for the sake of vocabulary—would be in the present in the occurrence of perhaps three months or even three days. It would be in the increase of vibration in the planet called Earth. Never fear. *At the darkest hour is the spark of the greatest Light.*

The blessings of the Universe would be upon those beings, for at the request of this being there would be the assistance in the turning to the Light. Would there be more?

> *It sounds like earth changes are going to solve a lot of problems.*

It would be that what we have been speaking of would not be so much in the vibration of the physicalness of the planet. It would be in the energies that in the past would have been an occurrence of three years—in the present would be three months. For there would be the enlightenment of the planet. In the enlightenment of the planet, those who would be requiring of themselves to experience

245

the Darkness before the Light, would be in the speediness of that experience.

There would be the trusting of the peoples of the planet called Earth, in the joy and the recognition that those beings going towards the pain of their own experience would be seeking the Light. And they would first be in the experience of their own Darkness. And we would be in joy — for they would be in the cycle quite quickly.

***

...when we carry the fulfillment of tradition, then we are One in the same with those who require the tradition to be fulfilled. It would simply be different manifestation. And who are we to say which would be correct? Who are we to say?

[Pretty Flower speaks with a married couple:] We have a problem with my parents. They have strong religious beliefs and we have a problem communicating with them. Is there anything we could do to bridge the gap, and bring them closer to us and our expected child?

There would be the belief, would there not? There would be the beliefs, over and over. And do they not know that this is the child, the very child who will be an upheaval to all of those beliefs? Though it might be in the unconsciousness of their beings—know, my dear friend, know within your being—that that would be the reason. That would be the reason—even though they know not themselves.

For they would be holding on to those traditions and those beliefs. And what would we be saying? There would be the birthing of the child who would be in the upheaval of the beliefs. Their very inner beings would be experiencing the upheaval—even as we speak. They would not be in the understanding of those words.

246

They would not even be in the understanding of why they must be so determined. For there would be within them the desire to embrace, to embrace you as you are. And yet there are the words, the traditions. They would be in the belief that the traditions would be a protection.

And, my dear friends, we are very well aware that they would be in the inhibiting of the beings. Never fear for the judgment of negative upon that occurrence. For there would be those beings who would be in the needing of the restriction of their beings. *They would be vibrating in the need of restrictions.* It would be proper, so to speak. For every being would be in the manifestation I AM. Every being.

Then there would be the recognizing, my dear friend, that upon the sight of the child—never fear—for the child would be beaming the Love. And upon the sight of the child there would be the placing aside of those fears, of those judgments. And they would be wanting to gather the child into their very own arms. When this is occurring, my friends, know that there is from the child the energies that would be in the assistance of those beings. That they would be releasing a little of the need to be restricted.

There would be the statement, my dear friend, that there would be nothing we would be doing to change those wonderful beings, for they are correct. *It is their manifestation I AM.* There would only be within your very own beings—understanding. Understanding of the way they would be manifesting.

Never fear. The child would be breaking the barriers, so to speak. And there would be the bestowal of the blessings of the two. For there was the recognition of the union—and the requirements of the union in tradition. There would be the statement from the great teachings of those beings, and of all beings, that the "requirements" have been met. And there would be the placing of the hand in the hat.

My dear friends, in every dimension there is the union of the beings. And there would be many who would be viewing the union. That the message would be sent through the dimensions—of the union. *That* is the tradition, so to speak. And it would be manifest in many different forms. That you would carry within the hearts of your being the fulfillment of the tradition—would be part of what we term to be the breaking of barriers.

Never fear. For when we carry the fulfillment of tradition, then we are One in the same with those who require the tradition to be fulfilled. It would simply be different manifestation. And who are we to say which would be correct? Who are we to say?

The Love of the parents is great. And the Love of the child for the parents is great. Never fear. Everything will resolve itself. Never fear. For you have asked and you would receive. For we hear everything. Everything. And you have remembered to ask.

***

The Story of the Three Children

Once upon a time there were three children. And they were gathering together that they might play. That they might play together. And they decided that they would go to the field and they would skip about in the field.

And as they were walking in the field they found that the grass was very, very tall. Very, very tall. Nearly over the tops of their little heads. And they were pushing aside part of the grass that they might be walking. And they decided that they would play in the tunnels which they made.

They were walking around and around. And one child went one way and another child went another way, and the third child continued. And they could hear each other playing. They were laughing and having fun. And what were they doing? They were attempting to gather together again, and they were playing.

And one child said, "Where would you be? Where are you, that I might be with you?"

And another child said, "I am over here."

And the first child said, "Over where?"

"Over here!"

It was quite a perplexing situation, so to speak, for they could not see above the tall grass. And they knew that they wanted to be together once again. And they did not know how.

And they continued and they continued and they continued making tunnels in the grass. Trying to find each other.

Children, in the innocence of their beings. They had not learned yet fear. They had not learned yet frustration. They simply were being. Knowing that they would be together. Trying to find the way. Trying to find the way.

And then one day one child found another, sleeping in the tall grass. And the child said to the other, "There you are. And I have been looking for you and looking for you and looking for you. And now we are together. Now we are together."

And the two children were filled with joy. And they did wonder, however, where would be the third? Where would be the other? Where would be the other? And how would we together find the other? How would we find that being?

And so the two decided that they would be calling the other. Calling, "Where are you? We are together and we are wanting you here. Where are you? Where are you?" And they heard not a sound.

And they were wondering and wondering how they would gather together. And they began to walk through the tall grass together. And they decided that they would place their little tiny hands together, that they would not be apart. That they would seek the other—together.

And they did walk and they did walk. And they did play and they did play. For they had not learned the tiredness of walking—they were playing. They were skipping about, for they knew within their beings that the three would be together. For they had begun together, had they not? Then they would end together—they always had! Why wouldn't they now?

So they were walking through the tall grass, having fun, skipping about, placing the flowers in their hair. And then they saw a hill.

And on top of the hill was a being. And they knew it was the other. The other—the third—on top of the hill. And they were in curiosity. For how could that being be on top of the hill, when we are all playing in the tall grass? How did that being get there?

"What are you doing up there," they said. "What are you doing up there?"

And the being smiled. And the being motioned to the two to come forward. "Come along up here."

And they wondered how they could get there. For they could see the mountain. They could see the hill. They could see where their friend was. And then they could see nothing else, for the tall grass hid the sight of the path. And they did wonder how they would get to be with their friend.

And then there came a tiny bird that sat on the shoulder. A bird with the feathers of blue. And the bird whispered in the ear of one child. And the child was filled with joy.

And then the bird went onto the shoulder of the other child, and whispered into the ear of that child. And *that* child was filled with joy.

And then they continued.

They walked through the tall grass.

They walked up the hill together.

And they found their friend at the top of the hill.

And then there were three together. That they began together and they ended together. Three.

And then there was the third saying, "I am so happy that you found your way."

And the two smiled at each other. And they said, "Our friend the bird told us." And the three were happy.

And at the beginning of the path, at the very beginning of the field, there was another being. It was a turtle. And he was placing his foot on the path—for the very first time.

And he saw way, way above, on the top of the hill, on the top of the mountain—he saw three beings. And they were filled with Light. And he said, "That is where I will go."

And he began. And he wondered what would be the secret of traveling through the maze—the field.

And there did come to him a tiny bird. And the tiny bird whispered in his ear that he would follow his nose and he would find the three.

And the turtle did say, "It must be more complicated than that."

***

Chapter 9

The Christos

*Every being would be the Master. Every being.
That we might be in the awareness of the expansiveness of our beings.*

We would be speaking, my dear friends, on the teachings on which
you would desire. For we are gathered together that we might share
from deep within our beings—the truths. What would we be speaking?

> *Please give your point of view on Christ's teachings in the
> Sermon on the Mount.*

Thank you, my friend. We would not be in the repeating of words;
however, as we have been speaking over and over, we are all One
in the same. That we are all One in the same. And here we are,
my dear friend, the Sermon on the Mount, so to speak, that we
would be speaking in the union.

There would be the messages coming forward through that
Being we have termed the Christos. The messages through that
Being, over and over, gathering the beings together. That as we
have heard, "The first would be last and the last would be first."
Yes, many words have been spoken that there would be the messages
that we are One in the same. That we are gathered together that we
might recognize within our beings—One in the same.

What we term to be the power without is the energies within our being—at hand, at our very hand—for our use, for our creation, for our manifestation. That there would be many "children" about who would be hearing the words in the form of simplicity. That the Light within their being would be opened. That there would be the spark of Light growing and growing.

And how would that occur? We would be in the speaking of the language in simplicity. In the stories. In the parables. In the synchronistic and rhythmic words, that there would be the opening. That those beings gathered about—for whatever reason they would be believing they would be gathered about—would be coming forward. That they would hear what they would be wanting to hear. What their spirit deep within their being would be wanting to hear.

For every being, regardless of their statements, would be seeking union and seeking the Light. Seeking the Light deep within our beings. Therefore the messages coming forward, the truth of the Universe coming forward, would be presented in the manner in which those beings might be receiving the truth—in the simplicity of form.

And what would be the truths? *That the entire Universe resides within our beings. That those that we believe would be different from our beings, are actually manifestations of our very own selves.* Every teaching—every teaching—whether it would be what we term the Sermon on the Mount; whether it would be the teachings from the People; whether it be one child speaking to another—would be opening that the manifestations of truths would be coming forward in the manner in which the people would be hearing—people in physical and spirit form. That they would be hearing the messages. That within their beings would be resounding the vibration, resounding the truths. That they might hear and experience within their very own beings—the truths.

We could be in dissertation of each and every statement. However, it would be simply and clearly stated that it would be the necessary mirror image of those beings, that they might hear the truths within their beings.

What would you be specifically wanting, that you would feel comfortable with the vocabulary coming forward?

Can you give information concerning each individual who is here now and if they were there at that time? And how they dealt with the situation—their personalities or the soul lesson?

My dear friend, we would be in the statement that you were sitting on the left side of the Great Christos. Not the first, and not the second, but the third seated. And that in the hearing of the words, my friend, the very center of your being would be opened. For you had come from very far. And you were even in spirit form with the comrades of those beings surrounding the Christos.

You would be in what we term the background. For you were hearing the information and you were feeling the resounding within your being, long before the words were spoken. And you were wondering, wondering, how this could be true. That you would be hearing within your being the very words that the Great Christos would be speaking.

As you were in the seating of that position, and as the words were coming forward through the Great Channeler of the Universe, you were in recognition of the great truths within your being. And there was the opening. There was the marriage. That there would be with the two—the Great Christos and your very own self—the marriage with the Father. That there were the three. And there was the recognition, if we would be speaking in what you term linear time, there was recognition of One in the same. One in the same.

And there was the slightest experience of lingering confusion. And the Great Christos turned, that the energies would be flowing directly through and to your very being. And you would be in the receiving of the energy that what would be confusion—would be receiving.

There was then the gathering of many about you, in the times to follow. For there were the words coming forward from your being. There were many—as it has not been written—during that gathering on the mount, who were in the spontaneous speaking of the truths. For the energies were raised that there would be the flowing of truths. And you, my dear friend, were in the opening. And there were many who would be in the following of your being

253

that they would be hearing the truths. For there were so many about the Christos, that it would be difficult in physical form to be in the Presence. And there were those who were learned beings, recognizing what would be occurring.

And there would be within your being the longing, the deepest longing to be with that Master. But the journey was beckoning you out amongst the people—that you would be in the speaking of the truths. And even as you turn to view the Master, you would be in the synchronicity of His viewing. And you would still be in the humanness of yourself—feeling the longing to be with the Master. And the Great Christos would be in the marriage of your very being once again, that the energies would increase that you would be in the experience once again. That you would be recognizing that you were One in the same with the Master.

And then began the journey where there would be the speaking of the words to many beings. Opening and opening that the words would be coming forward. There would be those who would be wanting you to be the manifestation of the Christos. And at that time you would have been in the statements that you were not the Christos. For there was deep Love within your being for the Master.

And there would be then the time when you would flee to the hills and the mountains, for there was the confusion in your being. For you recognized that you and the Master were One in the same. However, there was still the deepest longing that you would be in the physical manifestation of that being. And in the caves, in the very well known caves of learning in the hills, you would reside. And there the Master would present Himself in physical and spirit form to your very being. And you would be in the weeping of joy in the presence of His being. And there would be the whirling and whirling of energies about your being, that you would be carried to His bosom—that there would be the marriage.

And over and over again, there would be this teaching, that you would allow yourself to recognize that *you* are the Master. The One whom you desire to be with you—would be your very own self. And that Master would be presenting Himself in your very presence over and over. That the energies of the vortex would be surrounding your being, raising the energies that you would be able to see and to know that you would be One in the same with the Great Master.

And that, my dear friend, would be the information that would be coming forward for your very presence—from that very source. That you would be in the recognition once again, that you are One in the same. One in the same. And that you were the third seated, that you were One in the same.

How about the other individuals in this room? How many here participated?

Would there be any who would be interested in that information? (The others indicate they would and Pretty Flower goes on to speak with another person:) There would be the remembrance that when we are in manifestation in physical form, we are presenting our manifestations as "masculine" and "feminine." However, we would be in the recognition that we are actually One, as in the vocabulary of androgenous.

Then we would begin. There would not be vocabulary for this particular vibration, however, we would be in the attempting of explaining. There would be the combination of handmaiden, servant, and lover—in very different energies than we have the meaning in the present. That being would also be in the cleansing, in the annointing, in the assisting of placing the garments. That it was a most holy position. To be even the confidant in the innermost feelings of the humanness of that Being, the Christos.

And at that time would be the woman manifestation. We have been in hesitation of saying that vibration for we are wondering if you would understand that in other dimensions we are presented in many different forms. That in this dimension you would be quite surely the man, and in another dimension you would be quite surely the woman. Would that be clear?

Yes. It would.

Thank you, my friend. Then we would proceed. That at that particular time with the Great Christos, the Master, there would be your

255

very own self. And that you would be in the caring of many of the personal items of the Master. For there would be much required, unknown to many.

There would be the washing of the garments. And there would be the washing with herbs, that there would be the cleansing in the softness of the garment. For there would be luminesence on the body physical of the Being called the Master. And there would be the washing and the cleansing of the garments.

There would be the annointing of the physical body of the Master with oils, of which you would be doing. Recognizing that there would be much we would be learning of annointing in this dimension. For in the mixing of the oils, would be the gathering of the essence about the being. For example, about the Great Christos, gathering the essence that it be in the mixture with the oil.

Why would we be in the annointing? That the energies in the physical—in the body physical—might be in the greatest flowing with ease. For there were the energies presented and there would be the "transformation." That there was the physical appearance of the being called the Master and then there would be in the vocabulary, even though it would be inadequate, would be "dematerialization." And then there would be materialization.

Therefore, in the annointing of the body physical with oils would be in the holiness of the being. In the holiness of the being we would be in recognition that it would be in the increase of the flowing of the essence of the being. That it would be total and complete in the physical manifestation. Therefore you would be in the annointing of the body physical.

There would be the placing in your hands the hair of the Great Being. For there would be through the hair the great messages of Love coming through your being. In that manner, there would be the receiving of Love through your being of the Great Christos. That there would be the preparation of the Christos. That there would be in symbolism, symbolism only, the gathering together of nourishment. That there would be recognizing of the presence of the body physical. And there would be the gathering of the essence of blossoms that they would be surrounding the garments.

There would be within your being the hearing of the Christos in humanistic form, in the real feelings, in the beseeching. For in the heart of the manifestation in physical form of that Great Being, there was the beseeching that every being be healed and filled with Light. *Beseeching.* For there was total and complete awareness of every part of every being, in physical and spirit form, coming forward.

And you would be hearing the words. And you would be recognizing the tears, the streams of Love flowing from the Great Christos on the cheeks. And you would be receiving the drops that they would not be on the ground. That they would be in your very hands, on your very fingertips. That you would be in the annointing of your very own body physical with the tears of the weeping for the people.

That there would be you, amongst all, who would be quite aware of the humanness of that Being. For when we are in physical form, we are in the marriage of physical and spirit—as human beings. One in the same. And you would be in the recognition of the humanness of that Being. And there would be deep Love within the very heart of your being for that Great Christos. For you would be knowing, in the humanness of your being, that part of the Great Master revealing Himself to you. That you might know we are One in the same. Once again, the very same teaching in many different forms. That we are One in the same. That in the humanness of our very own beings, we are One in the same with the Great Christos.

There would be gathering about your being those other beings who would be the followers of the Christos. The followers who would be, in their humanness, weary of journeys. And you would be speaking in the Lightness of your being with those young journeyers. And you would be speaking of the truths. And they would be hearing your voice as if they would be hearing the bells within their ears. And you would be speaking that they would be hearing that there would be other methods of traveling. For you were in the awareness of annointing and the awareness of being. And you would be in the awareness of the transformation of the Christos that there would be the materialization and the dematerialization of that Being. And you would be in the Lightness of your being, suggesting that those followers of the Christos be learning that their journey would be as the breath. As the breath.

That the Christos did carry you through three dimensions. That you would be learning the carrying of the body physical from one dimension to another. That you were so filled with Light, you would know you would be in the traveling and in the spirit of that Master.

And then there would be the teaching that you would recognize that you are—once again—One in the same. One in the same with the Master. That then there would be the traveling in every dimension of your very own self. Would you be wanting more?

No, I think that will be it for now, thank you.

Thank you, my friend.

[Pretty Flower now turns to another person and says:] Would it be fearful to hear the words that you are the Mother of the Great Christos? We would not be wanting to be shocking your being. However, we are gathered together not by what we term to be the accident. Remember, we are One and All, every being. We are One and All. And we would be in the statement that you have been in the manifestation of that woman.

At that time, there was the recognition long before the receiving of the information. The recognition that you would be in the vibration of the One. And you carried your body physical from the presence of family and friends, that you made the journey alone. Of course we are not in the hearing of this story. However, you, as that woman, carried your body physical separate from the others—that you would be in the preparation. That you would be in the Presence.

Even though we have been hearing of the "conception" and "spirit," we would be in the statement, my dear friend, that the Great Christos presented Himself before you as the Androgenous Being. One in the same—the grandness. And before your very eyes He did come to the form as the Child—through every dimension— and there before you presented Himself as the Child. That you would be in the awareness of your being—of the totality of His being. That there was in the remembrance of gathering the Child, that there was the One. And that you are in the Lightness of being, meaning in the Light of your being—that there would be the marriage of the Child. And even as you held the Child, the vibration of Light from your being carried you through every dimension in simultaneous breathing, my dear friend. Simultaneous breathing.

And then you did decide that you would be in the manifestation of the body physical for the Mother of the Great Master. That there would be in physical form, the three, that there would be the Mother. And there from the beginning of time was the seed planted and grown of the Mother. That there would be the new age within the vibration of the teachings of the Christos.

There was the knowledge within your being, even in the growing of the body physical, of the Child in what we would term to be the age of eight and then twelve. Even in that age you did see before your very eyes and the knowingness of your being, that in other dimensions there was the traveling of the Being known as the Man. That there would be in other dimensions, the teaching and the receiving of vibrations—even as the form of the young Being of eight would be vibrating in the dimension in which you resided.

And this you did see and this you did know. That there would be the recognizing within your being, that even as the Child would be in your very arms, there would be in other dimensions the Being known as Androgenous Being, the Being known as the Man, simultaneously. That there would be many manifestations of body physical across the planet called Earth; in many other dimensions.

For there has been in many different civilizations the presentation of the appearance of the Great Teacher—the Great Being filled with Light. And now we do know that in every dimension would be One in the same—the Christos. One in the same. For we, as human beings, have the belief of linear time and we are trying to be "figuring out" according to that belief. It would be misconception.

There would be in your very being the recognizing from the very moment that you held the body physical of that Child, that there would be the carrying of the body physical to the earth from which it came. It was the awareness within your being in the very second that you saw before your very eyes, total and complete, the story of the Being. There was the awareness of Light-beings in that vibration that you would be recognizing the totality of what we term to be the manifestation of the Plan, so to speak.

[Pretty Flower goes on with another "lifetime" as she continues talking with the same person:] There would then be the recognizing of your being in the dimensions in which you reside in the temples, that there would be the turning of the energies from the temples—that they would be in the Light of the day. That those teachings that would be in the secret, would be coming forward—in the Light of the day, in every dimension. For you did recognize in those times that the teachings were dormant, so to speak—"without life." And you were longing and longing for the living teachings. *The living teachings.*

And you did come forward and receive the living teachings. And then my dear friend, in every dimension you did hear the living teaching. And in every dimension you did come forward from the temples and into the Light of the day. That you would be in the living teaching, vibrating as One. Recognizing once again that we would be One in the same—by the very teaching of the living Master presenting to you from the manifestation of Child to Being, from Being to Child, before your very eyes, that you would be in the knowing of the teaching. One in the same. One in the same. Would you be wanting more?

> *[The woman asks:] I would like to know "why"? Why was I chosen?*

There would be the statement, my friend, when one being dips their hand into the water, every being is dipping their hand into the water. It would be the teaching. For you would be recognizing that you would be in the manifestation of that being—the Mother. And every being would be the Mother. Every being. Every being would be the Master. Every being. That we might be in the awareness of the expansiveness of our beings.

We have the belief that in *that* dimension it would be quite a special time. We are in the awareness, however, in the present dimension it is the same. The same. There would only be the difference in belief. In belief. Would that be clear?

> *I think so.*

260

As human beings we wonder, "Why I, amongst all of these beings—why was *I* the one to be chosen?" And there would be the statement that there would be the man walking down the street. He is walking down the street for everyone. For he *is* everyone. There would be the being who would be the Mother. The Mother. That every being might be experiencing the Mother. That there would be the child, swimming in the waterfall, that every being might be the child in the waterfall. That there would be the being in the annointing of the One, that every being might be in the annointing of the One. Would that be clear?

> *Yes. In my meditation I found myself to be in what I believe was Qumran. The next minute I felt myself going over the wilderness. And the next minute I was at the foot of the crucifix. I felt this journey—and I felt tremendous sorrow, as if all the preparation was for naught. And that the people around me couldn't be trusted. And I kissed the Master's forehead. But I couldn't feel any special relationship, other than this tremendous sorrow.*

There was in the humanness of your being—the sorrow. The manifestation of the sorrow of human beings, my friend. The great sorrow. For there was the recognition within your being of the parting of the spirit from the physical. And even though the teachings had been before your very being of the One, to the One, to the One—even though you saw that the being would be in every dimension—you still would be in the experiencing of your very own self. That you would be in the recognition of the truths.

That you were—yes, my friend—in that very position beneath what we term to be the cross. That there would also be the recognition that there is more. That, yes, you did feel the hollow shell. And yes, you did place your lips on the forehead.

That you would even be in the experience, as you are, of viewing what we term to be the "picture" in other dimensions. That the spirit of your being would be viewing the hollowness. For you would be in the residing in spirit form with the Christos in other dimensions, even as that would be occurring. Therein would reside the part of your being called the awareness of conscious manifestation. Would that be clear?

> *Yes.*

Would there be more?

> *No, thank you. I'm sure the others in the group would like to hear about themselves.*

However, would there be more?

> *Well, Okay. Edgar Cayce and others say that the soul called Jesus and the soul called Mary, who was His mother, were twin souls. Is this what we're discussing?*

It could be. There would be many who would be in the speaking of the truths. However, there would be the remembrance that in each speaking would be the presentation according to the vibration of those beings present.

And there would be the statement that when we are in the belief of what we term to be "twin souls," that we are viewing the limitedness of our beings. For there would be the expansiveness that we are much more than twin souls—that we are each other. However, in the context of the statements of those truths, it would be necessary for those beings to be hearing the concept of twin souls.

Remember, when we are reading the truths presented through another being, we are hearing the truths presented through that being. And we try to marry ourselves to those words.

Remember that we would be within ourselves—that we would hear the truths from within. That we would know what the truths would be. For many would be speaking the vibrations of truths through *their* own being.

> *Thank you.*

Thank you, my friend.

262

[Pretty Flower continues on with the events of that dimension:]
You would be gathering the truths of the experiences. And you did
carry in the satchel upon your very back, the papers of writing,
carrying the information to many who would be in physical separation of the occurrence. And you did find, my dear friend, that even
in the carrying of the words to those beings, there would be the
opening of the papers. And you would be as you would be, reading
to groups of beings gathering about. That they would hear of the
Light and hear of the teachings.

And you would be seeing that even in the reading of the truths
and the experiences, there would be those beings who would be
opening with Light. By the hearing of the teachings. And you then
did recognize within your being, that you were in the carrying of
the truth. That you were in the speaking of the truths.

Then there did come the time when you recognized that there
would not be the need to be speaking of the written words. That
you would be opening. That from your very being would be the
speaking of the truths. And you did wonder and wonder how you
could be in the speaking of truths, the very same truths.

And in the room in solitude, you would be in the prayer of
your being, in the purification of your being. For you were in the
wondering how this could be occurring.

And there appeared before your being three luminescent beings,
that they would be in the speaking to your being. They would be
the three closest with the Christos. That you would see and you
would know that it would not be only with the Master that there
would be the manifestation of the truth—that it would be with *every
being*. Every being.

And you did see and you did hear. And in the beginning of
the experience you were in the fearfulness of your being. For you
did have the belief that perhaps you were in the wrongness of being,
carrying the written words and telling of the great teachings. And
the three luminescent beings would be in the surrounding of your
being. That you would be in the experience of the raising of energies.
And in the experience of the raising of energies, you did recognize
that you and the three beings would be One in the same.

And you still had the longing—for you were wondering within

the depths of your being, "How dare I even want more?" And you did want more. You did want to be in union with the One. And there appeared before your very being—luminescence of the gold. And you did view. And you did stand directly in the Presence. And you recognized the Presence. And you would be asking that you be in communion, in the Presence. And there would be in the center of the three the golden luminescent Light within which you would be in the standing of your being. That you would experience through the center of your being the luminescence and the vibrating of the essence I AM.

And you did experience and you did receive the teachings. And there were within the room the dimensions of energies flowing about and flowing about. And you did receive, in the totality of your being, the teachings presented in every dimension. And you did recognize in the simplicity of your being that you would be in the teachings.

And even in this present vibration you are in the knowing deep within your being—even though you would not be in the speaking. For you are in the awareness of the teachings in every dimension. And you would be in the recognition of the occurrence within the center of the three luminescent beings—the marriage of the One. And that you did carry those messages forward and continue even in the present dimension—by the very vibration of your being.

Those beings who gather about you are in the recognition of the peace that flows through your being. And they would be in the closeness of vibration. There would be many who would be wanting to be in the physical touch of your being for they would be wanting to experience the peace flowing through your being. And you would at times be "acting differently"—that they would know that you would be human. And even as you would be having fun, there would be within your being the recognition that you would be vibrating in many other dimensions at the very simultaneous time, of course.

There would be many who would be hearing the words coming forward from your being. That they would be in the hearing of the simplicity of the practicality. For you know the truths to be the truths however they would be manifested. And you would be in the speaking. Would there be more?

No. Thank you.

Thank you, my friend. We are in the enjoyment of the physical manifestation of your being.
[Pretty Flower to another woman present at the gathering:] Hello, my friend.

[Woman:] Hello.

There would be the statement that in physical form, you are not. And there you would be the guardian of the Light. It would be in spirit form, and there would be in each dimension the gathering of the manifestation of the balls of Light. That you and two others would be in the caretaking of the balls of Light in the dimensions.

There would be many who would be opening in the receiving of the truths. And even though we have the belief of fairies, of angels, so to speak, there would be those beings of luminescence who would be barely in form. That they would be in the caretaking of the Light of the Universe.

For in the grandness of the speaking of the truths, it would be as if we would be viewing that there would be luminescent "eggs" about the planet. That they would be in the beginning of opening. And that you would be with two others in the caretaking of those "eggs," in the caretaking of the Light. For it is your choice to be in physical manifestation when there would be times of transition in the planetary dimensions. And you would be recognizing the beginning of the sparks of Light.

And you did manifest, my dear friend, in the times after the Master, for there were great transitions occurring. The truths spoken by those beings would be, in one time or another, folding into the planet that they would return once again. And there would be the times of Darkness and the times of Light. That when there would be the beginning of the times of Light—you did manifest your very being. For you would be in the assistance of those beings coming forward. That they would be recognizing what actually would be occurring in the openings. In the openings.

And here you are in the present manifestation, in the time of the great openings—from Darkness to Light.

***

Chapter **10**

A Time For Uniting

As human beings we gather together that we might become One.

With our will or without our will, there is a marriage which is occurring even in the present—now. As we gather together we would be in the fulfillment of our beings. For as human beings we gather together that we might become One. As human beings we fulfill our purpose by allowing the union of physical and spirit to come forward, to be within our being. That we might manifest I AM. That we might open and allow the union to manifest. That we might be One. One in the same.

***

There would be no such thing as straying from the path. The path would be wherever we place our feet.

We would be in the process of learning what our own truth would be. The truth of our being. The truth of our journey within. It would be learning to trust those feelings, for you have been quite correct.

267

There would be no such thing as straying from the path. The path would be wherever we place our feet. It would be I AM. However we manifest is I AM. There would not be enlightened beings and those beings on the way to enlightenment. That would be a belief, my dear friend. For we would be I AM, as we are.

There are those beings who believe that we would be in the process of traveling through different levels; that we would be seeking the teachings. However, the journey would be within and it would be of our creation. Those beings who have experienced their truth in their journey through what has been termed "levels," would be speaking the truth of their beings. However, we have the choice. We could be as a carbon copy of their journey, attempting to be page 32. And it would be quite a struggle, for we would be attempting to be in the repeating of another's journey.

There would be those beings who would be believing that their truth would be the only truth. However, there would be the statement: We would be here on the planet called Earth for *union,* that we would gather together. When there would be the statement that "we are the only way," what would be occurring? Separation. Blessed are the beings who would be gathering together in union.

***

There is not one being on the planet called Earth that is not a member of the very same family.

Have I known my present family in the past?

My dear friend, there is not one being that we have not known, for we are everything. We recognize the question—yes, yes, we recognize the question. And we would be in the statement that there would be the belief of "past." It would be a belief, my friend. Everything is occurring in the "now." Everything is occurring as we speak.

Why is it that we seem to be most familiar with some beings and not with others? Because we have not opened ourselves to that dimension. *We vibrate with every human being in physical and spirit form—every second of every breath—right now.* Right now, my friend.

There have been many who have gathered together in different groups, so to speak. We would be saying of the family that those beings have gathered together as explorers in the mountains of Europe. Even in the exploring there was the seeking of fulfillment. And did it come? Temporarily it did—for those explorers climbing the mountains, seeking to reach the top of the mountain. And what occurs? The explorers reach the top of the mountain—and then what? Seeking, seeking—to be fulfilled.

It would all be an expression of the explorers. Even though the many have traveled across and about the planet called Earth, there would be the recognition that that which is sought is within. And there would be the message to those beings and to your very own self that everything in the physical dimension is fantasy. We would be seeking elusive dreams when we seek without. When we decide to release ourselves from the burdens of the physical plane and go within, then the dimensions open within our very being and we would be in the discovery of the greatest exploration. For in the dimensions within—untold adventure awaits us.

There would be the statement to the members of the family: When we seek outside of ourselves for the fulfillment, we are on an unending journey of disappointment. When we recognize that within our very being resides I AM—when we open to I AM—then we are fulfilled *from within.* Everything that we require a being from outside of ourselves to fulfill, we find empty—for we require perfection. From deep within our being vibrates fulfillment.

There would be in the country of France the members of the family, as children, going to school together. In those times there would be the recognition of the Light within. Playing together. And there would be the separation of those children. Three going one way, two going another way—and one passing to another dimension quite early. And even then the children knew that they were together, vibrating. Remember, my dear friend, when we speak of family, we can be speaking of our particular family about our being or we can be expansive. And we can remember that when we speak of family, we speak of the entire Universe. There is not one being on the planet called Earth that is not a member of the very same family. We have been taught as children to be separate. And we would be in the statement that it would be a time for uniting—becoming One.

***

It would be in the union of beings that there would be the recognition of self.

My husband died about ten years ago. And I've released him. I understand that we've been together many times. However I've met a young man who reminds me so much of my husband. He walks like him and talks like him. Would it be possible that there is a connection between my husband who is dead and this young man?

First, as we are well aware that you know, my friend, it would simply be the body physical that would not be vibrating. And we would be in the recognition also that the past is the present.

Then we would be in the statement that there has been the residing of that young man and your very own self and the being whom you call to be your husband in several dimensions together. In one occasion that being would be the son of that man whom you call to be your husband. And there would be two times in the dimensions where that being would be in the residing with yourself as your very own husband.

It would be in the union of beings that there would be the recognition of self. When we view another being and we say that that being reminds me of another, how do we know that? The familiarity of the energies and the presentation of the manifestation. We would be in the recognition that the reason we recognize those traits would be that they would be our very own—that we recognize

270

in each of the other. Our very own that we recognize in each of the other.

***

...we would be in the group hearing a being speaking of the truth of themselves, in the recognition that we are viewing the mirror image of our own selves.

[Pretty Flower speaks to a person about the study group they are in and the purpose of the group.]

We would be in the statement that first we are the reflection of each other. We are the mirrors of each other, gathering together. We would be easily accepting that statement, especially when we view the beauty of another being. When we view the Love pouring forward from another being, it would be the recognition—the mirror of our very own selves.

And when we view another being who would be in the statement of something that would be disagreeable to our very beings, *that* being would be a mirror of our very being. It would be, as a group, considering to be getting to know self. When we open to be receiving others, we are getting to know self. It would be taking a risk in speaking the truth—as the group. Taking a risk and speaking the truth.

In gathering together there have been many purposes set forward: That in gathering together we might know the spirituality of our very own beings, that we might pray together, that we might meditate together, that we might learn to receive each other's vibration in the Love of our being. There could be many, many reasons for gathering together, and we would be in the statement that *it would all be for union*. It would all be for union in One.

Then we would be in the stating of taking a risk. That when we gather together, we would be in the statement of the truth of our being. Not how we wish we would be, not how we are planning to be once we become more spiritual than we are, but how we would be vibrating in the present. What would be the *real* feelings? What would be really occurring within?

For there would be many statements in written material of the teachings. And many have gathered about that they would be reading and studying the material. It would not be incorrect. However, it would be placing ourselves "on hold." For we would be hearing the messages. And then what would occur in some instances? We would practice forming ourselves to fit the information presented. It would be trying to fit ourselves into the pair of shoes that are too tight.

And what would be the experience of the group? It would be: What have I experienced within my being? Even though I have not written a book or a manuscript. That each member of the group would be vibrating within the truth of their being. *Truth is truth.* There is not a greater truth or a lesser truth. It is the truth.

And there would be in the group the statement of truth of self. The slightest taking of the risk. That we would be in the statement of the truth of our very own selves. Then we would be in the group hearing a being speaking of the truth of themselves, in the recognition that we are viewing the mirror image of our own selves. For we are everything.

When we are hearing the truth of another being, we are getting to know ourselves. It would then be, within the being, the expression of the truth of self. And in the group, the receiving of the truth.

For as human beings there would be coming forward within each being, the judgments. It would not be correct or incorrect. It would be the fact that the judgments would be coming forward: Would the truth of this being be correct or incorrect? It would be a natural occurrence. And we would then be reminding our very own selves that we would be hearing the truth—and the truth is the truth. The truth of that being.

Then we would be in the recognition of that being and the vibration of that being. And we would be in the permission that we would be in the loving of that being, in the gratitude of that being. That that being would be sharing part of our very own selves—with our very own selves. That we would be getting to know I AM.

When we view parts of ourselves in the secrecy of our being, we would be hiding at times. Sometimes in a gathering of beings we hear the presentation of thoughts. And what do we do? We have a view that is quite different. And what do we do with that view at times? We rephrase the vocabulary, that it might be accepted when we make the statement. It would be part of being a human being. However, we would be in the encouragement of stating the truth—that it might be received within the group. For then there would be the marriage of One. And we would be in the recognition of I AM deep within our beings. Never fear. When we open to be speaking the truths of our being it is an unending situation. It would be continuing and continuing.

When we are in the judgment of our being, as we have stated before, there would be the statement: "I have tried not to be this way over and over again and I am still this way. I have tried to change myself and I cannot seem to change that part of my being." Whether we have verbalized it in a group or whether we have thought it in our very own minds, it has been the truth that every being at this gathering, at one time or another, has wished that part of their being would cease to be in existence. It would perhaps be the anger. It would perhaps be the judgment of the unholiness of the being.

We would be in the statement: When we view part of our being and we say, "I do not want to be that way," we are vibrating in the separation of our being. And what would we be doing? We would be denying I AM. For we are everything.

And what would we be doing in the union? We would be saying, "Welcome home." Welcome home to that part of our being that we have been denying. For when we deny, what do we do? In the very next step we are doing what we are trying not to do. Do we not, my friends? Of course. And we would continue to be that way as human beings until we "welcome home" that part of our being.

Then, my friends, we have the choice of how we would manifest I AM—how we would manifest our very own selves. In denying,

273

we have no choice. For it would be begging to be welcomed home. Begging to be part of I AM. That we would not be denying our very own selves. When we say "Welcome home," then we have the choice in the manifestation of self.

When we view and we hear another speak and we think, "How wonderful," we are hearing our very own selves. When we hear another speak and we think, "That cannot be correct," we are simply in denial of self. "Welcome home," for we have been hearing our very own selves.

And when we hear our very own self and we think neither that it would be correct nor incorrect, we are vibrating I AM. We are in receiving of self. Neither would be correct nor incorrect. Every being is in the manifestation I AM.

***

For we can be about and until the being opens, we are simply about. And when the being opens, then the marriage is complete.

I'm presently very much involved in the teachings of an entity called Lazaris.

Yes, my friend.

I would like to give all of my time to it. I feel a great urge and personal need to learn and study the teachings that he brings forth, which I feel are of the greatest importance to all of us at this time.

And there would be the encouragement of that participation—however, with the understanding that what we view, and what we hear, and what we see that resounds within our being—when we hear something or read something that resounds within our being—the reason that it would be resounding within our being would be the recognition that it is our very own creation, that we would be viewing our very own selves.

For when we hear the words, and we see, and we vibrate, there would be that part of the human being that then would be seeking without—reaching and reaching for those truths and for the understanding of those statements. And there would be the recognition that the originator of those statements would be I AM—within the very being.

When we seek without—we are misguided at times, for we have the belief that it is quite different from that which is within. And we would be in the statement that it would be correct to be vibrating in that particular circumstance with that wonderful being— with the remembrance, my friend. With the remembrance that everything that we attempt to be on the outside would be fantasy. When we are within our very own being and we vibrate I AM, then we are fulfilling purpose.

It would not be correct or incorrect to be in this creation called fantasy. Sometimes we attempt to call it a reality—one in the same. It would not be correct or incorrect. However, it would be in the fulfillment of purpose that we recognize that deep within—I AM. That there would be the statement: I OPEN MYSELF TO THE AWARENESS I AM. And then, my friend, whatever we do is the manifestation I AM. Whatever we choose to do, *in any dimension*, would be in the fulfillment of purpose in the manifestation I AM.

I feel as if I was in the desert so long.

We *are* the desert, my friend.

—perhaps, but lost in the desert. Lost and seeking and lonesome.

Yes, my friend.

And this is the closest I've come to perhaps reaching that point where I'll be home. I know there's a path to take, but I don't know which one will take me there.

275

When there is the desire to be "home," and we open to the fulfillment of that marriage, then anything we choose to do would be the correct path. And you have chosen, for that would be the beginning of the marriage of One. Never fear for your choice. For when we have the purpose at hand—everything we do would be towards the fulfillment of the purpose. It would be quite correct, my friend.

Wonderful.

Yes, my friend.

Do you recall our meeting one evening, you and I?

Yes, my friend. When we recognized each other, so to speak.

Where do we go from there?

We are here.

You are there *and I am* here.

I am here and you are here.

I see.

There would be the recognition, my friend, that in every dimension we vibrate together. In every dimension. When you are walking on the path *we* are walking on the path together.

We are so much of the earth, we don't feel it.

There would be the statement that when we open ourselves to the recognition of the marriage in every dimension, then we open ourselves to the awareness. Know that when you are on the path, we are on the path together. Never fear. When you feel the opening of your being, recognize that we open together. Recognize.

276

Is there a process, is there a way? Is there anything that I can do in order to open up?

Yes, my friend. You have just done it. It would be the simple statement:

I OPEN MYSELF TO THE AWARENESS *I AM.*

I OPEN MYSELF TO THE TOTAL AND COMPLETE FULFILL-MENT OF PURPOSE.

I OPEN MYSELF TO THE MARRIAGE OF ONE.

I OPEN MYSELF TO THE RECOGNITION IN EVERY DIMEN-SION *I AM.*

I OPEN MYSELF TO THE AWARENESS IN EVERY BREATH, I CREATE THE BLESSINGS OF THE UNIVERSE.

I OPEN MYSELF TO THE ABUNDANCE OF THE UNIVERSE.

I OPEN MYSELF TO THE JOY OF THE UNIVERSE.

I OPEN MYSELF TO THE GIVING AND THE RECEIVING OF THE ENTIRETY OF THE UNIVERSE.

I OPEN MYSELF TO THE HEALING POWERS OF THE UNI-VERSE, THAT ALL WHO COME IN CONTACT WITH ME MIGHT BE HEALED, WITHIN AND WITHOUT, BY THE MERE PRESENCE, BY THE MERE THOUGHT, BY THE MERE TOUCH OF THE GARMENT.

I OPEN MYSELF TO THE OVERFLOWING OF THE BLESS-INGS OF THE UNIVERSE, THAT ALL MIGHT BASK AND BATHE IN THE LIGHT IN EVERY DIMENSION, FOR *I AM.*

I OPEN MYSELF THAT I MIGHT BE THE BEARER OF LIGHT, THAT ALL MIGHT SEE THE LIGHT I AM.

I OPEN MYSELF TO THE MANIFESTATION OF THE TRUTHS OF THE UNIVERSE, FOR I AM THE EMBODIMENT OF TRUTH.

I OPEN MYSELF THAT I MIGHT RECOGNIZE THAT EVERY-THING ABOUT ME IS *I AM.*

I OPEN MYSELF TO THE TOTAL AND COMPLETE RECEIV-ING OF MY ENTIRE BEING, THAT I MIGHT RECEIVE *I AM* IN EVERY DIMENSION. FOR IN RECEIVING IS GIVING, AND IN GIVING IS RECEIVING, THAT THOSE WHO ARE ASKING WOULD RECEIVE—THAT THEY MIGHT GIVE.

FOR WHEN WE RECEIVE WE ARE IN FULFILLMENT. AND IT WOULD BE AN UNENDING FLOW. THAT WE WOULD BE IN THE RECEIVING AND IN THE GIVING IN ONE BREATH, EFFORTLESSLY—WITHOUT JUDGMENT, WITHOUT DIRECTION—JUST ALLOWING THE FLOW. ALLOWING.
Would there be more?

No, everything has been given.

Everything has been received.

Thank you very, very much. God bless you.

Thank you, my friend. Thank you, my friend. We are most happy to be sharing the physical vibration once again. Never fear, we are never apart.

I enjoyed that.

We would be in the enjoyment also. *For we can be about and until the being opens, we are simply about. And when the being opens, then the marriage is complete.* Have the awareness in your being that there has been a healing in every dimension. The burdens have been lifted in every dimension. It would be complete in every dimension. The blessings of the Universe have come forward. The blessings of the Universe reside within your being.

***

...when you are in the journey... remember, my friends, everything you see—every being— is part of your very being.

[The following is taken from a workshop Pretty Flower held with a group of people.]

278

We are happy to be gathered together, my dear friends. We're quite a few in number. There would be many gathered together in physical and spirit form that we might open our very own selves. That we might first experience our very own selves—who we are, how we really vibrate. That we might recognize our very own selves. *That we might be in union together.*

For we have been speaking of union and we have been speaking of many teachings. *That as we are gathered together there is a marriage that is occurring, even as we speak and breathe.* We would be experiencing that of which we speak. Experiencing. That in our vibration upon the planet called Earth, as we place our feet upon the path, we might recognize the marriage, we might recognize the union. That we might remember every part of our being. That we might be receiving every part of our being. Receiving—every part of our being.

So we would begin. And we would be wondering *who* we are. We are in great recognition as human beings as to what we believe we should be, who we think we are, where we are going, what would be the goal, and what would be the rules to which we are in great attempting to follow.

We have been in the discussing of many beliefs at many gatherings. And therein lies the answer of who we are. Who we are. How we manifest. How we choose to manifest. And here we are—human beings—spirit beings, in marriage with each other. And we have been teaching how we would be I AM. We would be recognizing here in this present vibration, together—I AM.

In this fine day we will experience together many vibrations that we might allow our sensitivities to grow. That we might allow ourselves to be aware—in many dimensions—that we might be getting to know who we are. Who we *are* that we might vibrate as One. Vibrate as One.

As human beings then, my friends, who are we? Have you viewed each other, my dear friends? Have you really viewed each other? Have you looked into each other's eyes? Please begin. See who you are. For therein lies the mirror of self. When we view another being and we see the beauty in that being and we vibrate and we think, "This is truly a mirror of my very own self," we are

279

indeed recognizing the beauty of our very own selves.

When we are viewing another being and we are in the statement, "How could that possibly be a mirror image of myself, I am not like that," then, of course, we are in denial of self. It would be quite simple. For as we have been learning, we are everything. How could we not be that one tiny person if we are everything? Everything. Here, in this very second, we are I AM.

When we say, "I do not want to be that way," what occurs? We *are* that way—the very first opportunity! And we keep trying not to be that way. And that part of our being is *begging* for union. And we would be in the teaching, "Welcome home. Welcome home." That we would receive every part of our being. That we might recognize I AM—everything—that we might be in conscious manifestation. When we are receiving every part of our being, then we have the choice. Then we have the choice.

Then here we are, once again, here we are, viewing each other. Viewing our very own selves. We would have two circles—here and here. (She indicates for those present to stand in two circles.) Come along. We would begin. There is no escaping now. (Laughing) We are mirrors of our very own selves, my friends. Now we are viewing ourselves. We are viewing our very own selves, as if we are viewing a mirror. Linger a moment with each other. Yes, my friends. Would you like to meet the rest of yourself? We would be mingling about that we would be viewing the other parts of our being. Perhaps forming a large circle; perhaps being together—that we would have the opportunity to be viewing every part of our being.

When you view each other in silence, remember, you are viewing a mirror; look deep, look deep. For we would be opening to the innermost parts of our being during this day. Look deep at every being. Look deep within.

Do not miss an opportunity to see your very own selves, and receive. Welcome home every part of your being. Remember, when you approach a being, you are approaching your very own selves. Look deep within your very own self. Receive your very own self. Welcome home.

Then we would begin, so to speak. It would be that we would be in a type of meditation. We would be opening that we might recognize part of our very own self. For we would be gathering together that we would know who I AM.

A Meditation on "Who I AM"

Then we would begin and we would be in the closing of our eyes—together. That we could be in any position, any position whatsoever. Closing our eyes.

That we would be releasing. That we would be releasing. That we would be releasing. That we might be allowing our very own beings to be. In this very moment, as we are. That we would be releasing the cares. That we would be releasing the concerns. That we would be releasing the wondering. That we would be releasing. In every dimension. In *every* dimension. Allowing our very own selves to be—to be as we are—in the present vibration.

That we would allow the awareness of self. That we would perhaps be thinking of the word "self." Self—self—self. That we would allow our awareness to travel inside self. Inside. Somewhere within, traveling about—inside. Within our beings. And we would allow our awareness to settle within. (Pause) Somewhere within— anywhere. Gently settling in the warmth of our being. Wherever we would be residing would be the center of this very moment in which we reside. In the center. (Pause)

In the center would be the blossom of life. Any blossom, any blossom. Any color. Any vibration. In the center. The blossom of Light. (Pause) In the center the blossom of Light would be the resting place of self. In the center of the blossom of Light would be the resting place of self. (Pause) In the center of the blossom of Light would be the resting place of self. (Pause) In the center of the blossom of Light would be I AM. In the center of the blossom of Light would be I AM. In the center of the blossom of Light would be *marriage*. In the center of the blossom of life would be marriage. In the center of the blossom of life would be marriage. Marriage of self. Marriage I AM. In the center of the flower of life would be the awareness I AM.

From the center of the flower of life would open a being of Light. From the center of the flower of life would flow a being of

281

Light. Flowing forward, filling our entire being. Flowing through every part of our being. Within and without. From the center of the flower of life flows I AM. Filling every part I AM. Overflowing. Overflowing. Overflowing. Moving forward. Going forward. Unending. I AM. I AM. I AM.

That we would carry this awareness, my friends, to the present—to the consciousness of our beings. That we would carry this awareness, my friends, to the consciousness of our beings. Bringing it forward. Bringing it forward. I AM, in the consciousness of our beings, coming forward. Coming forward. And when we open our eyes, once again, we would view who I AM. Coming forward, viewing each other. Carrying forward the consciousness of who I AM. That we might be aware. Opening our eyes. Coming forward. Viewing our very own selves. Viewing who I AM. Once again, I AM. Once again, I AM. Once again.

*

Hello, my dear friends. Do we see who we are? I AM. When we view out there for I AM, we are seeking in fantasy. Seeking in fantasy. The journey is within. Who I AM. If we were to be introduced now, what would be the statement? Would there be the wondering of how would we be in the definition of self? Would we be the mother? Or the healer? Or the father? Or the sister? Or the brother? Or the teacher? Or the student? Or the friend? Well—we are I AM. I AM.

We would be in the statement, my friends, when you are in the journey from here to there, remember, my friends, everything you see—*every being* — is part of your very being.

Remember the expansiveness of self. Opening to I AM. Opening to the greatest powers of the Universe. Opening. That we might allow it to come forward as human beings. As we are. Not as we would be some day. As we are, right now. With our questions. With our confusion. With our beliefs. With our blockages. With our beliefs about blockages. With our beliefs about the Light. With our beliefs about Love. Every part of our being. Everything. That is who would open—human beings. As we are. In the present.

Remember, my friends, every being is in manifestation I AM. How else would we be saying it? Every being is in the manifestation of God. Every being. However they would be. And when we view a being, we are viewing our very own self—something we have been trying to escape for a very long time.

***

We gather together that we might view each other eye to eye. That we would know that we are One in the same...

[Relating to physical sensations that a woman is experiencing, she asks:] Pretty Flower, sometimes I feel jolts of energy through me, especially in a gathering like this. Would you explain that?

It would be jolts of energy flowing through your being. (Laughter)

Well, is it normal? No one else seems to shake like I do.

[Pretty Flower asks the group:] Would there be another being here who would be feeling energy flowing through their being sometime during this gathering? [Most people raise their hands.]

But I don't see others shaking—and I sit here and shake.

Yes, my friend. For some are conductors and some are receivers. And then we are receivers and then we are conductors. For in the gatherings there would be balance. It would be as we have been stating, "in the second." Everything is different every second.

If we were to say, my friend, that you would be the receiver, then how long through your lifely vibration would you be believing that you would be the receiver? Perhaps for a very long time! And we would be in the statement: It would be for this second.

That yes, my friend, we are receiving and giving in the same breath. In the same breath. There are many who experience the energies of the Universe from within their being in very many different forms, for we are vibrating within our beliefs.

Never fear, for it would be what you term to be "normal." Would we be terming anything that occurred here this very day to be what we term to be "normal"? (laughter from all) My friend, what occurred here today *is* normal. Yes, my friend. That we might unite.

We gather together that we might view each other eye to eye. That we would know that we are One in the same and that we are correct. Yes. And one comes out from one closet and dares to say, "I am feeling shivers of energy flowing through my being." And another being says, "That is exactly what I have been experiencing." And what occurs? Then we know.

It is correct to be "out in the open," my friends. To dare to be—to dare to be. For the time is now, my friends. The time is *now*.

***

For everyone, it would be the time of becoming One.

[A woman talks about a group she belongs to that has cautioned her about the channeled material she has been studying because the channels "may not be of the Source—a true Source." The woman continues:] I said I disagree because I felt that these channels were bringing the Light to the people and I saw nothing wrong with it. I began thinking that the literature is so beautiful and that it's lovely to continue studying it. But now I have a quandry. I wonder, should we just follow our inner self or is it good to belong to a group?

284

It would be correct to be following ourselves. And whether we believe that we belong to a group or not, in fact, there is a marriage occurring with every being with whom we come in contact.

As far as the consciousness of the group is concerned, there would be the question once again: Would the purpose of the statement be to unite or to divide? If it would be to unite, then we would feel correct with our vibration within. If it would be to divide, then perhaps for some it would be correct.

For you, my friend, it would be correct to be with those beings who would be in the way of uniting. Where there would be room *for everyone*—no matter how they would be. For then we would be welcoming ourselves. For everyone, it would be the time of becoming One.

***

Everything, every movement of the Peoples, was for purpose. ...every movement was the teaching.

A psychic told me that in one lifetime in the 1800s I had been a white man on my way to San Francisco, and I had met three Indian medicine men. They said we had been together in Atlantis. So they took me under their wing and initiated me in their teachings. And then as I traveled about the settlements, I shared what I had learned. This fascinates me. I wondered if I would meet them again or if there is some way I could tap into whatever they had taught me?

Would you be in the receiving of those teachings?

Yes. How could I do that?

We would have a transference of energies and we would begin. We would step aside that the Warrior would enter and be in the teaching.

285

Oh, I'd like that. Yes.

[Pretty Flower goes through a transition, allowing the energy of the Warrior to come through. The Warrior now states:] So you come forward once again that there would be the teaching of three.

In the greatness of the Mother Earth would be the center of the Universe. In the teaching would be the receiving of the center of the Universe. In the teaching of old, would be the placing of the feet in what we have termed to be in the desert, upon the planet, upon the Earth. That we would be in the statement of our being that we would be traveling to the center of the Earth. When we are in the center of the Earth—we create.

There would be, in the time which you have spoken, our gathering together that there would be the teaching of the Peoples. And that we three, in the form of what you have termed to be "magic," presented the teaching for your very self.

That we did gather together from our very own satchels, that we would create the bag of medicine that you would carry around your being. Within the bag of medicine would be the dried blossom, which would be for the purpose of the traveling from one dimension to another. That there would be the awareness of self in the entire Universe.

And there would be the great teachers coming forward. And your being was in the receiving of the teaching.

There would be the teaching of the twirling about that there would be the releasing; that there would be the traveling to the Great Teachers who had been in the Land of the Holies. In the Land of the Holies would be the teaching of the rhythm of the Earth. The rhythm of the Earth. For when we place our feet upon the Earth, we would be in the recognition of the rhythm of the Earth.

There have been many teachings. There have been many beliefs that the tribes of old were those Indians who had strange beliefs and some had magical powers.

We would be in the statement: We are the Peoples of the Earth. And that in the time which you have spoken there was the teaching, for you had within your being the vibration of Light. That you were, so to speak, as from above. For there would be above the peoples on the planet called Earth the plateau of truth, where we would be residing in spirit form. That we would be viewing the peoples of the planet. That we would be viewing the tribes. And that we would be in the teaching of those beings in the tribes of the truths, as they would be receiving them.

And as you had been traveling, we saw that you were from above, even though the memory was faint.

There was the teaching of gathering of roots. That there would be traveling to the side of the mountain. And there would be the speaking to the mountain. That the mountain would receive the energies of your being. That you would enter. And then there would be the marriage of the mountain and the being.

There would be then the statement of the need of the root and the asking of guidance to the root. And then there would be the path of Light to the root.

There on the side of the mountain would be the bulging of the Earth. That there would be the statement to the great Mother Earth that there would be the opening that we might receive the great root.

And the Earth would be moving and there would be the parting of the Earth. There would be the root. And there would be the asking of the Earth for the releasing of the root. That the Earth would be releasing of the root, that we would receive. And there would be the releasing of the root that we would simply place our hands within, and lift the vibration of the great root—the holiness of the Earth.

And there would be then the place of abiding of the root. That we would be in the singing of the chanting to that place where the root had been in the abiding. We would be in the singing of the cleaning and of the holiness of the Earth. And we would be in the holiness of breath. And then we would be in the covering.

Everything, every movement of the Peoples, was for purpose. Every movement for purpose. The gathering of the root—every movement was the teaching. That there was not the walking without awareness of placing the feet upon the vibration of the Earth. That there was not the gathering of nourishment without the speaking to the Earth that she would release the nourishment. That there was not the drinking of the water without the asking of the blessings

287

that they would be fulfilled within our being. That there was not the ingestion of the plant—and the fruit of the plant, without the traveling within the plant to be aware, to be in the marriage of the plant. Then there was the removal of the essence of our being and then the receiving of the fruit of the plant. *There was not one thing that was not done without purpose and awareness.* Not one thing.

And that great teaching was received by your being. That you would be in the rhythm of the Universe. That you would be in the purpose of your being. That there would be not one movement and not one word that would be without purpose.

That there was the teaching of those creatures of the desert that they would be One in the same. That there would be the residing in the very same place without fear. For with the power of the man would be the power of the Universe—I AM. And his creatures would bc in the sameness of the power. For the teaching would be in the recognition of the sameness of all creatures.

That upon the soles of the feet was the inscribing of the teaching of walking. That there would be the receiving of the roots of the Earth.

There would be the recognition that the teachings coming forward would be in the practice of your daily vibration, for that time is *now.* Teachings are not words. They are in the doing. In the doing.

[Pretty Flower's energy returns and she says:] Never fear for the teaching of the Warriors. Never fear. For there has been the teaching on many dimensions. Sometimes the truth escapes our being. Sometimes the truths are spoken in silence. Never fear.

***

In every single thing that ever exists in the vibration of this dimension—and in any other dimension—would be the vibration of One.

[Pretty Flower speaks with a man about his feelings for Jesus and his soul's purpose.]

The Great Christos—with whom you would be sharing the Love of the Universe—would be residing within the very self. For the I AM would be *everything*. And there would be the recognition that when we seek, we are seeking our very own selves. For we have been told that we would do this and more, my friend. And it would be a fulfillment of the marriage of One. That the Great Christos would be in the residing of the being. For in the center would be I AM. Everything. Everything.

And we have chosen that there would be the manifestation of the Christos. That even in the writing there was the remembrances of those times and the wondering: "How could I know this to be the truth? Did I live with that Being? Did I vibrate in His Presence? How do I know these things to be true? How do I know that the very vibration within my being is vibrating in remembrance?" It would be that we would all be One in the same.

When the Master places His feet upon the planet called Earth, every being places their foot upon the Earth. When the Master ascends, every being ascends. We are One in the same. When you place your hand in the water, the Master places His hand in the water. One in the same. When you breathe the breath and the blessings of the Universe come forward, the Master is breathing the blessings of the Universe. One in the same. One in the same.

The questions would be answered for it would be true even though there would be the wondering, "How can I know?" Yes, my friend, One in the same, we would all be. That would be the purpose for vibration in the present. That we would allow that vibration to come forward more and more, recognizing the vibration in every being. In every manifestation. In every vibration. In every belief and every nonbelief. In every receiving and in every denying. In every single thing that ever exists in the vibration of this dimension—and in any other dimension—would be the vibration of One. Of that very Being—of the One.

And there would be those blessed to be in the presence of your very being, for they would be wondering what would be the great Light flowing from within. And there would be the recognition within your being that it would be truth. That it would be alive and vibrating within your very being.

The blessings of the Universe flow forward from your being—within and without, in every dimension.

***

The Story of the Child and the Sage

Once upon a time there was a child. And the child was born on the planet called Earth. And the child grew. And the child grew. And the child knew of his being—the essence of his being.

And there came to the awareness of the child, the wondering. The wondering, "Why would I be here on this planet called Earth? Why would I be here?"

And the child would open his eyes. And the child would see.

And what would the child see on the planet called Earth? He would see the birds. He would see the clouds. He would see the depth of the sea. He would feel the Wind Spirit upon his cheek. He would feel the Earth beneath his feet. He would feel the vibration within his being.

And he would be wondering, wondering, "What would be the purpose? Why would I be here on the planet called Earth?"

And there would appear to that young child several visions.

The first vision would be of the mountain. That there would be from the top of the mountain, the flowing. The flowing. It would appear to be as if it were a cloud flowing from the top of the mountain. And the little boy would be wondering, wondering.

And then there would be the second vision. There would be in the depths of the sea a deep blue light, growing and growing. And growing and growing.

And the third vision of the young boy, the child, would be the great star from the sky, floating to the Earth in the brightness of its being. To the Earth. Floating to the Earth. And when the great star floated to the Earth, the Earth was illuminated. Illuminated. And the boy saw.

And the last vision of the boy was of the Earth itself. That there was a bulge in the Earth. And there was an opening in tne

290

Earth. And the Earth gave forth birth of itself. That there was a great flame coming forward from the center of the Earth. And the burning grew and grew. And the boy saw. And the boy saw.

And then the Sage appeared to the boy. The great Sage. And what did the Sage say to the great boy? He viewed the boy and he knew the visions.

And the boy viewed the Sage. And in his being he requested the answer. "Why am I here on this planet called Earth? For I have seen the vision."

And the Sage viewed the boy. And with his being he replied, "You have viewed the birth of the Earth. You have viewed the Light of the Universe in the darkness of the sea. You have viewed the truths of the mountain flowing forward into the valley. You have felt the Wind Spirit upon your cheeks."

And the boy remembered the visions well. And the boy breathed the Earth. And the boy drank the Light.

And the truths of the Universe poured forward from the mountain. And the wideness of the truths surrounded the fire of the Earth. And the blueness of the Light of the Universe, from the very depths of the sea, filled the center of the flame.

And there was the opening of the Universe. There was the pulsebeat of the Universe. There was the Oneness of the Universe.

And the boy stood in the center of the Light of the Universe. And the Light grew. And the Light grew. And the flames grew. And the flames grew. And the truths grew. And the truths grew. And the boy became the Sage. And the Sage became the boy. And the Universe expanded. And the Light shone brighter and brighter. Brighter and brighter.

And the beings knew—above the Earth, beneath the Earth, within the Earth, upon the Earth—of the Light of the Universe. Of the fire of the Universe. Of the truths of the Universe. Of the Sage of the Universe. Of the child of the Universe. One in the same.

***

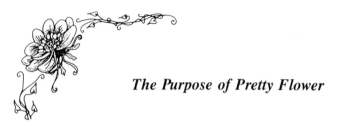

The Purpose of Pretty Flower

This manifestation of energies would be for the benefit of your being. When we are not here, we are not. We are I AM.

There would be a gathering of beings. We would be vibrating. We would be vibrating in the dimensions which we have heard described "above the planet called Earth." Vibrating. When we view the spark of Light within the being on the planet called Earth, we would be dipping into the Light that it would grow and grow.

We would be in this manifestation that there would be the fulfillment of hope on the planet called Earth. The fulfillment of hope. We have been in the manifestation many times, with many beings in this very similar manner, that there would be the recognition of truth.

When we gather together in what seems to be personality, we are gathering together the creation of your beings that we would manifest. That we would show you your very own selves and the Light of your selves. Where there are beings gathered together and they say, "I feel the power—I feel the energies coming forward from the very hands of the vessel," what would be occurring? We would be *sharing* with your very beings what flows through *your* beings, that you might know. We would be gathering together that we would be in the creation of this energy that we would share with your very being.

However, when we are not here, we are not. We are not gathered together in another dimension in this particular energy. We are I AM. Everything. We would then be with you in the petals of a flower, in the song of a bird, in the wind upon your very cheeks—that would be where we would reside. For as you are I AM, then we are I AM.

293

EILEEN ROTA's experience as a psychic child and her 15 years of channeling led to the energy known as Pretty Flower which first spoke through Eileen in 1984. Her story is told at length in Henry Leo Bolduc's book, THE JOURNEY WITHIN: PAST LIFE REGRESSION AND CHANNELING (Inner Vision Publishing, 1988). Many of Pretty Flower's early channeled messages are excerpted in Bolduc's book.

Eileen was also featured in the article, "Are Children More Psychic in the July, 1986 issue of *Venture Inward,* published by the Association for Research and Enlightenment in Virginia Beach and in the book AWAKENING YOUR PSYCHIC POWERS by Dr. Henry Reed (Harper & Row, 1988). In addition, stories from Pretty Flower are being published in the periodical, *Spirit Speaks.*

Sand Castle Publishing
P.O. Box 629
Virginia Beach, Virginia 23451
(804) 425-0996

ORDER FORM

☐ Gift Order

ORDERED BY: (Please Print)

Name _____

Address _____

City _____

State _____ Zip _____

SHIP TO: (Fill in only if different from "Ordered By")

Name _____

Address _____

City _____

State _____ Zip _____

How Many	Title	Price Each	Total Price
	WELCOME HOME	12.00	
	Tape 1 - Meditations from WELCOME HOME 60-minute Audio Cassette Tape (see description following page)	8.00	
	Tape 2 - Stories from WELCOME HOME 90-minute Audio Cassette Tape (see description following page)	8.00	

Shipping and Handling Charges (U.S. only)	SUBTOTAL
Regular Shipping First Item .... $1.50 *Each* additional item .... $ .50	Virginia Residents Add 4.5% Sales Tax
☐ I can't wait 3-4 weeks for Book Rate. Please send by Air Mail. I'm enclosing $3.00 for the first item; $2.00 for *each* additional item.	Add Shipping & Handling Charge (See chart at left)
Canadian orders (surface mail) USA shipping charges plus 20% of Merchandise Total. Overseas orders (surface mail) USA shipping charges plus 25% of Merchandise Total.	**TOTAL ENCLOSED**

Prices subject to change without notice.

Make check or money order payable to Sand Castle Publishing. (Please: no cash, stamps or CODs.) Foreign orders payable in U.S. currency only.

Wholesale Inquiries please direct to Riverrun Press, Box 367, Piermont, NY 10968

PRETTY FLOWER AUDIO CASSETTE TAPES

Hear Pretty Flower's own voice sharing meditations and stories as they were recorded live. These tapes include the following meditations and stories from this book:

TAPE 1 - Meditations from WELCOME HOME
(60-minute tape $8.00)

Includes: Meditation to Meet the Child Within (page 70)
Meditation for Conscious Manifestation (page 130)
Meditation on the Healing Powers of the Universe (page 164)

TAPE 2 - Stories from WELCOME HOME
(90-minute tape $8.00)

Includes: A Story of Pocket (page 24)
A Story of Three Gifts (page 76)
A Story of Purpose (page 148)
A Story of Wings (page 184)
A Story of Decision (page 227)
A Story of the Three Children (page 248)

Please note: Tapes are excerpted from the actual sessions at which Pretty Flower told these meditations and stories. Audio quality may vary from one excerpt to another.

I'd like to help make Pretty Flower's teachings available.

Here are some of my local metaphysical (or other) bookstores:

Store Name   City & State

_____

_____

_____

Please send information on your books and tapes to these friends:

Name   Address   City   State   Zip

_____

_____

_____

_____

_____

_____

Sand Castle Publishing
P.O. Box 629
Virginia Beach, Virginia 23451
(804) 425-0996

ORDER FORM

☐ Gift Order

ORDERED BY: (Please Print)

Name _____

Address _____

City _____

State _____ Zip _____

SHIP TO: (Fill in only if different from "Ordered By")

Name _____

Address _____

City _____

State _____ Zip _____

How Many	Title	Price Each	Total Price
	WELCOME HOME	12.00	
	Tape 1 - Meditations from WELCOME HOME 60-minute Audio Cassette Tape (see description following page)	8.00	
	Tape 2 - Stories from WELCOME HOME 90-minute Audio Cassette Tape (see description following page)	8.00	

Shipping and Handling Charges (U.S. only)	
Regular Shipping First Item .... $1.50 *Each* additional item .... $ .50	SUBTOTAL
☐ I can't wait 3-4 weeks for Book Rate. Please send by Air Mail. I'm enclosing $3.00 for the first item; $2.00 for *each* additional item.	Virginia Residents Add 4.5% Sales Tax
Canadian orders (surface mail) USA shipping charges plus 20% of Merchandise Total.	Add Shipping & Handling Charge (See chart at left)
Overseas orders (surface mail) USA shipping charges plus 25% of Merchandise Total.	**TOTAL ENCLOSED**

Prices subject to change without notice.

Make check or money order payable to Sand Castle Publishing. (Please: no cash, stamps or CODs.) Foreign orders payable in U.S. currency only.

Wholesale Inquiries please direct to Riverrun Press, Box 367, Piermont, NY 10968

PRETTY FLOWER AUDIO CASSETTE TAPES

Hear Pretty Flower's own voice sharing meditations and stories as they were recorded live. These tapes include the following meditations and stories from this book:

TAPE 1 - Meditations from WELCOME HOME
(60-minute tape $8.00)
Includes: Meditation to Meet the Child Within (page 70)
Meditation for Conscious Manifestation
(page 130)
Meditation on the Healing Powers of the
Universe (page 164)

TAPE 2 - Stories from WELCOME HOME
(90-minute tape $8.00)
Includes: A Story of Pocket (page 24)
A Story of Three Gifts (page 76)
A Story of Purpose (page 148)
A Story of Wings (page 184)
A Story of Decision (page 227)
A Story of the Three Children (page 248)

Please note: Tapes are excerpted from the actual sessions at which Pretty Flower told these meditations and stories. Audio quality may vary from one excerpt to another.

I'd like to help make Pretty Flower's teachings available.

Here are some of my local metaphysical (or other) bookstores:

Store Name   City & State

_____

_____

Please send information on your books and tapes to these friends:

Name   Address   City   State   Zip

_____

_____

_____

_____

_____

_____